ELDERLY ALCOHOLISM

ABOUT THE AUTHOR

Michael Beechem, MSW, Ph.D., is a faculty member in the Division of Social Work and Aging Studies at the University of West Florida. He serve for nine years as the University's Director of the Center on Aging and continues to administer the Aging Studies Program. Before his current appointment, he assumed several positions in varied social services agencies providing substance abuse and mental health services. In addition, he served as the Director of Mental Health Outreach Services for a five-county region in South Texas. Dr. Beechem is an engaging speaker who has conducted numerous workshops and talks in the grieving process within the context of elderly alcoholism.

ELDERLY ALCOHOLISM

Intervention Strategies

By

MICHAEL BEECHEM, M.S.W., PH.D.

University of West Florida
Pensacola, Florida

Charles C Thomas

PUBLISHER · LTD.

SPRINGFIELD · ILLINOIS · U.S.A.

Published and Distributed Throughout the World by

CHARLES C THOMAS • PUBLISHER, LTD.
2600 South First Street
Springfield, Illinois 62794-9265

©*2002 by* CHARLES C THOMAS • PUBLISHER, LTD.

ISBN 0-398-07285-X (hard)
ISBN 0-398-07286-8 (paper)

Library of Congress Catalog Card Number: 2002020644

*With THOMAS BOOKS careful attention is given to all details of manufacturing
and design. It is the Publisher's desire to present books that are satisfactory as to their
physical qualities and artistic possibilities and appropriate for their particular use.
THOMAS BOOKS will be true to those laws of quality that assure a good name
and good will.*

Printed in the United States of America
TH-R-3

Library of Congress Cataloging-in-Publication Data

Beechem, Michael Henry.
    Elderly alcoholism : intervention strategies / Michael Beechem.
        p. cm.
    Includes bibliographical references and index.
    ISBN 0-398-07285-X -- ISBN 0-398-07286-8 (pbk.)
    1. Aged--Alcohol use. 2. Alcoholism--Treatment. I. Title.

HV5138.B43 2002
362.292'084'6--dc21   2002020644

This book is dedicated primarily to my wife, Ruth, whose support for my alcoholism recovery is continuous. Too, it is she who word processed the manuscript and offered numerous suggestions to enhance its quality. Included in the dedication are my children, Eric and Amy, whose personal sacrifices made recovery possible. My Mother, Mabel, must also be included in the dedication for encouraging me to keep a journal of my feelings and experiences in treatment, which I hope will someday appear in book form

FOREWORD

Elderly Alcoholism: Intervention Strategies represents an important contribution to those interested in improving the lives of older adults. The field of alcohol and aging is a challenging one for researchers, policy makers, practitioners, older adults and their family members. With the aging of the population, one would think that this problem would be of greater interest as the baby boomers reach their later years. Yet, risky or excessive use of alcohol by the elderly has remained a "hidden problem," with relatively few older adults being screened for alcohol problems and far fewer finding their way to treatment. Perhaps this is due to the fact that many older adults no longer consume alcoholic beverages, let alone abuse them, or due to an ageistic view that alcohol is but one of a few pleasures left for an elder. More likely, the older adult lacks the visibility of the younger alcohol abuser and is less likely to be admitted to treatment.

The history of the field of alcohol treatment for older adults is not very old itself. In the late 1960s and early 1970s studies focused on the epidemiology of the problem. In the 1980s the focus seemed to be on treatment issues such as the need for elder-specific treatment programming. In the 1990's policy and best practices in the field were being discussed. These include the Treatment Improvement Protocol Manual (number 26) produced by a national panel of experts for the Center for Substance Abuse Treatment (CSAT) of the Substance Abuse and Mental Health Services Administration (SAMHSA). Recent research has focused on less costly alternatives to formal treatment, i.e., brief physician advice and brief interventions.

In the past few years, several books have been published on various aspects of treatment of the older problem drinker, but Dr. Beechem's contribution offers a wider array of topics of interest to a wide audience. He has written this book based on his experience as a professional counselor and an academic, as well as from his personal perspective.

This book will be resource for students, and for professionals in the gerontological, addictions, social work, mental health, nursing, and medical fields. Rather than presenting a limited focus on treatment, Dr. Beechem offers the reader a wide array of issues and information. The book summarizes the various models of alcoholism and how they relate to the older adult. It describes various precipitants for drinking problems in old-age, including "loss-grief theory." It addresses the issues faced by many professionals such as identification and assessment of the problem and how to work with special populations, perhaps the least known area in this relatively new field. The book also addresses the critical issue of relapses and the relationship of alcohol to suicide. Rather than just summarize the literature, Dr. Beechem traveled to locations in the U.S. and Canada known for the innovative programs for elders. He took the time to interview the program directors, researchers, and others to learn what made their treatment programs different from others.

We need to advocate for improved substance abuse treatment and its availability for our older citizens. *Elderly Alcoholism: Intervention Strategies* is an important contribution and can only help us to become more aware of the scope of the problem and what to do about it.

Lawrence Schonfeld, Ph.D., Professor,
Department of Aging and Mental Health
Louis de la Parte Florida Mental Health Institute
University of South Florida
Tampa, Florida 33617

PREFACE

As a beginning professional counselor in the early 1970s, I fervently avoided accepting clients with presenting problems suggesting substance abuse. On November 29, 1989, after innumerable, but futile, efforts to convince a university administrator that I was not an alcoholic, I decided to enter a thirty-day residential treatment program not with sobriety as a goal but, instead, to prove once and for all that I was not an alcoholic so that the administrator's incessant nagging would finally stop.

After a full hour of disclosing my seemingly endless beverages of choice to the facility's intake worker, the nurse took my rapidly escalating pulse and blood pressure. As she charged to the medicine cabinet for anticonvulsant medication, my tenacious grip on alcoholism denial started to crumble. Although nowhere near the acceptance stage, this very incident, day, and year indelibly inaugurated the beginning of my successful alcoholism recovery. With a certain sense of pride, I can now proclaim that "My name is Mike, I am a grateful recovering alcoholic."

Enthusiastic with prospects to start anew, I accepted a faculty position at The University of West Florida to coordinate the Aging Studies Program and to teach substance abuse courses. New to the community, I was invited to join a community mental health subcommittee to assess the seriousness of elderly alcoholism, the "hidden disease." After some six to eight months of study, all fourteen committee members concurred that alcoholism was rampant among the elderly in the Pensacola community. Like many fact-finding committees, the group disbanded with their mission completed, despite a rapidly growing elderly alcoholic population largely untreated. In all likelihood, the very same situation could be documented in countless communities throughout our country.

Primarily because of my teaching and research focus on gerontology, substance abuse, and the grieving process, I decided that this book should appropriately integrate those areas. It was further determined that as an interdisciplinary supplementary text, both undergraduate and graduate students in the physical and behavioral sciences would be served. Despite the book's structure, which conveniently includes study questions for students' learning needs, it was purposively written with professional counselors in mind. As a reference book for professionals, including nurses, physicians, and others who provide services to an elderly clientele, it has practical value in focusing on the interplay between alcoholism and the aging process.

I would be remiss not to include my rationale for interspersing Beetle Bailey cartoons throughout. As a mere private with a career duration of two years, nine months, four days, and sixteen hours, I can readily identify with the lowly, yet lovable Private Beetle Bailey; but, it is General Amos Halftrack, whose alcoholic behaviors are highlighted. I selected twenty-three cartoons depicting the "mischievous" General Halftrack who superbly exhibits many alcoholism behaviors. I tried to match appropriate cartoons with situations. For example, in the cartoon with the General rationalizing that his alcoholism allows him to tolerate increased amounts of alcohol, he asserts, "the brain's ability, eh? About time I got some credit!" I, therefore, inserted this cartoon in Chapter V, Difficulty in Identification ("Hidden Alcoholism"). Then, again, there were cartoons that did not necessarily fit that well, but because they represented typical behaviors of elderly alcoholism, they were included.

With a strong sense of indebtedness and gratefulness, this book was passionately written for the purpose of perhaps making some contribution to the professional counseling community that supported me to recover successfully.

Michael Beechem

ACKNOWLEDGMENTS

I am very appreciative to those persons who contributed immeasurably toward the overall quality of my book. First, I must give substantial credit to the reviewers whose constructive criticism led to needed revisions. Those reviewers include:

General Reviewers:
Dr. James Boren, Northeastern State University
Dr. Richard Doelker, The University of West Florida
Dr. Richard Ager, Tulane University
Dr. Katherine van Wormer, University of Northern Iowa
Medical Reviewer: Dr. Michael Acromite, M.D., Naval Air Station, Pensacola, Florida
Spirituality Reviewer: Rev. Arnold Hendrix, Graduate Student, The University of West Florida

My thanks to several students who were especially helpful. Gregory Kimbriel, Cynthia Jones, and Linda Torres ordered reading materials considered essential from various universities. Students Angela Bernard, Laura Leonard, Erin Robinson, and Karen Smith provided important student perspectives about the book. Another student, Sarah Nasca, proved enormously helpful in selecting and developing appropriate case studies and study questions.

A special thanks goes to Connie Works, who generously provided support in completing the manuscript when my wife contracted acute leukemia and was no longer able to continue her important role. Without Connie's invaluable support, the finished product would have been substantially delayed.

CONTENTS

Chapter

Chapter

Chapter

Chapter

Chapter

Chapter

ELDERLY ALCOHOLISM

Chapter I

INTRODUCTION

It would be repetitious with other researchers if we were to say the problems of elderly alcohol abuse needs further verification of its extent and treatment implications. The problem may continue to be overlooked due to the older problem drinker's lack of visibility. However, as the number and proportion of older people increase, alcohol abuse in the elderly is likely to become less hidden.

Schonfeld & Dupree, 1990, pp. 5–9

SERIOUSNESS OF THE PROBLEM: DIVERGENT VIEWPOINTS

Not a Problem

Elderly alcoholism has slowly been recognized as a serious health problem. Based on a population of 100 patients sixty years and older in a psychiatric hospital, Gaitz and Baer (1971) determined that 44% of the sample population was alcoholic. Although a large number of alcoholics was identified within the psychiatric population, the study concluded that elderly alcoholism for the general population is not at high levels and that the "percentage of people who drink excessively declines with increasing age," which they attributed to increased maturity, responsibility, reduced drive, less social involvement, fewer social pressures, and less affluence (Gaitz & Baer, April 1971). Conversely, other researchers insist that if there is a decline in elderly alcoholism, it is attributable to a high mortality rate among alcoholics; that is, many die from alcoholism-related ailments before they reach old age (Abrams & Alexopoulos, 1987). Leading researchers in elderly alcoholism are divided over whether elderly alcoholism declines, increases, or remains the same.

Problem is Serious

Generally, recognition that elderly alcoholism is a serious health problem has gained support from researchers in recent years. Butler, Lewis, and Sunderland (1991) insist that many elderly alcoholics are unreported, because many drink in the privacy of their homes. They estimate that 10 to 15 percent of elderly older than sixty are alcoholics (Butler, Lewis, & Sunderland, 1991). According to Bienenfeld (1987), most research studies identify at least 10 percent of Americans older than age sixty-five as having a "drinking problem," whereas at least 8 percent of elderly drinkers are "alcohol-dependent" (Bienenfeld, 1987). According to Levinthal (1996), "there is a widely held belief that alcohol abuse is not much of a problem with the elderly. Unfortunately, that is a myth" (Levinthal, 1996, p. 587).

Elderly alcoholism researchers commonly regard the elderly population to be the most vulnerable age group for alcoholism. Generally, the elderly are exposed to life events that frequently cause high stress levels, including chronic illness, spousal care giving (especially for Alzheimer's disease), poor health, ageism (or rather, the low status arbitrarily proscribed by society), and the depression associated with difficulty in grieving losses that occur in rapid succession. These and other factors will be subsequently addressed throughout this discussion on elderly alcoholism. Estimates of the number of elderly alcoholics vary considerably, from a low of 2 percent to a high of 20 percent, and this wide variance will likely continue as long as a precise data collection instrument remains undeveloped. Schuckit (1977) insists that precise data are lacking on the number of alcoholics, but he estimates that elderly alcoholism ranges from 2 to 10 percent of the elderly population (Schuckit, 1977). Researchers face difficulty in arriving at a definitive number of alcoholics for various reasons. As previously stated, many alcoholics drink at home; too, the institutionalized elderly are typically excluded from the statistics.

ALCOHOLISM DEFINED

Alcoholism is a broad term with varied meanings. In 1956, the American Medical Association (AMA) acknowledged alcoholism to be a disease. The Diagnostic and Statistical Manual IV (RTDSM-IVRT) (2000) identifies the conditions that constitute chemical dependency, of which alcohol is included. Geraldine Miller (1999) delineates these conditions for alcohol dependency:

To meet the criteria for dependence, the client must have a maladaptive use pattern causing some type of impairment with at least three of the following occurring within one year: tolerance; withdrawal; more or longer use than planned; desire without ability to cut down or control usage; time spent on obtaining, using, or recovering from the substance; impact on activities that are social, occupational, or recreational (do less or not at all); and continued use in spite of physical or psychological problems related to use.

Neither the World Health Organization (WHO), which publishes the International Classification of Diseases, nor the American Psychiatric Association (APA), publishers of DSM-IVRT, uses the term alcoholism. Both organizations, instead, establish the syndromes: alcohol dependence and alcohol abuse. The DSM-IV (4th edition) includes both alcohol dependence and alcohol abuse. The omission of the term alcoholism was an effort by the AMA and WHO to avoid confusion from the numerous varied understandings of alcoholism.

Character Defect Theory of Alcoholism

Once the leading explanation for alcoholism, the theory continues that alcoholism is attributable to a personal character defect that can only be removed through a moralistic, religious treatment orientation. Katherine van Wormer (1997) writes that:

> In the United States, there are religiously oriented shelters and halfway houses (missions) for recovering alcoholics or reformed drunks. Funded by private donations, churches, and community resources, treatment is in the form of preaching, praying, and work therapy. Drunkenness has long been viewed by major North American religions as sinful behavior. The criminal justice system takes a punitive stance toward those who commit offenses while intoxicated. Despite the official disease-model rhetoric, there is in the United States an undercurrent of moralism that coexists with the belief that the alcoholic is suffering from a disease.

ETIOLOGY: ALCOHOLISM AS A DISEASE

Both the WHO and the AMA classify alcoholism as a disease, which serves to dispel the myth that alcoholics exhibit character defects and must be dealt with harshly and punitively. Instead, the benefit of viewing alcoholism as a disease gives impetus to the need for treatment, and, in addition, the disease classification serves to lessen the deep sense of shame so deeply instilled in alcoholics. There is near unanimity of agreement among alcoholism counselors that alcoholics are generally more receptive and motivated toward a supportive treatment regimen; hence, an increased probability of successful treatment outcomes occurs if the alcoholic is not preoccupied with the deep feelings of shame and guilt associated with the disease. Alcoholism counselors also argue that for the alcoholic to successfully recover feelings of shame and guilt associated with years of alcoholism must be overcome. They also need to be motivated to affect lifestyle changes.

NATURE VS. NURTURE

Nature:

In the latter 1950s, WHO and the AMA established that alcoholism was a disease and that it runs in families; that is, there is a genetic predisposition to the onset of alcoholism. One study, the well-known twin studies, compared twins who had been separated through adoption. A significantly high incidence of alcoholism was reported in twins who had been separated from their biologically alcoholic parents and adopted into homes where alcoholism of the adopted parents was absent.

Nurture:

The opposing argument postulates that environmental "stressors," if not managed effectively, will likely lead to alcoholism. Related to stress theory is another theory that maintains that unresolved loss-grief issues, if not adequately addressed and grieved, will likely precipitate alcoholism.

Each position no doubt has merit in explaining alcoholism. The alcoholism counselor's task should be to individualize each case and apply the most relevant and applicable theories. The debate concerning nurture vs. nature continues as an endless and unabated intellectual exercise with purists establishing polarized positions that may not optimally serve the best interests of recovering alcoholics. As Butler, Lewis, and Sunderland (1991) aptly assert, "A balance must be struck between that which the individual can control and that which is beyond his control" (p. 209).

ALCOHOL ABUSE

According to the DSM IVRT (2000), alcohol abuse syndrome is characterized as either: (1) the continuous use of alcohol for at least one month despite the knowledge of having a persistent or recurring physical problem or some difficulty in social or occupational functioning, or (2) the recurring use of alcohol in situations (such as driving) when alcohol consumption is physically hazardous.

Alcohol dependence syndrome is characterized as alcohol abuse that also involves any three of the following seven situations:

1. Consuming alcohol in amounts over a longer period than the person intends.

2. A persistent desire of one or more unsuccessful attempts to cut down or control drinking.

3. A great deal of time is spent drinking or recovering from the effects of drinking.

4. Alcohol consumption continuing despite knowledge that drinking either causes or exacerbates recurrent physical or psychological problems.

5. Important social, occupational, or recreational activities given up or reduced because of alcohol.

6. Marked tolerance or the need to drink more than before to achieve previous levels of intoxication.

7. Symptoms of alcohol withdrawal or the consumption of alcohol in order to relieve or avoid withdrawal symptoms. (*Diagnostic and statistical manual of mental disorders*, 4th ed., 2000)

PROBLEM DRINKER

Throughout the elderly alcoholism literature are frequent references to problem drinking, as if it were a diagnostic category. Like the term alcoholism, problem drinker is a nebulous, overused term that has many varied interpretations. As a former patient in an alcoholism treatment facility, the author recalls a counselor criticizing the use of the problem drinker designation. Like many euphemisms, there is the tendency to cushion the traumatic impact of the real meaning through word substitutions. Such euphemisms as passed on for died, golden age for old age; problem drinker for alcoholic, may serve to prevent acceptance and acknowledgement of the actual condition and/or life transition and therefore perpetuate denial. Counselors generally maintain that life transitions are more likely to be successful when participants perceive the transition realistically, which likewise requires succinct word designations to describe the life transitions. That is, successful life transitions are likely contingent on the participant's acceptance rather than denial of the life transition; hence, the problem drinker designation may perpetuate denial of the disease, alcoholism. Physicians are well aware of the problems associated with disease denial. For example, the diabetic is unlikely to comply with a strict medical regimen, including daily insulin and a strict diet, because of disease denial.

Alcohol's Effects on the Elderly

Generally, the combination of the aging process and alcohol consumption poses potential health risks. Alcohol tends to cause stronger reactions in the elderly largely because they metabolize alcohol slower than younger people, allowing the alcohol to remain in the bloodstream for a longer duration. Alcohol, especially alcohol abuse, causes particularly strong reactions (drug interactions) for those elderly administered medications. According to Lawson (1989), the interaction of medication drugs and alcohol can contribute to confusion, sedation, and, in some cases, death (Lawson, 1989).

Adams (1997) writes:

> Many medications have a potential for adverse interactions with alcohol. A number of different mechanisms can cause such interactions. Some medications alter the metabolism of alcohol, causing higher blood levels than expected. Alcohol, on the other hand, alters the metabolism of many drugs, affecting the levels of these drugs in the body. Alcohol can also interfere with the effectiveness of medications and exacerbate their side effects.

Adams further points out that even moderate alcohol use among the elderly can lead to interactions between drugs and alcohol. Despite of the evidence of serious problems occurring from the misuse of alcohol and medications, Adams further writes, "data are lacking on actual adverse events resulting from such interactions" (Adams, 1997, pp. 185–205). Alcohol's adverse effects on the elderly will be further discussed in Chapter III.

CATEGORIES OF ELDERLY ALCOHOLICS

Elderly alcoholism researchers have identified three broad categories of elderly alcoholics: early onset, late onset, and intermittent.

Early-Onset Alcoholism (EOA)

When onset of alcoholism occurs before old age, it is termed early onset alcoholism. Researchers, however, vary considerably on when old age starts; the onset of old age has been variously designated as ages fifty, fifty-five, sixty, and sixty-five. Because aging is an individualized process, the age designation will likely vary; that is, either some people age prematurely or experience delayed aging symptoms. Early onset and long-term alcoholism are interchangeable terms to describe elderly alcoholics who have extensive histories of alcohol dependence. Schonfeld and Dupree (1991), highly respected elderly alcoholism researchers, assert that early-onset alcoholics "are often well known to the service delivery system and they constitute 70 percent of elderly alcoholics" (Schonfeld & Dupree, 1991, p. 587).

Late-onset Alcoholism

Beechem (1997) reports:

> The terms late-onset, late-life and "reactive" alcoholism are used inter-changeably and the consensus among researchers is that late-life alcoholism is precipitated by people becoming overwhelmed when faced with several losses simultaneously and, lacking sufficient coping resources, they resort to alcohol abuse–hence, the term "reactive" alcoholism. Therefore, for the "reactive" alcoholic, onset of alcoholism occurs in old age as older people tend to experience disproportionately more losses than other age groups. (p. 400).

Researchers commonly report that late-onset alcoholism is precipitated by traumatic loss and unresolved loss-grief issues (Robertson, 1991). The Finlayson, et al (1988) study with a sampling of 211 elderly alcoholics con-cluded that 81 percent of his late-onset alcoholics experienced stressful life events that precipitated alcoholism (Finlayson, Hurt, Davis, & Morse, 1988). Another study found that widowers were more likely than widows to become late-onset alcoholics (Stachler, 1991).

Because of the shorter duration of the disease process for late-onset alco-holism, the treatment outcomes are generally more successful than early-onset alcoholism, in which the disease process has continued unabated over a prolonged duration. Chapter IX will address recommended treatment strategies for late-onset alcoholics. About 30 percent of elderly alcoholics comprise this classification.

Intermittent alcoholic

Another elderly alcoholism designation and the least known and recognized is intermittent alcoholism. The intermittent alcoholic abuses alcohol before reaching old age, but his drinking behaviors don't advance to alcoholism until old age, when his drinking behavior is sufficiently severe to be clinically termed alcoholism (Zimberg, 1978).

SERIOUSNESS OF ELDERLY ALCOHOLISM UNDERESTIMATED

Generally, researchers agree that elderly alcoholism is underestimated as a serious disease, and numerous factors are noted:

- The elderly are generally underrepresented as clients/patients in the health care system, especially in alcoholism treatment. For various reasons the elderly simply do not avail themselves of the health services available. In 1989, the National Institute on Drug Abuse and the National Institute on Alcohol Abuse and Alcoholism conducted a nationwide survey of alcoholism treatment centers and concluded that "of 383,525 clients only 22,235 (5.8%) were 55 or older" (Schonfeld, 1991). Siegel and Davidson (1984) reported that the percentage of elderly sixty-five and older (5.8%) is substantially lower than the total U. S. population. For those persons sixty-five and older, the percentage in 1997 was 13 percent (U.S. Bureau of the Census, 1993).

- Considerable alcoholism is simply unreported, primarily because many elderly do not evolve through the social service system. (Based on a survey conducted by the Community Drug and Alcohol Commission [Pensacola, Florida.] Seventy-six percent of the elderly drink only at home. (Community Drug and Alcohol Commission).

- Misdiagnosis by health professionals is common because behaviors exhibited by alcoholics typically mimic those behaviors so characteristic of acute dementia, especially memory loss and disorientation. One researcher reported that some behavioral symptoms of elderly alcoholism mimic "medical and behavioral disorders, leading to misdiagnosis" (Atkinson 1991).

If the elderly person poses a management problem for the caregiver, who is typically a relative or a close friend, there is a tendency to encourage alcohol consumption, a form of enabling. Disconcertingly, enabling behaviors are often not limited to relatives and close friends; one research study surveyed the perception of elderly substance abuse by professionals and concluded that health care professionals generally regard elderly substance abuse with a "relatively low level of concern" (Brown, 1982). As a guest on a local call-in television show addressing elderly alcoholism issues, one caller berated the host and me "for daring to pick on those old folks. Why don't you just leave them alone and let them do what they want." Unfortunately, this pervasive attitude is shared by not only the general public but also by health care professionals.

Drinking inventories typically do not include age-specific items. The Michigan Alcoholism Screening Text (MAST), a commonly used inventory to identify elderly alcoholism, includes twenty-four items but none that is age specific. Such interrogative questions include:

> Have you ever been arrested, or taken into custody, even for a few hours, because of other drinking behaviors? Have you ever been arrested for drunk driving, driving while intoxicated, or driving under the influence of alcoholic beverages? Have you ever been seen at a psychiatric or mental health clinic or gone to any doctor, social worker, or clergyman for help with any emotional problem, where drinking was part of the problem? Have you ever gotten into trouble at work or school because of drinking? (Seizer, 1971)

Not only are these questions generally irrelevant to elderly persons' lifestyles, but the interrogative nature of the questions predictably causes client defensiveness, thereby compounding the difficult task of successful treatment intervention.

The practitioner must recognize that the elderly generally experience life events and situations that are specific to the aging process. The development of a utilitarian inventory to identify elderly alcoholics is tantamount to an understanding and sensitivity of the aging process. Drinking inventories that fail to address life events that are germane to the aging process are inadequate diagnostic tools for the elderly. In Chapter IX, an elder-specific inventory will be introduced.

The numerous contributing factors that cause the seriousness of elderly alcoholism to be underestimated, explain why elderly alcoholism is also referred to as "hidden alcoholism."

MONETARY VS. HUMAN COSTS

The *Journal of the American Medical Association* reported in 1989 that hospital charges to Medicare for alcohol-related admissions was $233 million. The AMA further reported that heart attack–related admissions were surpassed by "alcohol-related medical complications" (Adams, Yuan,

Barboriak, & Rimm, 1993). "But a more serious problem relates to the loss of the human potential and quality of life" (Beechem, 1996).

SUMMARY

Estimates vary among researchers as to the prevalence of elderly alcoholism, from a low of 2 percent of the elderly population to a high of 20 percent. Alcoholism researchers generally concur that the seriousness of the problem is downplayed because of several factors: (1) the elderly are the least represented in alcoholism treatment, because they tend not to avail themselves of treatment; (2) elderly alcoholism is unreported, because they tend not to evolve through the social service system; (3) misdiagnoses; (4) enabling behaviors by professionals and relatives; and (5) the inadequacies of drinking surveys because of the omission of items germane to elderly life events.

The AMA's recognition in 1956 that alcoholism is a disease is especially noteworthy because it downplayed the "character defect" theory; yet, debate continues whether nature or nurture is the more influential in the onset of elderly alcoholism. Although both nature and nurture may play significant roles in the onset of early-onset alcoholism, late-onset alcoholism seems to be more influenced by nurture; that is, stressful environmental factors associated with the aging process.

GLOSSARY OF TERMS

Ageism: Negative feelings and/or attitudes about the elderly and old age.

Alcoholism: Is generally considered a disease characterized by alcohol dependency and significant impairment, including dysfunctioning.

Early-onset alcoholism: A designation for those elderly whose onset of alcoholism occurred before old age.

Etiology: The study of the causes of diseases, i.e., alcoholism.

Genetic predisposition: Within the context of alcoholism, offspring of alcoholics have a substantially greater probability of becoming alcoholics because of inheriting the genetic make up.

Intermittent alcoholism: A designation for those elderly who abused alcohol before old age, but whose onset of alcoholism was in old age.

Late-onset alcoholism: A designation for elderly whose onset of alcoholism occurred during old age. Term used interchangeably with "reactive alcoholism," "late-life alcoholism," and "hidden alcoholism."

Nature vs. nurture: Terms used to refer to the influences of genetics (nature) and the environment (nurture).

STUDY QUESTIONS

1. Identify the factors contributing to elderly alcoholism.

2. What characteristics define (constitute) an alcohol-dependent person?

3. Describe the three categories of elderly alcoholism.

4. Explain the rationale for discouraging use of the term "problem drinker" in alcoholism-treatment settings.

5. Identify factors that tend to precipicate late-onset alcoholism.

6. What is the underlying meaning behind the term "hidden alcoholism?"

7. Identify and explain the factors that contribute toward the seriousness of elderly alcoholism to be underestimated.

REFERENCES

Abrams, R.C. & Alexopoulos, G.S. (1987). Substance abuse in the elderly: Alcohol and prescription drugs. *Hospital and Community Psychiatry, 38*(12), 1285–1287.

Adams, W.L. (1997). Interactions between alcohol and other drugs. In A. M. Gurnack (Ed.) (1997). *Older adults' misuse of alcohol, medicines, and other drugs: research and practice.* New York: Springer.

Adams, W.L., Yuan, Z, Barboriak, J.J., & Rimm, A.A. (Sept. 8, 1993). Alcohol-related hospitalizations of elderly people: Prevalence and geographic variation in the United States. *JAMA, 270*(10), 1222–1225.

As we grow older: Alcohol and medications. Pamphlet by Community Drug and Alcohol Commission, Pensacola, Florida.

Atkinson, R.M. (1991). Alcohol and drug abuse in the elderly. In R. Jacoby and C. Oppenheimer (Eds.), *Psychiatry in the elderly*, Oxford: Oxford University Press, 819–851.

Beechem, M. (1997). Beechem risk inventory for late-onset alcoholism. *Journal of Drug Education, 27*(4), 397–410.

Bienenfeld, D. (Aug. 1987). Alcoholism in the elderly. *American Family Physician, 36*(2), 163–169.

Brown, B.B. (1982). Professionals' perceptions of drug and alcohol abuse among the elderly. *The Gerontologist, 22*(6), 519–24.

Butler, R.N., Lewis, M., & Sunderland, T. (1991). *Aging and mental health: Positive psychosocial and biomedical approaches* (4th ed.). New York: MacMillan Publishing Company, 209.

Diagnostic and Statistical Manual of Mental Disorders, 4th Ed RT. (2000). Washington, DC: American Psychiatric Association.

Finlayson, R., Hurt, R.D., Davis, L.J., & Morse, R.M. (1988). Alcoholism in elderly persons: A study of the psychiatric and psychosocial features of 216 inpatients. *Mayo Clinic Proceedings, 63*(8), 761–768.

Gaitz, C.M. & Baer, P.E. (April 1971). Characteristics of elderly patients with alcoholism. *Archives of General Psychiatry, 24*, 372–378.

Lawson, A. (1989). Substance abuse problems of the elderly: Considerations for treatment and prevention. In G. Lawson & A. Lawson (Eds.), *Alcoholism and substance abuse in special populations* (pp. 95–113). Rockville, MD, Aspen Systems.

Levinthal, C.F. (1996). *Drugs, behavior, and modern society.* Needham Heights, MA: Allyn & Bacon.

Miller, G.A. (1999). *Learning the language of addiction counseling.* Boston, MA: Allyn & Bacon.

Robertson, N. (Feb-Mar 1991). Under the influence: The intimate enemy. *Modern Maturity*, 27–28, 30, 65.

Schonfeld, L. (Jan./Feb. 1991). Research findings on a hidden population. *The Counselor*, 20–26.

Schonfeld, L. & Dupree, L.W. (1990). Older problem drinkers–long-term and late-life onset abusers: What triggers their drinking? *Aging (361)*, 5–9.

Schonfeld, L. & Dupree, L.W. (1991). Antecedents of drinking for early- and late-onset elderly alcohol abusers. *Journal of Studies on Alcohol, 52*(6), 587.

Schuckit, M.A. (1977). Geriatric alcoholism and drug abuse. *Gerontologist, 17*(2), 168–174.

Selzer, M.L. (1971). The Michigan alcoholism screening test (MAST): The quest for a new diagnostic instrument, *American Journal of Psychiatry, 3*, 176–181.

Siegel, J.S. & Davidson, M. (1984). Demographic and socioeconomic aspects of aging in the United States: Current population reports, special studies series P-23, No. 138. Washington, D.C.: U. S. Department of Commerce, Bureau of the Census.

Stachler, C. (1991). *Men and grief.* Oakland, CA: New Harbinger Publications, Inc.

U.S Bureau of the Census. (1993). Population Projections of the United States by age, sex, race, and Hispanic origin, 1993-2050. *Current Population Reports*, pp. 25–1104. Washington, DC: U.S. Government Printing Office.

Van Wormer, K. (1997). *Alcoholism treatment: A social work perspective.* Chicago: Nelson-Hall Publishers.

Zimberg, S. (1978). Treatment of the elderly alcoholic in the community and in an institutional setting. *Addictive Diseases: An International Journal, 3*(3), 417–427.

Chapter II

LOSSES AS PRECURSORS OF ELDERLY ALCOHOLISM

Psychosocial factors must also be examined as possible determinants of drinking among the oldest segment of the population.

Jung, 1994, p. 260

ANTECEDENTS

In a relatively short time period the "extended family" structure, so firmly a mainstay of stability in rural United States at about the turn of the twentieth century, was transformed into a so-called modern nuclear family. The elderly family members in preindustrial United States were very likely assured respect and high status as the eminent storytellers and transmitters of culture. Through storytelling, the elderly would pass on from one generation to another ways of doing things. A poem, song, recipe for a traditional dish, or perhaps proper social conduct was taught to a younger generation; thus, the miraculous transmission of American culture continued.

For the respected family elder, there was a sense of self-worth, as the cultural leader of the household conveyed family traditions to multiple generations within the family. The esteemed elder's role, highly revered and treasured, came to an abrupt halt virtually overnight as agrarian America was met head-on by a world phenomenon: the Industrial Revolution. Seemingly overnight, some 90 percent of households abandoned their farms and flocked to the rapidly swelling cities to run the factories' machines. The elders' once lofty status was suddenly diminished by the unyielding roar of the factories as denizens scurried about ambitiously, if not mindlessly. To make room for this newfound "progress" their once-revered elders were "warehoused" to "old folks homes" and other convenient institutional arrangements so as not to impede the progress of an industrious, fast-paced America in action.

LOSSES COMMONLY FACED IN OLD AGE

Definitions of loss abound, but none is stated with quite the eloquence of Judith Viorst (1986), a psychoanalytic therapist, whose ambitious undertaking, *Necessary Losses,* may well be the definitive research on loss. In the following passage, Viorst captures the all-encompassing nature of loss:

> When we think of loss we think of the loss, through death, of people we love. But loss is a far more encompassing theme in our life. For we lose not only through death, but also by leaving and being left, by changing and letting go and moving on. And our losses include not only our separations and departures from those we love, but our conscious and unconscious losses of romantic dreams, impossible expectations, illusions of freedom and power, illusions of safety–and the loss of our younger self, the self that thought it always would be unwrinkled and invulnerable and immortal. (p. 2)

The elderly face disproportionately more losses than any age group. Although outwardly appearing able to accept losses that inevitably accompany old age, it takes a toll. Katzenbaum (1995, p. 336) coined the term "bereavement overload" to describe situations faced by the elderly, in which multiple losses are experienced in rapid succession and the capacity to effectively grieve is diminished. Schneider (1984, p. 17) writes that "As individuals get older, they lose more and more members of their family, friends, and peers." Lowy (1991, p. 207) asserts that multiple losses tend to cause the elderly to be "more vulnerable to successive losses."

Schneider (1984, p. 5) has identified two types of losses, external and internal. External losses are those that "have an external, or discretely recognizable, aspect. These include relationships, objects, and aspects of the environment." Natural disasters, abuse, and changes in living are also losses included within this category. Internal losses are often difficult to identify, because they are unrelated to external feelings that are readily observable. They include self-worth, self-esteem, self-concept, body image, libido, feelings of powerlessness, hopelessness, and loss of control. Schneider subsequently formulated a loss-grief model, which includes the physical, behavioral, spiritual, emotional, and cognitive components. This model could effectively be used by alcoholism counselors in assessing the client's overall functioning.

GRIEF: A REACTION TO LOSS

There is a common tendency to use the terms grief, bereavement, and mourning interchangeably, although distinct differences require delineation, especially for professionals providing elderly alcoholism treatment services.

Bereavement. The verb bereave is defined in Webster's Dictionary as "to take away from, to rob, to dispossess." Grief is the act of separation. Simply defined, bereavement is the event of loss.

Grief. Grief is the affective, feeling reaction to loss as expressed by such emotions as confusion, guilt, sadness, disgust, relief, sorrow, anger, and even self-pity. Bereavement, the act of loss, precedes grieving; or, as the late Richard Kalish (1985, 182) succinctly stated, "you can't grieve without being bereaved."

Mourning. Mourning is the outward expression of grief (feelings) and bereavement (separation and/or loss) (Kalish, 1985, p. 182). Examples would include black clothes worn at funerals, the funeral wake, a black arm-band symbolizing and honoring the deceased, and, in some cultures, the consumption of alcoholic beverages at a wake.

The Grieving Process

In some ways the grieving process is akin to the "flight or fight" response used by stress theorists to describe how stress increases the hormonal level when the body prepares to either fight or flee a stressful situation. Counselors need to alert their clients who are grieving losses to manage "life stressors" effectively through good nutrition, exercise, and sufficient sleep, because the immune system is often depleted from the energy exerted in the grieving process and is therefore highly vulnerable to physical ailments. An understanding of the mind-body interplay is vital to a health-prevention strategy, which will be further discussed in Chapter IX.

The grieving process can be likened to flu; that is, you have to get worse before you get better. A Cherokee elder once sagely advised me that "Wisdom comes from the bad times, not from the good times." The attainment of successful grief resolution poses one of life's greatest challenges that clients can use as a character-building strategy. The grieving process should not be viewed as something to be ignored and scorned but instead accepted as an opportunity to bring about successful closure to loss-grief reactions.

A major task for the recovering elderly alcoholic is to face the numerous losses associated with both the aging and the disease (alcoholism) processes. The attendant losses associated with aging are in themselves challenging; but with the additional losses associated with alcoholism, the recovering alcoholic has an overwhelming challenge that requires a counselor well versed in loss theory and the aging process to assist in the grief work.

Grief Features of Elderly Grieving

Worden (1991) has identified the following grief features commonly experienced by the elderly that need to be addressed by counselors.

Interdependence: Because of long-term marriages in which various tasks had been delegated to each partner, widowhood poses a challenge. The widow is commonly frustrated with business matters that were previously assigned to her deceased husband; and the widower often feels disconnected from a viable social network his deceased wife had provided (p. 128).

Multiple losses: As discussed previously, the elderly often experience what Katzenbaum (1995, p. 336) refers to as "bereavement overload."

Personal death awareness: Older people will often experience in rapid succession many deaths involving friends, relatives, children, and siblings. Considering the trauma associated when faced with several deaths, it is understandable that a preoccupation with one's own death would ensue.

Loneliness: The loneliness associated with widowhood is largely attributable to older people living alone after a spouse or other family dies.

Role adjustment: Role adjustment is especially challenging for older people facing widowhood and effective intervention is needed to assist in their adjustment.

Support groups: For the elderly whose social network may be depleted, a support group can provide the needed "human contact," especially for those who are lonely and living in relative isolation from others.

Touch: Intervention through touch can be therapeutic for older people, and especially therapeutic for those facing widowhood.

Reminiscing: This intervention strategy has therapeutic benefits in resolving grief issues. In Chapter IX, we will discuss reminiscing therapy, also called life review therapy, to elaborate on its practical application in working with recovering alcoholics.

Discussing relocation: Rather than making decisions independently of the elderly, they should be engaged in the planning and decision-making processes concerning possible relocation, especially decisions about relocating to nursing homes, independent-care facilities, or other living arrangements.

Skill building: When virtually everything is done for you, the elderly develop a sense that they cannot do anything by themselves, and their self-esteem and sense of self-worth suffer. There is frequently a tendency to view the elderly as incapable of performing even the simplest of tasks and to, therefore, assume the control and responsibility of completing tasks that the elderly are able to do for themselves. It is important for the alcoholism counselor to educate caregivers not to establish enabling roles and instead to empower the elderly alcoholic to accept responsibility in performing those tasks for which they are capable. In effect, the locus of control should be returned to the elderly client to enhance self-esteem and self-worth.

The alcoholism counselor needs to focus on these grief features to individualize a treatment plan for the elderly recovering alcoholic.

Loss-Grief Theory

If losses are not addressed and subsequently grieved, the bereaved will likely face depression. Typical of many bereaved, they take their cue from others to "snap out of it," an approach encouraging repression, or "stuffing" of the feelings associated with the loss. Mental health professionals recommend that people work through their grief, because repressed unresolved loss-grief issues will inevitably result in some form of depression because the emotional pain associated with loss will not magically disappear. Has the factory mentality, after years of intense industrialization, caused Americans to treat people mechanistically, something that can be turned on or off at will? Human behavior is more complex than a mere light switch. Carol Staudacher (1991, p. 43) alerts one to the dangers associated with repression of feelings, which "can lead directly to alcohol misuse among both men and women" elderly. She identifies the elderly person facing widowhood as especially vulnerable. Gender-specific differences in grieving will be discussed in Chapter VI.

Psychosomatic Disorders: The "body-mind" connection

Whenever introducing the concept of psychosomatic disorders in class discussions, students will invariably suggest that it's a psychiatric disorder "that's in their head." The notion that the mind and the body are inseparable and operate interdependently with one another is a difficult concept to grasp. The stress theorist, Hans Selye, long ago forewarned the mental health community that "stressors," if not managed effectively, may lead to psychosomatic disorders. As the following passage and case study will demonstrate that in working with the elderly alcoholic, therapy should not be at the exclusion of the physical component. Herr and Weakland (1979) aptly describe the mind-body interplay in the following:

> . . . an elder may be in conflict with his son over some sort of matter; the conflict serves as an environmental stressor that acts through the nervous system on the cardiovascular system to cause high blood pressure. The high blood pressure (hypertension) is *real.* It can be objectively observed using the proper instruments and is clearly recognized to be dangerous to health. The conflict could have provoked other psychosomatic responses; for example, instead of high blood pressure, the elder (or his son) might have developed a stomach ulcer, colitis, or asthma. Any of these illnesses could be real in the sense that they would be observable using the proper diagnostic equipment and are potentially dangerous. In any event, *psychosomatic illness* should not be thought of as simply "being in the mind," since specific body tissues are demonstrably affected. (p. 234)

Norman Cousins (1986), who lived several years after he had been diagnosed as terminally ill, attributed his added longevity to his innate ability to manage the forces of the mind and body through a strong belief system.

> Over the years, medical science has identified the primary system of the human body—circulatory system, digestive system, endocrine system, autonomic nervous system, parasympathetic nervous system, and the immune system. But two other systems that are capable in the proper functioning of a human being need to be emphasized: the healing system and the belief system. The two work together. The healing system is the way the body mobilizes all its resources to combat disease. The belief system is often the activator of the healing system. The belief system represents the unique element in human beings that makes it possible for the human mind to affect the workings of the body. How one responds—intellectually, emotionally, or spiritually—to one's problems has a great deal to do with the human body functions. (p. 205)

Although only in recent years has disease been attributable to psychosomatic and stress-related origins, Kenneth Pelletier (1982, p. 7) reported in the 1950s the following illnesses to have psychosomatic features: peptic ulcer, mucous colitis, ulcerative colitis, bronchial asthma, atopic dermatitis, urticaria and angioneurotic edema, hay fever, arthritis, Raynaud's disease, hypertension, hyperthyroidism, amenorrhea, enuresis, paroxysmal tachycardia, migraine headache, impotence, general sexual dysfunctions, sleep-onset insomnia, and alcoholism. It is noteworthy that Pelletier, a Ph.D. medical researcher, included alcoholism among the aforementioned list. His position is that alcoholism may be precipitated by unmanaged stress, which is diametrically opposed to the American Medical Association's position that insists alcoholics are genetically predisposed to alcoholism. Assuming that both alcoholism theories are credible, it behooves the alcoholism counselor to individualize each client's specific treatment plan.

Grieving Process Model

Elisabeth Kubler-Ross is considered by many health professionals to be the pioneer in the field of death and dying and the first to formulate a model to assist the dying through the grieving process. Increasingly, alcoholism counselors recognize that recovering alcoholics need to move beyond denial to acceptance of the disease to attain successful treatment outcomes. The following is an adaptation of Ross' model to assist the recovering elderly alcoholic to work through losses.

Denial

As successfully recovering alcoholics and their counselors will verify, denial of alcoholism is one of the major obstacles to overcome for successful recovery. It is a common defensive, coping strategy used by the alcoholic who has become indelibly reinforced through several years of drinking. "No, it can't be me. I can't be an alcoholic" is a typical response to an intervention.

Anger

As Kubler-Ross (1969, p. 50) asserts, "When the first stage of denial cannot be maintained any longer, it is replaced by feelings of anger, rage, envy, and resentment with recovering alcoholics." Many counselors discover that recovering alcoholics are commonly beset with deep feelings of loss time, usually elapsing several years when their lives have been utterly unfulfilling. As the grieving process evolves, feelings of anger are appropriately replaced by more "tender" feelings and emotions such as sadness and disappointment. Even though anger is used to mask feelings of disappointment, sadness, and being hurt, it serves, at least temporarily, as a substitute for the genuine, repressed feelings. In the initial stages of recovery, it is common for the recovering alcoholic to feel a strong sense of anger in having been a "drunk" for so many years.

Bargaining

Kubler-Ross (1969) reports that usually the grief worker is not always able to identify this stage, because it commonly is the client's silent pact with God, which he unlikely will share with anyone, including the practitioner. It is not unusual for recovering alcoholics to suggest to the practitioner that "maybe I can still drink if I just don't drink too much and just stop before I get drunk." In a real sense, this reaction could also be construed as a form of denial.

Depression

Kubler-Ross (1969) reports that in the stage of depression, feelings of numbness or stoicism, anger, and rage replace a sense of deep loss. One of the most intense losses experienced by many recovering alcoholics is the loss of their alcoholic lifestyles and beverages of choice. Despite the recovering alcoholics' recognition of the debilitating effects of alcohol, there remains a deep sense of loss for their beverage of choice and, for many, beverages of choice. Their reactions are not unlike clients who resist changing manipulative behaviors; however dysfunctioning the behavior is, it offers a semblance of familiarity and security. Alcoholics are apprehensive and fearful about the prospects of losing alcohol in their lives, especially for early-onset alcoholics who conceivably have been drinking heavily for forty, fifty, or sixty years. In the past, the recovering alcoholic has been able to effectively mask such intense feelings as sorrow, sadness, and loss through alcohol, which numbs the intensity of the feelings. The role of neurotransmitters and how they serve to keep feelings from entering a conscious level will be discussed in Chapter III.

Some types of depression may be normal and healthy, whereas other types may be psychopathological. This temporary condition needs to be communicated to the client to allay likely feelings of apprehension and fear.

Acceptance

Kubler-Ross (1969) described this stage as free of depression and anger. For many elderly recovering alcoholics, a deep sense of elation is felt, as well as pride to at last be sober and successfully controlling this insidious disease. However optimistic and hopeful the recovering alcoholic is with the prospects of finally gaining a sense of control in his or her life, it is essential for the counselor to encourage the client to temper his enthusiasm with the "one day at a time" affirmation, because in the early stages of recovery, there is the probability of relapse. To help the elated and euphoric recovering alcoholic to temper his enthusiasm, a sponsor is highly recommended. An elderly sponsor who understands the many dimensions of alcoholism and the aging process should be considered. Typically, the alcoholic will assume an "I can do anything attitude" at the onset of alcoholism, but conventional counseling requires the client to defer to a "higher power." The recovering alcoholic will likely be reminded that alcoholism is associated with arrogantly trying to solve problems independently of others and is instead encouraged to embrace a "higher power." A discussion on the controversy concerning a "higher power" will ensue in Chapter X. As a former faculty member at a southwestern university, a group of us invited Kubler-Ross to visit our campus to lecture on death and dying. I engaged Kubler-Ross in a discussion concerning the grieving process in our 1 1/2 hour drive from the airport to the university. In response to my inquiry about people misunderstanding facets of her five-stage model, Elisabeth, as she asked to be addressed, offered that she had not explicitly described certain components of the model in her book. She expressed the individualized nature of grief and that not everyone evolves through the process in set ways; that some do not experience all five stages, and that some stages may be experienced that were excluded in her model, and that the bereaved may not have evolved through the stages in the same order. She further expressed a concern about the negative associations with the depression stage, a stage that is typically characterized by reflection. I suggested that reflection may be an appropriate substitute for depression, to which she replied in the affirmative.

SUMMARY

The status of the elderly diminished along with their once prominent role in the extended family as the United States was transformed from an agrarian to an industrial society. Accompanying a lower status was the unrealistic task of grieving multiple losses associated with the aging process.

Common practice is the interchangeable use of the terms bereavement, grief, and mourning despite distinct differences that need to be recognized by the counselor who will assist recovering alcoholics through the grieving process. Uppermost in importance, the counselor must recognize that successful alcoholism recovery is contingent on resolution of loss-grief issues.

Excluding the elderly from decisions concerning their lives is common, especially decisions concerning new living arrangements. Instead, the locus of control needs to be returned so that the elderly are able to be involved in decisions that influence their quality of life.

The interplay between the mind and the body needs to be in harmony with one another to function interdependently. Stress researchers, Hans Selye and Norman Cousins, demonstrate how disharmony and dysfunctioning of the mind and body will predictably result in psychosomatic disorders and a breakdown of the immune system, thus leading to both emotional and physical health problems.

Dr. Elizabeth Kubler-Ross' stage theory describing the grieving process is discussed within an alcoholism recovery context. The alcoholism counselor has a challenging and important role in assisting the elderly recovering alcoholic through the grieving process because successful treatment outcomes are contingent on grieving the countless losses associated with the aging process.

GLOSSARY OF TERMS

Bereavement: The act of separation, or the event of loss.

Bereavement overload: Term coined by the gerontologist Robert Katzenbaum to describe elderly persons overwhelmed with having experienced numerous losses in rapid succession.

Fight or flight response: Stress theorists use this term to describe one's reaction to stress; that is, the person subjected to stress can either remain in the situation and fight the "stressors" or go into flight and escape.

Grief: The affective (feeling) reaction to loss as expressed with emotions including confusion, sadness, disgust, relief, sorrow, anger, and self-pity.

Mourning: The overt expression of loss and grief including funeral wakes, black clothes, and armbands.

Reminiscing: Refers to reminiscing therapy, whereby the elderly client is encouraged to disclose his or her life story, sometimes used interchangeably with life review therapy.

STUDY QUESTIONS

1. Explain how the transformation from an agrarian to an industrialized society largely influenced the demise of the status of the elderly, which in turn led to large-scale institutionalization.

2. Differentiate between Schneider's internal and external types of losses and how they may serve to precipitate both early- and late-onset alcoholism.

3. Identify the dissimilarities between bereavement, grief, and mourning within an alcoholism recovery context.

4. Explain the mind-body interrelationship and its role in elderly alcoholism.

5. Explain through examples why the elderly are vulnerable to losses.

REFERENCES

Cousins, N. (1986). *Human options.* New York: Berkley Publishing Group.

Herr, J.J. & Weakland, J. H. (1979). Counseling elders and their families: Practical techniques for applied gerontology. New York: Springer Publishing Company.

Jung, J. (1994). *Under the influence: alcohol and human behaviors.* Belmont, CA: Brooks/Cole Publishing Company.

Kalish, R.A. (1985). *Death, grief, and caring relationships* (2nd ed.). Monterey, CA: Brooks/Cole Publishing Company.

Katzenbaum, R.J. (1995). *Death, society, and human experience* (5th ed.). Needham Heights, MA: Allyn & Bacon.

Kubler-Ross, E. (1969). *On death and dying.* New York: MacMillan Publishing Co., Inc.

Lowy L. (1991). *Social work with the aging: The challenge and promise of the later years* (2nd ed.). Prospect Heights, IL: Waveland Press, Inc.

Pelletier, K.R. (1982). *Mind as healer, mind as slayer: A holistic approach to preventing stress disorders.* New York: Delta Publishing Co.

Schneider, J. (1984). *Stress, loss and grief: Understanding their origins and growth potential.* Baltimore: University Park Press.

Staudacher, C. (1991). *Men & grief: A guide for men surviving the death of a loved one, A resource for caregivers and mental health professionals.* Oakland, CA: New Harbinger Publications, Inc.

Viorst, J. (1986). *Necessary losses: The loves, illusions, dependencies and Impossible expectations that all of us have to give up in order to grow.* New York: Fawcett Gold Metal.

Worden, J.W. (1991). *Grief counseling and grief therapy: A handbook for the mental health practitioner.* New York: Springer Publishing Company.

Chapter III

HOW ALCOHOL ABUSE INFLUENCES
THE AGING PROCESS

After nearly three days of "drying out," I began my three-hour
shift to provide support for Sam, the sixty-eight year-old man
who had been admitted for treatment of acute alcoholism.
Unlike before, each body part seemed to shake in unison, as if
attached to a machine that induced electrical shocks to its subjects. A psychiatrist friend had once described the effects of
shock treatment, and this man's physical withdrawal reactions
were not unlike the description.

The day they brought him here he was drunk and non-con-
versant, and placed in the "detox room." The second day, he
was listless, except for an occasional scream that "I'm dying,"
which may have served as the only evidence to the dozen or
so patients who voluntarily maintained an around-the-clock
vigil by his bed to support him through alcoholism withdrawal that he was, in fact, alive.

Patient at Valley Hope, OK, December, 1989

Alcohol provokes the desire but it takes away the performance.

Shakespeare

Alcohol abuse significantly influences the aging process; that is, it has a
direct influence on how the elderly age biologically, cognitively, and
psychosocially. Because of its individualized nature, alcohol abuse influences the aging process to varying degrees.

As discussed in Chapter I, the seriousness of elderly alcoholism is underestimated, caused in part, by physicians' misdiagnoses. A common mistake,
even among health professionals, is to confuse alcoholic behaviors with the
aging process because the biological symptoms of alcoholism frequently
mimic acute dementia. Hartford and Thienhaus (1984) explain this confu-

sion when they write that:

> It is not unusual for the problem of alcoholism to blend into pathology that may arise as the sociological consequences of the aging process. The actual incidence of alcoholism in the elderly ranges from 15 to 25%. Even with knowledge that alcoholism is relatively common, it can be extremely difficult to differentiate the problem of aging and other medical or psychiatric conditions in the elderly person from alcoholism. (p. 253)

BIOLOGICAL AGING

Alcohol abuse influences all of the body's systems, especially the gastrointestinal system. With decreased amounts of gastric alcohol dehydrogenase (ADH), an enzyme that functions to metabolize the alcohol, the stomach is unable to metabolize as much alcohol as it did before old age. With decreased gastric ADH, the elderly person experiences an increase in blood alcohol concentration (BAC) (Lieber 1995). A slower metabolic rate increases the duration that alcohol is in the stomach, and, therefore, intensifies the toxic effects of alcohol. One research study concluded that women produce about 60 percent less ADH in the stomach than men (Levinthal, 1996). Unlike the stomach, where alcohol metabolism is not significantly altered, the alcohol burden on the liver is increased (Smith, J. W., 1982).

With increased amounts of alcohol entering the bloodstream, virtually all tissues of the body are subject to damage (Smith, J.W., 1982). One report attributes gastrointestinal and liver problems to alcohol abuse:

> ... the liver is particularly endangered by alcohol. Here, alcohol converts to an even more toxic substance, acetaldehyde, which can cause substantial damage, including cirrhosis in 10% of people with alcoholism. Liver damage is more common and develops more quickly in women than in men with similar histories of alcohol abuse. Within the GI tract, alcohol can contribute to the cause of ulcers and pancreatis, a serious infection of the pancreas. On a minor scale, it can cause diarrhea and hemorrhoids.

According to Standridge (1998), elderly alcohol abuse has an especially devastating effect on the gastrointestinal system, causing gastritis, peptic ulcers, and diarrhea, as well as upper alimentary canal cancers. Early-onset alcoholics contract liver cirrhosis more commonly than late-onset alcoholics because of the prolonged duration of alcoholism in the stomach (Standridge, Nov. 1998).

CARDIOVASCULAR SYSTEM

The elderly are at high risk for serious complications associated with cardiovascular disease, because alcohol is a central nervous system depressant that impairs cardiac efficiency even with a single drink. Elderly alcoholics are especially vulnerable to alcohol cardiomyopathy, which is potentially fatal (Standridge, Nov. 1998). Cardiomyopathy is characterized by cardiac enlargement and low cardiac output and commonly occurs with chronic alcoholics. In spite of the obvious threat of death, alcoholic cardionyopathy is treatable in the early stages through "prolonged bed rest, digitalis and diuretic drugs, total abstinence, and correction of nutritional defects" (Brigden, 1972, pp. 187–201). Brigden, a highly regarded cardiologist and medical researcher, asserts that "cardiomyopathy occurs in only a limited number of alcoholics. However, the great variation in alcohol tolerance is well known, and is due in part to variation in levels of alcohol dehydrogenase activity which is probably genetically determined" (Bridgen, 1972, p. 197).

Esophagus

Even moderate alcohol consumption has an adverse effect on the lower esophageal sphincter, the muscle that prevents the "backward flow" of acid into the esophagus from the stomach. But with the characteristically heavy drinking of alcoholics, acid is more apt to come into contact with the esophagus and, hence, damage its lining. As the esophagus becomes inflamed, the passage becomes narrow, thus making food more difficult to pass. The narrowing of the passage, and the pain associated with swallowing, is likely to contribute to malnutrition (Marsono, 1993).

Neuromuscular System

Neuromuscular problems are common among elderly alcoholics and can be observed in weak legs, gait problems, and frequent falls, which may lead to fractures. For most people older than forty, especially women, the body loses its ability to absorb calcium efficiently, which contributes to increased bone fractures in old age. Coupled with bone loss associated with the aging process, alcoholism "accelerates this bone loss and may lead to compression fractures of vertebrae" (Moniz, 1994).

Interaction with Medications

Because of major physiological changes associated with the aging process, coupled with the tendency for physicians to overprescribe medications to elderly patients who pose management problems, the interaction of alcohol with prescribed medications creates a serious health problem.

The aging process causes a decline in body water content and lean body mass along with an increase in body fat content. Combined with alcohol, these physiological changes bring about a "higher blood alcohol level among the elderly." According to Burkle (1995), it is not adolescents who have the highest death rate from drug interactions but, instead, the elderly who represent 51 percent of drug-related deaths, although the elderly comprise slightly less than 13 percent of the total U.S. population.

The potentially fatal interaction of alcohol and medications can pose serious problems for the elderly, especially because the elderly are prescribed upward of 25 percent of all prescription medications (Atkinson & Kofoed, 1982).

Disulfiram

Disulfiram, the scientific name for Antabuse, should not be administered to the elderly person who is trying to successfully recover, because the side effects associated with disulfiram administration can present risks that can lead to death (Hartford & Thienhaus, 1984). Van Wormer (1997, p. 78) describes the symptoms associated with the administration of disulfiram (Antabuse):

> Once Antabuse is ingested, if a person drinks, a severe physical reaction of nausea, flushing, and shortness of breath occurs. Even if alcohol is placed in the skin, such as that contained in perfume, a strong reaction will occur. Although consumption of alcohol is dangerous to most alcoholics who have injected antabuse, some chronic alcoholics will "brag" that they can drink freely, with no negative consequences. There is as yet no substantiation of these claims, however, in the literature.

Elderly Alcoholic Women Vulnerable

Gender-biased research, which has resulted in disproportionately more research data about men, has caused a dearth of information about the effects of medication interaction on elderly women. That is, with more male researchers who tend to be motivated to learn about themselves, there is considerably more medication interaction data about men than women.

According to Mellinger, Balter, and Manheimer (1971), elderly women have a substantially higher use of sedatives, stimulant drugs, and tranquilizers. The researchers warn that alcohol combined with these drugs may cause severe side effects and cross-tolerances.

Recent research studies show that women metabolize alcohol differently than do men and that they are, therefore, more vulnerable to alcohol-related organ damage. As discussed early in this chapter, the elderly generally have decreased amounts of gastric ADH, the enzyme that metabolizes alcohol. Women also have less ADH, so elderly women are especially vulnerable to the ill effects of alcohol damage. Coupled with the decrease in ADH levels for elderly women, women generally contain less body weight than men of comparable weight, resulting in higher concentrations of BAC for elderly women. According to the National Institute on Alcohol Abuse and Alcoholism (Oct., 1994), women are more apt to have liver and brain damage from alcohol abuse:

Liver damage: Compared with men, women have alcohol-induced liver disease develop over a shorter period of time and after consuming less alcohol.

Brain damage: Views of the brain obtained by magnetic resonance imaging (MRI) suggest that women may be more vulnerable than men to alcohol-induced damage.

COGNITIVE AGING

Although most experts concur that many elderly generally undergo cognitive changes associated with the aging process, there are varying theories, if not confusion, concerning the extent to which alcohol influences cognitive functioning. Beresford (1995, p. 331) writes that the "extent to which lesser cognitive problems are caused or worsened by the extended use of alcohol among elderly persons is not clear." Part of the confusion relates to the unsettled controversy concerning whether there should be a clear distinction between alcohol-induced dementia and Wernicke-Korsakoff's syndrome, or whether these disorders are of the same spectrum. There clearly is significant overlap in the features of these disorders (Smith & Atkinson, 1997). Although some researchers maintain that Wernicke-Korsakoff's syndrome, or "wet brain," is caused by a thiamine deficiency, other researchers believe that alcohol also has an influence (Van Wormer, 1997).

One school of thought classifies the two conditions as one, but as "successive stages in the recovery of a single disease process. Stated in another way, Korsakoff's psychosis is the psychotic component of Wernicke's disease" (Victor & Martin, 1991, p. 94).

Wernicke-Korsakoff's syndrome, evident in approximately 20 percent of alcoholics, is characterized by confusion, disorientation, and an inability to "sustain physical, or mental activities." Because of the extreme "cognitive personality deficits" caused by Wernicke-Korsakoff's syndrome, most of its victims require institutionalization (Chafetz, 1983). Some researchers will separate Wernicke's syndrome from Korsakoff's psychosis, whereas others combine the two, hence Wernicke-Korsakoff's syndrome. Van Wormer (1997) is careful to separate the two and their symptoms accordingly. She writes that "Wernick's syndrome is characterized by paralysis of normal eye movements, mental confusion, and problems with walking and balance" whereas Korsakoff's psychosis, caused by brain damage, affects the "memory function" (p. 94-985). Confabulation, characterized by the alcoholic changing the events of a story, or embellishing, to compensate for an inability to recall the actual specifics surrounding the event, is frequently symptomatic of Korsakoff's psychosis (Rivers, 1994). Katherine Van Wormer, a social worker and author, eloquently describes her father, who has Korsokoff's psychosis:

> Confined to a bustling and surprisingly cheerful nursing home, he has the "run of the place" and is the manager of the television electronic control device. Although his legs are numb from peripheral neuropathy, in his mind he is the outstanding tennis player of his middle years and youth. Moreover, he has recently signed a contract with Hollywood to film a movie at his house. Believing that he has been only temporarily confined for a mysterious leg problem, he has no awareness of the recent past or of the future. Every detail, however is recorded from the long ago, so that the visitors can share in reminising about what to others would be ancient history. For my father, there is no sense of time or loss. (Van Wormer, 1997, p. 96)

Pathological Intoxification

Chafetz (1983, p. 84) identified the following behaviors as symptomatic of pathological intoxification:

- Dramatic and sudden onset
- Impaired consequences
- Confusion and disorientation
- Illusions, transitory delusions, and visual hallucinations
- Impulsive and aggressive activity carried out to the point of destructiveness
- Rage, anxiety, and depression
- Frequent suicide attempts

"Blackouts"

Undoubtedly, one of the most difficult phenomena to understand is the alcoholic blackout, whereby varying durations of time periods are not recalled. Although not included in the alcoholism definition, many alcoholism counselors use the alcoholic blackout as a significant criterion for alcoholism. It has been reported that for an alcoholic blackout to occur, the person needs to have developed a physical tolerance for alcohol (Van Wormer, 1997). Wegscheider-Cruse (1989, p. 62), the well-known author on alcoholism, insightfully captures the implications of an alcoholic blackout:

> The onset of blackouts is a frightening development. It can cause personal and job problems that are costly and hard to explain because neither his companions nor the victim himself has any clue that the blackout is happening. He talks and acts normally, does not lose consciousness, and may not even show any signs of intoxication, but for the period of the blackout nothing is written on his memory. He can make promises, hear class assignments, negotiate business deals, incur debts, and have no idea afterward that he has done so.

The alcoholic blackout varies in duration from a few minutes to several hours, and for some it will last for days. It is not unusual for an alcoholic to experience blackouts after ingesting as little as 60 grams of absolute alcohol even though not exhibiting the behaviors associated with intoxication (Rivers, 1994).

Neurotransmitters

Natural neurochemical changes take place within the brain that affect behavioral changes, but certain substances, alcohol in particular, change the natural chemical process. Alcohol abuse will alter the release of neurotransmitters, which, in turn, will lead to adverse behavioral reactions. The problem is not with neurotransmitters per se but with the role of alcohol in "mimicking the action of neurotransmitters" (Goldberg, 1997). The brain is comprised of various neurotransmitters that transmit messages chemically, hence neurotransmitters are often called "chemical messengers." Alcohol abuse has a major role in the brain functioning of neurotransmitters, affecting the chemical substances that transmit messages from cell to cell. There are three key neurotransmitters that are especially influenced by alcohol abuse: gamma-eminabutyric acid (GABA), norepinephrine, and serotonin (Kinney & Leaton, 1995).

GABA:

GABA is an inhibitory neurotransmitter within the central nervous system (CNS). Alcohol's initial influence increases the inhibitory effects, but with alcohol abuse, its function is substantially decreased and is therefore described as a "social lubricant because with its ability to lower inhibitions and anxiety it gives one courage in social situations" (Beach, 1999). In addition to alcohol, antianxiety drugs including Xanax, Valium and Librium also influence GABA's functioning by inhibiting the cell firing and thereby are apt to cause memory loss (Avis, 1996). Carrol (2000) cautions that when the normal functioning of the neurotransmitter GABA is disrupted, "convulsions may occur" (Carroll, 2000).

Norepinephrine:

The neurotransmitter, norepinephrine, has a major role in mood states, whereby low levels can cause depression. Kinney and Leaton (1995) write that alcohol "hastens the breakdown and removal from the body of norepinephrine" (Kinney & Leaton, 1995, p. 43). People with depression, especially the elderly, should be alerted to the probability of clinical states of depression being exacerbated because of the concurrent use of alcohol and antidepressants (Kinney & Leaton, 1995).

Serotonin:

Through alcohol abuse, the serontonin level is lowered, causing behaviors associated with depression, anxiety, poor impulse control, aggressiveness, and suicide (Kinney & Leaton, 1995). Both norepinephrine and serotonin function to provide optimal levels of mood, so when alcohol upsets this balance, it can cause either manic behavior when the mood swings upward or depression when the mood swings downward (Levinthal, 1996). The serotonin neurotransmitter is influenced by alcohol and is primarily associated within "sleep and sensory experiences" (Van Wormer, 1997, p. 94). "Serotonin regulates patterns of sleep and emotionality" (Levinthal, 1996).

Alcohol and Sexuality

Sexuality:

Alcohol abuse has a major influence on the quality of sexual functioning in both men and women. The belief that only men experience sexual dysfunction and that women are spared of this malady may have it's origins in gender-biased research, whereby male researchers are preoccupied with learning about themselves. Covington (1991) draws on gender-specific socialization theory to assert that men are conditioned from youth to be "aggressive, physically combative, independent, nonemotional, and outwardly oriented;" whereas women learn to be "passive, dependent, emotional, and oriented toward relationships" to explain why men tend to be sexually aggressive and women sexually passive. These gender-specific differences, she insists, will influence "one's sense of self-worth," which is contingent on "healthy sexuality." Covington (1991) continues her argument by suggesting that because women have been socialized to satisfy male sexual needs, their own sexual needs remain unmet. She writes that:

> Many recovering female alcoholics and drug users spent so many years focusing on the needs of their partners that they do not have any idea what would be sexually gratifying for them (Covington, 1991, 75).

> Even though, in the general population, only 30 percent of women report experiencing an orgasm during intercourse, it is still the preferred sexual activity among men and for many is synonymous with 'having sex." (Hite, 1976)

Another source of female sexual dysfunctioning relates to posttraumatic stress disorder (PTSD) from sexual trauma. To lessen the emotional fear associated with sexual abuse, female victims will resort to alcohol and drug abuse (Khantzian, Halliday, & McAuliffe, 1990). One study reports that anywhere from one fifth to one third of women have been subjected to sexual abuse (Russell, 1986). Teusch (1997) insists that women recovering from substance abuse need to have sexual abuse-related issues addressed in "an integrated treatment approach" (Teusch, 1997).

It is widely accepted by addictionologists that male sexual dysfunctioning is often associated with chronic alcoholism. Although alcohol has generally been thought to be an aphrodisiac because of its inhibitory lessening effects, "chronic alcoholism will likely cause sexual dysfunctioning. In the short term, before onset of alcoholism, alcohol may enhance sexual functioning due to a "lack of impulse control," but further research is needed to definitively arrive at this conclusion. Shakespeare's insightful assertion that alcohol "provokes the desire, but it takes away the performance" thus has clinical relevance hundreds of years henceforth (Fishbein & Pease, 1996, p. 111). Fishbein and Pease (1996, p. 111) advise that "alcohol may cause atrophy of the testicles, and sperm production becomes impaired due in part to lowering of testosterone levels." The task of differentiating the biological from the psychosocial features of aging continues to pose a challenge, especially related to male impotence, because the symptoms clearly overlap. Nowhere is the interplay between the "mind and body" more apparent than with impotence.

Because impotent men and anorgasmic women comprise a large segment of recovering elderly alcoholics, sexual dysfunctioning needs to be integrated into their treatment regimen.

Alcohol And Depression

As discussed in Chapter II, unresolved loss-grief issues are common antecedents to clinical depression. The male alcoholic is primarily affected by depression after onset of alcoholism; whereas for women the reverse is true as depression tends to precede alcoholism. Whether depression precedes or follows alcoholism, one fact is undisputed: alcohol, a CNS depressant, effectively intensifies depression.

Alcohol And Suicide

A close relationship clearly exists between alcoholism and suicide, and because suicide is disproportionately high among the elderly, this interplay will be further elaborated on in Chapter XII.

SUMMARY

Alcohol abuse influences the aging process with specific attention to the cardiovascular and neuromuscular systems. Even moderate alcohol intake can adversely effect the elderly, especially elderly women, largely caused by reduced gastric ADH levels in elderly women. ADH is the essential enzyme that metabolizes alcohol; alcohol remains in the bloodstream for longer durations, thus causing pathological damage to vital organs.

The potentially fatal combination of alcohol and medications is stressed. Although some medications are inhibited when combined with alcohol, other medications are strengthened when combined with alcohol, thus causing death. Disulfiram (Antabuse) is also potentially fatal to alcoholic patients when combined with alcohol. Alcoholism counselors are urged not to use this drug as a treatment strategy with elderly clientele.

Alcohol influences behavior as a result of chemical changes associated with the neurotransmitters GABA, norepinephrine, and serotonin. Neurotransmitters are the "chemical messengers" that, when combined with alcohol, will effect behavioral changes, including the lowering of inhibitions, anxiety, alertness, wakefulness, and depression.

Although discussed only briefly, there is a relationship between alcoholism and suicide.

GLOSSARY OF TERMS

Acetaldehyde: A colorless, flammable substance that is highly toxic and can cause substantial damage, including cirrhosis of the liver, ulcers, pancreatitis, diarrhea, and hemorrhoids. Acetaldehyde was a chemical in its original form before conversion.

Anorgasmic: An inability to achieve the climax of sexual excitement.

Blackout: Memory lapses, whereby one is unable to recall events that occurred while drinking alcohol. Although not formally included in the criteria for alcoholism, many counselors regard the alcoholic blackout as indicative of alcoholism and/or physical dependency.

Cardiomyopathy: A diagnostic term designating myocardial disease characterized by cardiac enlargement and low cardiac output. The disease occurs in chronic alcoholics.

Confabulation: Behavioral characteristic of Wernicke-Korsokoff's syndrome whereby the alcoholic will change the events of a story.

Cross-tolerance: A condition in which the effects of drugs are reduced because of the use of other drugs representing the same drug class.

Dementia: A brain disorder characterized by impairment of cognitive functioning.

Digitalis: Its dried leaves are used to treat cardiomyopathy.

Disulfiram: The scientific name for Antabuse is administered to recovering alcoholics to prevent the oxidation of acetaldehyde, thus resulting in high concentrations of this substance in the body, causing severe discomfort. Used occasionally in alcoholism treatment, because when combined with alcohol it produces an adverse physical reaction.

Esophageal sphincter: A muscle that prevents the backward flow of acid into the esophagus from the stomach.

Gamma-aminobutyric acid (GABA): An inhibitory neurotransmitter located in the brain. GABA's function is reduced because of the effects of alcohol abuse considered a "social lubricant" with its ability to lower inhibitions and anxiety.

Gastric alcohol dehydrogenase (ADH): An enzyme that metabolizes alcohol.

Gastrointestinal system: Refers to the system that includes the stomach and intestine.

Norepinephrine: An excitatory neurotransmitter that can cause depression when at low levels caused by alcohol abuse. Sufficient levels are required to maintain alertness and wakefulness. This neurotransmitter regulates appetite and waking.

Pathological intoxification: Indicated by dramatic and sudden onset, impaired consequences, confusion, and disorientation; illusions, transitory delusions, and visual hallucinations; impulsive and aggressive activity carried out to the point of destructiveness; rage, anxiety, and depression; frequent suicide attempts.

Peripheral neuropathy: Referring to pathological changes and/or functional disturbances in the peripheral nervous system.

Serotonin: A neurotransmitter that inhibits activity and behavior. Low levels caused by alcohol abuse contribute to depression, anxiety, and suicide. Like norepinephrine, serotonin influences mood levels and may have a role in manic depression and depression when its levels are lowered from alcohol abuse.

Thiamin: A component of the B-complex group of vitamins.

Vertebrae: Referring to the thirty-three bones that comprise the vertebral spine column.

Wernicke-Korsakoff's syndrome: An alcohol-induced dementia characterized by confusion, disorientation, and confabulation of events.

STUDY QUESTIONS

1. Explain ADH's function and its effectiveness when the elderly, especially elderly women, consume alcohol.

2. How does alcoholism influence the cardiovascular and neuromuscular systems?

3. Explain VanWormer's rationale for treating Wernicke-Korsakoff's syndrome as two separate conditions, hence Wernick's syndrome and Korsakoff's psychosis.

4. Describe the relationship between alcoholism and an "alcoholic blackout" and its effects.

5. How does alcohol abuse affect the normal functioning of the GABA, epinephrine, and serotonin neurotransmitters.

REFERENCES

Alcohol and hormones. (October 1994). *Alcohol Alert.* National Institute on Alcohol Abuse and Alcoholism, No. 26, 352.

Atkinson, R.M. & Kofoed, L.L. (1982). Alcohol and drug abuse in old age: A clinical perspective. *Substance and Alcohol Actions/Misuse*, 353–368.

Avis, H. (1996). *Drugs and life*, (4th ed.). New York: WCB/McGraw-Hill.

Beach, R. (Nov., 1999). Seminar at University of South Alabama, Hattiesburg, MS.

Beresford, T.P. (1995). Alcoholic elderly: Prevalence, screening, diagnosis, and prognosis. In: Beresford, T. & Gomberg, E. (Eds.), *Alcohol and aging: Looking ahead*. NY: Oxford University Press.

Brigden, W. (1972). Alcohol cardiomyopathy. *Cardiovascular Clinics, 4*(1), 187–201.

Carroll, C.R. (2000). *Drugs in modern society* (5th ed.). New York: McGraw-Hill.

Chafetz, M. (1983). *The alcoholic patient: Diagnosis and management, Vol. I & II.* Oradell, NJ: Medical Economics Company, Inc.

Covington, S.S. (1991). Awakening your sexuality: A guide for recovering women and their partners. San Francisco, CA: HarperCollins.

Fishbein, D.H. & Pease, S.E. (1996). *The dynamics of drug abuse.* Needham Heights, MA: Allyn & Bacon.

Goldberg, R. (1997). *Drugs across the spectrum.* Englewood, CO: Morton Publishing Company.

Hartford, J.T. & Thienhaus, O.J. (1984). Psychiatric aspects of alcoholism in geriatric patients. In J. T. Hartford & T. Samorajski (Eds.), *Alcoholism in the elderly.* New York: Raven Press

Hite, S. (1976). *The Hite report.* New York: Macmillan.

Khantzian, E.J., Halliday, K.S., & McAuliffe, W. E. (1990). Addiction and the vulnerable self. In Straussner, S., & Zelvin, E. (Eds.), *Gender and addictions: Men and women in treatment.* New York: Guilford.

Kinney, J. & Leaton, G. (1995). *Loosening the grip: A handbook of alcohol information* (5th ed.). St. Louis, MO: Mosby–Year Book, Inc.

Levinthal, C.F. (1996). *Drugs, behavior, and modern society.* Needham Heights, MA: Allyn & Bacon.

Lieber, C.J. (1995). Disorders of alcoholism. *New England Journal of Medicine*, 333, 1058–1065.

Marsono, L. (1993). Alcohol & malnutrition. *Alcohol World Health & Research, 17*(4), 284–291.

Mellinger, G.D., Balter, M.B., & Manheimer, D.I. (1971). Patterns of psychotherapeutic drug use among adults in San Francisco. *Archives of General Psychiatry, 75,* 385–394.

Moniz, C. (1994). Alocohol and bone. *British Medical Bulletin, 50,* 67–75.

Rivers, P.C. (1994). *Alcohol and human behavior: theory, research, & practice.* Englewood Cliffs, NJ: Prentice-Hall.

Russell, D. (1986). The secret trauma: Incest in the lives of girls and women. In Straussner, S., & Zelvin, E. (Eds.), *Gender and addictions: Men and women in treatment.* New York: Guilford.

Smith, J.W. (1982). Neurological disorders in alcoholism. In Estes, N.J. & Heinemann, M.E. (Eds.), *Alcoholism development, consequences, and interventions.* St. Louis: Mosby.

Standridge, J. (Nov. 1998). *Alcohol abuse in the elderly.* Internet article: http://www.sma.org/medbytes/gm_9.htm

Teusch, R. (1997). Substance-abusing women and sexual abuse. In Straussner, S., & Zelvin, E. (Eds.), *Gender and addictions: Men and women in treatment.* New York: Guilford.

van Wormer, K. (1997). *Alcoholism treatment: A social work perspective.* Chicago: Nelson-Hall Publishers.

Victor, M. & Martin, J.B. (1991). In Wilson, J.D., Braunwald, E., Isselbacher, K. J., Petersdorf, R.G., Martin, J.B., Fauci, A.S., & Root, R.K. (Eds.), *Harrison's principles of internal medicine* (12th ed.). New York: McGraw-Hill, Inc.

Wegscheider-Cruse, S. (1989). *Another chance: Hope and health for the alcoholic family* (2nd ed.) Palo Alto, CA: Science and Behavior Books, Inc.

Chapter IV

THEORIES OF AGING

... that older people prefer to disengage from life, to withdraw into themselves, choosing to live alone or perhaps with only their peers. Ironically, some gerontologists themselves hold these views.

Butler, 1975

We turn older with years, but newer every day.

Emily Dickinson

Germane to the effective formulation of an elder-specific treatment plan for the recovering alcoholic is the counselor's assessment of the client's reactions to societal expectations and perceptions of the elderly in contemporary United States. These essential issues and questions must be explored by the alcoholism counselor for each client. Some answers may lie within the forthcoming theories on aging that describe how people evolve through the aging process. Clearly no single theory explains the dynamics of aging because of its individualized nature. Nonetheless, certain features of these theories may provide insight into how the aging process and its attendant challenges and difficulties may precipitate and/or exacerbate elderly alcoholism. The following aging theories are described: activity theory, disengagement theory, modernization theory, labeling theory, exchange theory, continuity theory, and phenomenological theory.

ACTIVITY THEORY

Activity theory, no doubt the best known of the aging theories, postulates that there is a positive correlation between high activity levels and high life satisfaction. Crandall (1991) maintains that there is a greater likelihood of high life satisfaction if the activity is informal and on "a frequent basis" (Butler, 1975). Activity theory assumes that major losses diminish one's self-concept and that frequent, informal activity cushions the losses' impact. The theory further postulates that to compensate for losses, the bereaved must replace losses with new activities maintained at the same level as undertaken in middle age. Although supportive of activity theory, Atchley (1991) maintains that older people do not need to substitute former roles and activities to age optimally. Instead, they can simply "redistribute their time, energy and emotional commitments among their remaining roles and activities," a process he refers to as "consolidation" (Atchley, 1991, p. 264). He further suggests that if older people, for whatever reasons, no longer partake in the same activities as they did when younger, that they need to find suitable substitutes. Atchley continues that "retirees are expected to find substitutes for work and bereaved people are expected to look for new friends and loved ones to replace those who have died" (Archley, 1991, p. 263). Similarly, alcoholism counselors typically recommend that the recovering alcoholic seek out new nondrinking friends to replace their former alcoholic friends who might precipitate a relapse. It would behoove alcoholism counselors to refer clients to support groups to address unresolved loss-grief issues.

DISENGAGEMENT THEORY

Disengagement theory is considered by many to be the antithesis of activity theory; rather than people replacing lost activities, proponents of this theory insist that the elderly should withdraw from society to assume a passive, dormant lifestyle. Disengagement theory, much like functional theory that stresses the need to establish social order, contains three basic propositions as described by Cockerham (1991):

1. A process of mutual withdrawal of aging individuals and society from each other is natural;
2. This process of withdrawal is inevitable; and
3. It is also necessary for "successful" aging. (p. 51)

Cockerham (1991) explains that disengagement is a process whereby the elderly voluntarily relinquish their roles to a younger generation so that continuity and stability of the social order survives (Cockerham, 1991). Lowy (1991) argues that disengagement theory as originally formulated by Cummings and Henry has been "misunderstood," and even though older people are forced to relinquish certain activities such as gainful employment through forced retirement, they do seek productive roles when provided. Lowy arduously attacks the assumption that older people are forced into institutions, because statistics show that only about 5 percent of the elderly reside in nursing homes (Lowy, 1991).

According to Atchley (1991), disengagement theory caused considerable controversy because of the long-time acceptance of the "conventional wisdom that keeping active was the best way to deal with aging" (Atchley, 1991,

p. 215). Discouraging social isolation for the recovering alcoholic is a major challenge, because discontinuing familiar behaviors, however dysfunctional, are likely to cause a sense of insecurity. The need to "engage" and to not "disengage" in meaningful social intercourse should be encouraged by counselors, because social isolation will likely contribute to relapse.

MODERNIZATION THEORY

Although Cowgill is probably the most notable proponent of modernization theory, it was first introduced by Simmons (1945) in his book *The Role of the Aged in Primitive Society* (Simmons, 1945). Modernization theory includes four influences and/or developments that purport to lower the status of those undergoing the aging process.

1. Health technology: Because of advanced health technology causing birth and survival rates to increase, the population of young persons will likewise increase and thereby make competition for jobs keener. At the same time, life expectancy increases as older people live longer. With the older segment of the population perceived as a threat for jobs, forced retirement is considered by some as the logical solution.

2. "Economic modernization/development:" Through increased knowledge there evolves the development of high-status specialized occupations in urban areas. Because younger people are generally mobile, they can compete more effectively than older people who are left behind in rural areas in low-status occupations.

3. Urbanization: As a result of younger people moving into the cities to seek better jobs, the extended family is disrupted, effectively causing the demise in status of elders by virtue of a younger generation no longer interdependent on their elders. Another contributing factor is that younger people residing in urban areas are close to sources for knowledge; that is, with increased knowledge a younger generation is able to assume the position of power once held by an older generation; thereby, a significant transfer of power has ensued (Crandall, 1991). Because high self-esteem and a healthy self-concept are essential for successful alcoholism recovery, the aforementioned developments can undermine the primary treatment goal, sobriety. With older and younger people in competition for alcoholism treatment services, the younger able-bodied workers who are needed to fill technical positions will likely be given preference over an older population whose job productivity is considerably diminished or, at best, in decline.

LABELING THEORY

Sociological labeling theory postulates that society's perception of an individual will influence behavior. For example, on field trips to nursing homes with my students, I ask them to closely observe interactions between residents and staff. Invariably, a staff member addresses the elderly resident in a condescending, childlike fashion. "Oh, honey, you shouldn't do that." Students invariably note that residents will react with childlike behavior. The perception of the nursing home resident as childlike and senile effectively supercedes the image of a proud, dignified, mature, older adult. Crandall (1991) astutely describes the impact of this parent-child interaction:

> . . . once an individual is given the status of "senile," it is this status to which others will respond first. Once labeled, it is difficult for us to change the label because our behavior is interpreted in light of the new identity. Often behavior that is contradictory to the label will be ignored and behavior that supports the new identity will be emphasized. For example, if an older person who has been labeled "senile" exhibits coherent behavior, this behavior will be ignored or minimized by the belief that the person is having a "good day." However, slips of the tongue, the forgetting of a date, or any change in habits or appearance will reinforce the "fact" of senility. Even successfully recovering alcoholics experience difficulty losing the alcoholism label. An eighty-one-year-old recovering alcoholic once disclosed to me that: "After six years of recovery, I "slipped" and had a few drinks, but that was it, just a few drinks. Yet, everyone who was aware of the "slip" said nothing and they didn't have to because I could see it on their faces. They were 'see I told you so looks'. Put it this way: They weren't looks of support, but instead of a reminder that once a drunk, always a drunk. (p. 106)

A major challenge in successful alcoholism recovery is coping with the stigma many people associate with alcoholism, and for the recovering alcoholic a negative perception can serve to reinforce poor self-concept and low self-esteem. It is of paramount importance that the elderly client acquire a positive self-concept and a healthy self-esteem to be sufficiently motivated to learn nonalcoholic behaviors and to recover successfully.

EXCHANGE THEORY

Exchange theory is based on an interdependent relationship between older people and the nonelderly, wherein rewards, both material and non-material including money, property, services, love, affection, information, labor, and respect, are exchanged with others. The participants in this inter-personal exchange negotiate on the premise that the rewards will be greater than the costs or at least of a comparable value. But older people negotiate in this system at a disadvantage, because, as Atchley (1991, p. 293) asserts, "Older people are often assumed to have less up-to-date information, obso-lete skills, and inadequate physical strength or endurance." This discrepan-cy in exchange abilities is reflected when the elderly, who are essentially powerless, try to negotiate in a competitive, capitalistic system that favors the "haves" over the "have nots" and that glorifies strength and loathes weak-ness.

An elderly person in need of alcoholism treatment may discover a bureau-cratic health system that neither encourages nor desires the elderly person to enter treatment (Dowd, 1975). Dowd, who developed exchange theory, identified the inherent inequities with which elderly clients are faced when negotiating for power in a society that does not value elderly resources. Dowd noted, however, that the affluent elderly fared well, whereas the impoverished elderly's exchange powers were diminished. Crandall (1991) suggests that the elderly who lack affluence and power have but one recourse to obtain needed resources, including "retirement income, medical insur-ance, and other benefits": they must assume passive, compliant roles rather than aging gracefully with their dignity and self-respect intact, clearly inap-propriate behaviors for successful alcoholism recovery (Quadagno, 1999). That is, the powerless elderly must assume compliant roles to merely receive a meager subsistent existence from the power elite in a society that extols strength and power.

Continuity Theory

Some theorists view continuity theory as "a more formal elaboration of activity theory" (Quadagno, 1999, p. 28). Continuity theory suggests that the "traits, interests, and behavior" one had before old age continue into old age, thus a person reacts to the aging process consistently to ways in which he or she adjusted to changes before old age (Cockerham, 1991, p. 56). That is, how people face challenges in middle age is indicative of how they will face challenges in their later years. The theory is not without controversy as Atchley differentiates normal from pathological aging. Atchley (1989, pp.

183–84) alludes to "usual, commonly encountered patterns of human aging. . . .It can be distinguished from pathological aging by a lack of physical or mental disease." What Atchley (1991) means by "pathological aging" perhaps can be discerned in his assertion that,

> The fact that alcoholism is related to deviance is dramatically illustrated by the finding that 53 percent of men and 30 percent of women over 60 admitted to a Texas psychiatric screening agency were diagnosed as suffering from alcoholism. (p. 319)

Atchley continues to disclose his narrow perception that there is a close correlation between elderly alcoholism and social deviance when he asserts that:

> Just about every textbook on deviance contains a section on alcoholism. Addiction to alcohol has probably been recognized as destructive to society's functioning for thousands of years. Chapter 12 discussed alcohol abuse as a form of escapism; here we look at alcoholism as it contributes to the elders as deviant. (p. 319)

PHENOMENOLOGICAL THEORY

Phenomenological theory assumes that everyone has a unique perceptual framework that was determined by one's specific socialization; that is, each person perceives and interprets world phenomena differently from others. Varying types of socialization and early-life experiences and events will determine one's world view. Because of the highly abstract nature of phenomenological theory, it would be difficult to subject this theory to vigorous scientific studies; the theory has, therefore, not received sufficient empirical testing (Crandall, 1991). Despite a lack of testing, there seems to be some relevancy to how elderly alcoholics may have perceived socially acceptable activity when they first began drinking at an early age, especially considering how impressionable young people are to alcohol advertisements for alcoholic products.

Phenomenological theory is significantly germane to understanding how gender-specific socialization in some situations perpetuates alcohol abuse in men. A more comprehensive discussion on the subject is presented in Chapter VI.

SUMMARY

This chapter described several theories of aging that identified societal attitudes and perceptions toward the elderly and society's values of the elderly. The elderly's reactions will provide invaluable information to the alcoholism counselor whose goal is to provide viable services to the recovering elderly alcoholic.

GLOSSARY OF TERMS

Activity theory: This theory postulates that older people need to assume activity levels and lifestyles comparable to those in middle age to attain high life satisfaction and a healthy self-concept in late life. Should active participation in a former role be impractical, then he or she should replace the lost role(s) with new ones at a comparable activity level. It needs to be stated that there are several, varied interpretations of activity theory.

Continuity theory: Was first developed by Robert Atchley and stresses the importance of personality in making successful adjustments to old age; that is, continuity of personality is required despite undergoing certain changes associated with aging.

Disengagement theory: This theory presumes that the elderly voluntarily disengage from former roles because of changes in the aging process, and that a transfer of roles and power are essential to maintain the social order.

Exchange theory: A theory that suggests that interactions between the elderly and nonelderly decrease because the former have fewer resources and of lesser value to exchange. The theory further suggests that the negotiators strive to maximize their rewards at the lowest costs that predictably put the nonaffluent elderly at a disadvantage.

Labeling theory: A theory that postulates that people act out ways in which society perceives and stereotypes them. The theory also includes the notion that one's sense of worth (i.e., self-esteem and self-concept) is contingent on society's stereotypes.

Modernization theory: This theory operates on the premise that through modern health technology, economic modernization, and urbanization the status of the elderly will decline.

Phenomenological theory: This theory purports that how one perceives and interprets phenomena is influenced by his or her specific socialization.

STUDY QUESTIONS

1. As an alcoholism counselor, how would you integrate activity theory into a treatment plan for an elderly alcoholic?

2. Explain the dissimilarities between disengagement and activity theories.

3. What three events influenced the modernization theory? Describe each event.

4. Through examples, show how labeling theory could affect the treatment outcome for an elderly alcoholic.

5. What are possible implications for the nonaffluent elderly person as a participant in an exchange theory negotiation?

6. Atchley describes elderly alcoholism as a form of deviant behavior. How might deviant perceptions of the elderly alcoholic influence treatment outcomes?

7. Of what possible relevance is phenomenological theory in age-specific alcoholism treatment?

REFERENCES

Atchley, R.C. (1989). A continuity theory of normal aging. *The Gerontologist, 29.* 183–90.

Atchley, R.C. (1991). *Social forces and aging: An introduction to social gerontology* (6th ed.). Belmont, CA: Wadsworth Publishing Co.

Butler, R.N. (1975). *Why survive?* New York: Harper & Row.

Cockerham, W.C. (1991). *This aging society.* Englewood Cliffs, NJ: Prentice-Hall.

Crandall, R.C. (1991). *Gerontology: A behavioral science approach* (2nd ed.). New York: McGraw-Hill, Inc.

Dowd, J.J. (1975). Aging as exchange: A preface to theory. *Journal of Gerontology, 30*(5): 584–594.

Lowy L. (1991). *Social work with the aging: The challenge and promise of the later years* (2nd ed.). Prospect Heights, IL: Waveland Press, Inc.

Quadagno, J. (1999). *Aging and the life review course.* New York: McGraw-Hill.

Simmons, L.W. (1945), *The role of the aged in primitive society.* New Haven, CT: Archon Books.

Chapter V

DIFFICULTY IN IDENTIFICATION ("HIDDEN ALCOHOLISM")

The National Institute on Alcohol Abuse and Alcoholism reported that it is more difficult to identify alcoholism in the elderly than with other age groups, because the retired elderly typically have limited interactions with "social, legal, and other networks, (sic, and) there are fewer opportunities for their alcohol abuse or alcoholism to be observed." Adding to the difficulties in identifying alcoholism, elderly persons are likely to visit primary health care facilities where the presenting problem may be symptomatic of alcoholism, such as depression, malnutrition, insomnia, cognitive problems, and loss of interest in life (National Institute on Alcohol Abuse and Alcoholism Report No. 40).

STEREOTYPICAL ELDERLY ALCOHOLIC

The stereotypical perception of the elderly alcoholic's appearance contributes to the identification difficulties. Anita Shipman, a substance abuse specialist who provides services to the elderly, explains that:

> The word "alcoholic" usually brings to mind a disheveled person who at the end of the day passes out on the bed in a room strewn with paper plates and unwashed clothes. That image is correct only a small percentage of the time. In fact, in some cases the alcoholic's home or apartment will be overly neat. Many people also assume that the alcoholism won't be hard to detect. Empty liquor bottles will be on the kitchen counter [sic, and] the person will have alcohol on his breath and by mid-day, you'll see him take a drink. Not true again. In about 100 cases of alcoholism that I have dealt with over the past two years as a geriatric substance abuse specialist, I saw only one person actually take a drink and I rarely smelled alcohol on any-

one's breath. Given the nature of the disease and the denial that surrounds alcoholism, it may be hard to detect. (SIRS, 1990, pp. 18–21)

To complicate the identification of alcoholics are the subtle symptoms exhibited by elderly alcoholics, which can make a definitive alcoholism diagnosis difficult. Blake (1990) insists that the difficulty associated with making an accurate alcoholism diagnosis is more "fundamental than just the lack of instruments specific to older persons" (Blake, 1990, p. 357). Common factors causing difficulties in identifying the elderly alcoholic relate to the behaviors exhibited by both the alcoholic and the family members, including shame, secretiveness, confusion, and accidents.

SHAME

Elderly alcoholics and their family members frequently experience a deep sense of shame associated with alcoholic drinking behaviors and are therefore reluctant to seek professional treatment. Also, the family members, although they may not be alcoholics, are part of the "family disease" and exhibit many of the alcoholic's behaviors, especially denial of the disease.

SECRETIVENESS

Unlike younger drinkers who are apt to boisterously announce that they are going to get "blasted" or "bombed out of my mind," the elderly alcoholic tends to drink secretively without announcing his or her drinking intentions. Coupled with the alcoholic family's interest to keep the disease a "family secret," there is less likelihood of finding help.

CONFUSION

Elderly alcoholics and their family members will often attribute symptoms of alcoholism to the aging process, including confused mental states associated with profound memory loss, extreme mood swings, and disorientation. Even physicians, and other health professionals, experience difficulty in differentiating the symptoms of alcoholism with the aging process because of the striking behavioral similarities.

ACCIDENTS

Statistically, there is a close relationship between a high incidence of accidental injuries and alcoholism. One study reported that 14 percent of the persons involved in vehicular accidents were elderly persons with high blood alcohol levels (Higgins, Wright, & Wrenn, 1996). Another report attributed alcohol as a major factor in older people suffering bone fractures from falls (Council on Scientific Affairs, 1996).

NONSPECIFIC PRESENTATIONS

The criteria commonly used to identify alcoholics are impractical for use with the elderly caused largely by physiological changes associated with the aging process. Moderate alcohol consumption preceding old age may not cause significantly observable problems, but for the older person, confusion, falls, emotional lability, and adverse drug interactions may be symptomatic of moderate alcohol intake (Bienenfeld, 1987).

Bienenfeld (1987) warns that nonspecific presentations may be clues for elderly alcoholism and that counselors should look for reactions to medications. Such medications as tolbutamide (Orinase), phenytoin (Dilantin), and warfarin (Coumadin) will increase metabolism as a result of the interaction of alcohol. Other nonspecific presentations include self-neglect, falls, injuries, confusion, lability, depression, unusual behavior, incontinence, diarrhea, malnutrition, myopathy, hypethesia (Bienenfeld, 1987).

As reported in Chapter I, some of the factors contributing to difficulties in identifying the elderly alcoholic include drinking at home, misdiagnosis, public apathy, enabling behaviors, and the failure of drinking inventories to include late-life events (*As we grow older*, Atkinson, 1991; Brown, 1982). Although drinking at home for many elderly provides a less-expensive alternative to bars and the dangers associated with night driving, it perpetuates the "hidden" nature of the disease, hence the term "hidden alcoholism." As an excuse for not answering the door, they may use poor health, and as retirees, they generally don't have jobs where their alcoholism may be revealed. Furthermore, they tend not to evolve through the social service system, specifically the legal system for drunk driving. Hence, the appropriately coined term, "Hidden Alcoholism," aptly applies (Hazelden Brochure, "How to Talk to an Older Person Who has a Problem with Alcohol or Medication"). The Hanley-Hazelden Center has compiled a practical list of behavioral symptoms that are symptomatic of elderly alcoholism to assist in identifying the elderly alcoholic:

- Prefers attending a lot of events where drinking is accepted, such as luncheons, "happy hours" and parties
- Drinks in solitary, hidden way
- Makes a ritual of having drinks before, with or after dinner, and becomes annoyed when this ritual is disturbed
- Loses interest in activities and hobbies that used to bring pleasure
- Drinks in spite of warning labels on prescription drugs
- Always has bottles of tranquilizers on hand and takes them at the slightest sign of disturbance
- Is often intoxicated or slightly tipsy, and sometimes has slurred speech
- Disposes of large volumes of empty beer or liquor bottles and seems secretive about it
- Often has the smell of liquor on his/her breath or mouthwash to disguise it
- Is neglecting personal appearance and gaining or losing weight
- Complains of constant sleeplessness, loss of appetite or chronic health complaints that seem to have no physical cause
- Has unexplained burns or bruises and tries to hide them
- Seems more depressed or hostile than usual
- Can't handle routine chores and paperwork without making mistakes
- Has irrational or undefined fears, delusions or seems under unusual stress
- Seems to be losing his or her memory ("How to Talk to an Older Person Who Has a Problem with Alcohol or Medications," Hazelden)

Physical Abnormalities Associated with Elderly Alcoholism

According to Huntington (1990), a geriatric nurse with a specialization in alcoholism treatment, the elderly alcoholic may have all, or at least some, of the following visible "stigmata" abnormalities:

1. Usually male (women show the same symptoms except for reproductive system changes).
2. Thin–other evidence of poor nutrition such as nail, hair, and skin changes. Fatigues easily, often ill with URI or GI upsets, wasted muscles, cracked lips, bleeding gums.
3. Jaundiced (yellowed) eyes and skin.
4. Bloated stomach, sometimes a positive fluid wave. May have caput medusae (visible vein pattern around umbilicus).
5. Lurching, uneven gait. Similar to "old salts" walk.
6. Croaking, raspy voice (especially noticed in women).

7. Swollen ankles. Often unclean feet, uncared for nails.

8. Multiple skin lesions, scabbing, pustules, or increased pigmentation. Multiple bruises or burns in various stages of healing (results of injuries while intoxicated).

9. Oversedated (concurrent use of prescribed or OTC medications). This may be from drugs needed to treat other problems or may be simply from the abuse of other available drugs. Often it may be the result of a prescription drug given for symptoms of depression or neurotic behavior when the underlying or complicating problem was undiagnosed alcohol abuse. This multiple abuse is especially common among female alcoholics who have often been prescribed valium, Xanax, serax, elavil, etc. for their "symptoms."

10. Males: enlarged breasts, decreased chest, pubic, axillae and extremity hair, atrophied testes

11. Many dilated capillaries, usually on face but also occasionally on backs of hand and tops of feet.

12. "Rum nose" (large, bulbous, bumpy, purplish).

13. Very poor dentition

14. Very poor hygiene

15. Smells of alcohol, difficulty focusing on questions or purpose of home care visits.

16. Demented, evidence of neuropathies.

17. Depressed (Huntington, 1990).

Innovative Programs to Identify the Elderly Alcoholic

The Community Older Persons Alcohol Program (COPA), an innovative client-centered approach to treatment, embraces a "holistic approach" that does not require alcoholism as a criterion for receiving services; but rather, the client identifies the problem, which may include housing, marital problems, and loneliness. Because of the shame associated with receiving alcoholism treatment, some of the barriers and stigma are allayed with this approach, thus making client identification less difficult. The principle of self-determination is considered uppermost by the COPA staff in identifying the presenting problem. Rather than requiring sobriety as the treatment goal, "the person's overall well-being and helping to maintain independent living is of primary importance" (Graham et al., 1995, p. 28).

Elderly Services, an innovative program to identify the elderly who are at risk for alcoholism, was instituted at the Community Health Center in Spokane, Washington. Elderly Services enlisted such nonmental-health types as meter readers and bank personnel to identify isolated and high-risk elders in the community. For example, an apartment manager identified a 69-year-old depressed widow whose children were living in the Midwest. She was experiencing loneliness and had a ten-year history of "periodic alcohol abuse," as well as other health problems. Elderly Services arranged to provide a new primary care physician, participation in a grief group, and homemaker and nutrition services. Elderly Services provided the following data about their clientele:

> The 400 people presented with such problems as chronic physical illness (71%), social isolation/lacking a support system (69%), environmental/social stress (67%), significant problems with personal care/activities in daily living (62%), denial of illness/ problems (60%), significant memory impairment (59%), emotional depression (56%), alcohol abuse (19%), and mood altering prescription drug abuse/misuse (9.5%). (Raschko, 1991, pp. 72–74)

It is of particular significance that alcoholism is identified only after the identification of other problems. A follow-up research project conducted by Elderly Services provided the following information:

> . . . that 64% exhibited early onset of abuse while 36% began abusing after the age of 60. The conditions they presented to the doctors who prescribed the drugs were chronic pain (44%); grief reactions (36%); and chronic anxiety (20%). (Raschko, 1991, pp. 72–74)

Of particular interest in the report is that "60% of all persons abusing/misusing prescription drugs were current or past abusers of alcohol" (Raschko, 1990, p. 39).

DIAGNOSTIC INSTRUMENTS ARE INADEQUATE

The Michigan Alcohol Screening Test (MAST), a widely used diagnostic instrument administered to a geriatric population, has been criticized for its alleged ineffectiveness to identify elderly alcoholism. This twenty-five item instrument fails to include late-life items to which an elderly population can relate. Although MAST has generally proven successful with a nonelderly population, its shortcomings are apparent when administered to an elderly population. Another version of MAST has been developed to counter criticism of its use with an elderly population. MAST-G, the geriatric version, is a twenty-four-item diagnostic screening instrument that includes "five underlying symptom domains: Loss and loneliness, relaxation, dependence, loss of control with drinking, and rule making" (Blow, Brower, Schulenberg, Demo-Damanberg, Young, & Beresford, 1992). Despite efforts to develop a more user-friendly instrument to identify elderly alcoholics, the revised MAST version is not without its detractors. DeHart (1997), an expert in assessing the utilitarian benefit of such screening instruments, asserts that "tolerance did not emerge as a factor in this analysis and does not appear to be a reliable indicator of alcohol abuse for older adults" (DeHart & Hoffman, 1997, p. 39). The following discussion offers a brief description of commonly used alcoholism screening instruments.

SELF-ADMINISTERED ALCOHOLISM SCREENING TEST (SAAST)

The SAAST is a thirty-seven-item inventory used to identify alcoholism in medical patients. Of the 1156 sampling size, 80 percent of 520 alcoholics were correctly diagnosed. The SAAST does not specifically address late-life events.

ALCOHOL USE DISORDERS IDENTIFICATION TEST (AUDIT)

AUDIT is a ten-item screening inventory to assess the degree of harm caused by alcohol consumption. AUDIT was developed by the World Health Organization and includes three questions relating to the amount and frequency of drinking, three questions relating to alcohol dependence, and four questions relating to problems caused by alcohol. AUDIT's primary strength is in its cross-national focus, but sensitivity and specificity data for the elderly are unavailable (DeHart & Hoffman, 1997).

CAGE

CAGE is a four-item screening inventory that does not specifically address late-life items. The four questions are: (1) Have you ever felt you should cut down on your drinking? (2) Have people annoyed you by criticizing your drinking? (3) Have you ever felt bad or guilty about your drinking? and (4) Have you ever had a drink first thing in the morning (eye-opener) to steady your nerves or to get rid of a hangover? One positive feature is the instrument's nonconfrontational nature (Allen & Columbus, 1995).

DRINKING PROBLEM INDEX (DPI)

The DPI purportedly measures elderly alcoholism. This seventeen-item screening inventory is designed to measure "adverse consequences from drinking, excessive consumption, dependence symptoms, and escapist drinking." DeHart (1997) suggests that further research data are needed to determine DPI's effectiveness in administering the instrument to an elderly population (DeHart & Hoffman, 1997).

BONS SCREEN

BONS serves as an acronym for blackouts, objections, neglect of responsibility, and shakes. This inventory was administered to a sampling of 310 women and 672 men who were medical and surgical inpatients in two hospitals. Ninety-nine percent of the sampling identified "at least one of the four items, compared to 7% of the patients with a history of alcohol dependence" (DeHart & Hoffman, 1997).

U-OPEN SCREEN

U-OPEN is an acronym for the inventory items addressing unplanned use, objections, preoccupation with use, use in response to emotional distress, and neglect of responsibilities. According to DeHart (1997), "with older adult alcoholics, this set of screening items appears to be more sensitive than BONS" (DeHart & Hoffman, 1997).

The National Institute on Alcohol and Alcoholism reported that scales such as the MAST are inappropriately administered to an elderly population because the inventory items are designed to "measure the prevalence of social, legal, and job-related problems" (National Institute on Alcohol & Alcoholism, p. 2). DeHart (1997) stresses that screening tests and/or inventories should not be used for diagnostic purposes; rather, their usefulness should be to identify persons for "in-depth interviewing and further diagnostic testing" (DeHart & Hoffman, 1997, p. 47).

There seems to be a need to develop an assessment tool that includes life events germane to an elderly population. To reiterate this need, Schonfeld and Dupree (1990) assert that "there is a need on [sic, for] screening assessments which relate to more later-life issues" (Schonfeld & Dupree, 1990, p. 361). Although lacking reliability and validity testing, the "Beechem At-Risk Inventory," a twenty-eight-item inventory, seeks to provide a user-friendly assessment tool to identify an elderly population who may be at risk for late-life alcoholism. The inventory identifies unresolved loss-grief issues that may precipitate late-life alcoholism (aka "reactive alcoholism"). With the use of a Likert scale corresponding to each loss item, the respondent is able to measure the extent to which he or she feels the particular loss at the moment (i.e., in the "here and now").

With an emphasis in recent years to intervene at the primary level, as opposed to waiting until the person has reached acute, chronic levels of alcoholism, this inventory has been useful in identifying vulnerable elderly persons who are at risk for alcoholism. That is, the respondent may not be alcohol dependent but may be vulnerable to alcoholism and/or alcohol-related problems because of a disproportionately high number of unresolved loss-grief issues. In spite of the absence of subjecting this inventory to the rigors of validity and reliability testing, it has nonetheless served as a useful guide to alert elderly persons to their potential for alcoholism.

Only those life events for the category designated "Age Fifty-five and Older" were considered. An average of sixty-six was established from the ninety-six respondents in the study. The highest score attained was a 112, and the lowest score was a thirty-two. As a result of this survey of ninety-six respondents, the following ranges were established to approximate the extent to which the respondents were at risk for "late-onset" alcoholism.

	Low	Moderate	High
Range of Scores	32–49	50–69	70 +
Distribution of scores	14	59	23

Loss–Grief Ranking Scale

The following sample demonstrates how a total loss-grief weighted ranking can be computed. A general range will indicate the respondent's overall loss-grief rating score.

Categories of Losses

(A) Age 54 and younger	1	2	3	4	5
(B) Age 55 and older	<Least			Most>	

Sample Sample Sample					
19. Loss of status and/or role		does not apply			
(A) Age 54 and younger					
(B) Age 55 and older				X	

The respondents marked this loss in the four (4) category, thus indicating that at the moment, he or she feels the intensity of the loss greatly, but a five (5) marking would have indicated even greater intensity of loss. Each category is computed by multiplying 1 X the degree of loss, e.g. 1 X 4 = 4 four would be the computed score for Item 19. All of the individual item scores are added together to arrive at a total score.

If, for example, this respondent's total score was 68, it would fall into the high-moderate category range of fifty to sixty-nine. It would behoove the counselor to then examine more closely those loss-grief items marked 4 and 5 scoring to identify possible unresolved loss-grief issues to discuss.

The Beechem At-Risk Inventory follows:

BEECHEM AT-RISK INVENTORY

Check the appropriate categories for each of the losses. Then for each of the losses, rate on the 1 to 5 scale the extent to which you are feeling each of the losses.

Categories of Losses

(A) Age 54 and younger	1	2	3	4	5
(B) Age 55 and older	<Least			Most>	

15. Loss of independence		does not apply			
(A) Age 54 and younger					
(B) Age 55 and older				X	

1. Loss of ability to remember details		does not apply			
(A) Age 54 and younger					
(B) Age 55 and older					
2. Loss of a driver's licence		does not apply			
(A) Age 54 and younger					
(B) Age 55 and older					
3. Loss of a goal or a dream		does not apply			
(A) Age 54 and younger					
(B) Age 55 and older					

Categories of Losses

		1	2	3	4	5
(A) Age 54 and younger						
(B) Age 55 and older		<Least			Most>	

4. Loss of security due to abuse						
(i.e., physical emotional, sexual)	does not apply					
(A) Age 54 and younger						
(B) Age 55 and older						
5. Loss of a social life/social network	does not apply					
(A) Age 54 and younger						
(B) Age 55 and older						
6. Loss of financial stability	does not apply					
(A) Age 54 and younger						
(B) Age 55 and older						
7. Loss of self-respect (negative feelings						
toward self)	does not apply					
(A) Age 54 and younger						
(B) Age 55 and older						
8. Loss of someone special through death	does not apply					
(A) Age 54 and younger						
(B) Age 55 and older						
9. Loss of transportation	does not apply					
(A) Age 54 and younger						
(B) Age 55 and older						
10. Loss of a close relationship or companion						
(e.g., marriage, friend, pet)	does not apply					
(A) Age 54 and younger						
(B) Age 55 and older						
11. Loss of good health	does not apply					
(A) Age 54 and younger						
(B) Age 55 and older						
12. Loss of self-confidence	does not apply					
(A) Age 54 and younger						
(B) Age 55 and older						
13. Loss of independence	does not apply					
(A) Age 54 and younger						
(B) Age 55 and older						
14. Loss of confidence in others	does not apply					
(A) Age 54 and younger						
(B) Age 55 and older						

Categories of losses

(A) Age 54 and younger	1	2	3	4	5
(B) Age 55 and older	<Least			Most>	

15. Loss of time (e.g., wasted time)	does not apply				
(A) Age 54 and younger					
(B) Age 55 and older					
16. Loss of sexual satisfaction	does not apply				
(A) Age 54 and younger					
(B) Age 55 and older					
17. Loss of status and/or role	does not apply				
(A) Age 54 and younger					
(B) Age 55 and older					
18. Loss of mobility	does not apply				
(A) Age 54 and younger					
(B) Age 55 and older					
19. Loss of balance/coordination/dexterity	does not apply				
(A) Age 54 and younger					
(B) Age 55 and older					
20. Loss of bowel control	does not apply				
(A) Age 54 and younger					
(B) Age 55 and older					
21. Loss of bladder control	does not apply				
(A) Age 54 and younger					
(B) Age 55 and older					
22. Loss of hearing	does not apply				
(A) Age 54 and younger					
(B) Age 55 and older					
23. Loss of vision	does not apply				
(A) Age 54 and younger					
(B) Age 55 and older					
24. Loss of physical appearance (or loss of attractiveness)	does not apply				
(A) Age 54 and younger					
(B) Age 55 and older					
25. Loss of spiritual life	does not apply				
(A) Age 54 and younger					
(B) Age 55 and older					
26. Loss of a home	does not apply				
(A) Age 54 and younger					
(B) Age 55 and older					

Categories of losses	1	2	3	4	5
(A) Age 54 and younger					
(B) Age 55 and older	<Least			Most>	
27. Other losses (specify)	does not apply				
(A) Age 54 and younger					
(B) Age 55 and older					
28. Other losses (specify)	does not apply				
(A) Age 54 and younger					
(B) Age 55 and older					
29. Other losses (specify)	does not apply				
(A) Age 54 and younger					
(B) Age 55 and older					

Family Physician in an Identification Role

According to alcoholism researchers Burge and Schneider (1999), the family physician must assume a key role in the identification of elderly alcoholics because "(1) alcoholism-related problems are prevalent in patients who visit family practices; (2) heavy alcohol use contributes to many serious health and social problems; and (3) physicians can successfully influence drinking behaviors." Because alcoholism affects virtually every aspect of an elderly person's life, and there is an interplay between the various systems, including the physical, emotional, social, and the spiritual systems, the family physician is in an ideal situation to identify the elderly alcoholic in the early stages of the disease process, if not before onset of dependency. Before a physician can effectively assume the role of identifying the elderly alcoholic, appropriate training on the physical and behavioral symptoms must take place. Burge and Schneider (1999) assert that:

> Excessive alcohol use can affect part of a person's life, causing serious medical problems, family conflict, legal difficulties and job loss. Family physicians, with training in biomedical and psychosocial issues and access to family members, are in a good position to recognize problems related to alcohol use and to assist patients with lifestyle changes. (p. 67)

Finlayson and colleagues (1988) recommend that the physician conduct a longitudinal history (i.e., a drinking history) to identify such losses as a spouse, a job through retirement, and other losses associated with "major life events" and learn about the person's coping strategies. The family physician is in an ideal position to identify alcoholism in elderly patients, because their alcoholism is likely symptomatic of poor health, as opposed to younger alcoholics whose symptoms are more apt to include a "high tolerance for alcohol, antisocial behavior, and job-related problems" (pp. 761–768).

Currently the U.S. Federal Government earmarks roughly 70 percent of its annual substance-abuse–related expenditures toward drug-enforcement–related services. With a mere 5 percent increase specifically earmarked toward training professional health care providers to identify elderly alcoholics, significant inroads would be realized. At present, the people who make decisions on money appropriations for drug-related problems are more oriented toward law enforcement than to prevention, education, and treatment.

Contrary to a widely held belief that nursing home residents generally do not pose alcoholism problems, the National Institute on Alcohol Abuse and Alcoholism suggests that alcoholism in nursing homes may be as high as 49 percent as several studies indicate (Alcohol Alert, No. 40, 1998). Problematic for researchers is to the virtual absence of scientifically based research studies to support the claim that alcoholism is in fact highly prevalent in nursing home facilities.

SUMMARY

Numerous factors were identified to explain difficulties in identifying elderly alcoholics, including confusion in distinguishing symtoms relating to the aging process with those from alcoholism. The professional health provider should look for nonspecific presentations that may indicate alcoholism, including negative reactions to medications, self-neglect, falls, injuries, confusion, mental lability, depression, unusual behavior, incontinence, diarrhea, malnutrition, myopathy, and hypethesia.

Two innovative programs to identify the elderly alcoholic were discussed. The Community Older Persons Alcohol Program (COPA) does not require that the client accept an alcoholism diagnosis as a precondition to treatment. The primary reported problem may, instead, be identified as financial, marital, or health related. Elderly Services of Spokane, Washington, another innovative program similar to COPA, is dependent on referrals from others—but unlike COPA, Elder Services is not limited to professional referrals, because they have trained nonprofessional types to identify those symptoms characteristic of elderly alcoholics.

Several instruments were reviewed for effectiveness to identify elderly alcoholism. Primarily because of the exclusion of late-life items, the instruments were considered inappropriate. It is imperative that a user-friendly instrument be designed that is nonconfrontational and contains late-life items.

GLOSSARY OF TERMS

Axillae hair: Under the armpit hair.

Caput medusae: Visible vein pattern around the umbilicus.

Elavil: A trade name for amitriptyline hydrochloride, an antidepressant.

"Family disease": Refers to the alcoholic's family members who may not be alcoholics but are adversely influenced by the disease.

Hidden alcoholism: Refers primarily to the late-onset alcoholic in which onset began in old age and was hidden or masked because of several factors.

Holistic approach: Term has many varied and sometimes confusing meanings. In this chapter, it is used to describe an alcoholism treatment program that addresses numerous issues, including loneliness, marital, and financial problems.

Jaundice: Characterized by yellowness of the skin and/or eyes caused by abnormality of bile flow in the liver.

Myopathy: A muscle disease

Neuropathies: Refers to functional disturbances and/or pathological changes of the peripheral nervous system.

OTC: Over-the-counter drugs that are not required by law to be sold on prescription only.

Phenytoin (Dilantin): Used primarily for most forms of epilepsy (except petit mal) as an anticonvulsant and cardiac depressant.

Serax: Trade name for oxazepam, a tranquilizer (especially for the elderly), issued for acute withdrawal symptoms for alcoholism.

Tolbutamide (Orinase): An oral hypoglycemic agent. Orinase is the trade name.

Umbilicus: Navel.

Valium: Trade name for diazepam, a tranquilizer. Used for alcoholism withdrawal and delirium tremens.

Warfarin (Coumadin): An anticoagulant.

STUDY QUESTIONS

1. Name nonspecific presentations that may be clues for elderly alcoholism.

2. What are some common factors that make diagnosis difficult and explain each.

3. Identify physical abnormalities associated with elderly alcoholism.

4. Show the extent to which each of the diagnostic screening instruments is applicable to identify the elderly alcoholic.

5. Explain ways in which the Beechem Inventory differs from the other diagnostic instruments.

6. In what ways can physicians assume an essential role in identification of elderly alcoholism?

REFERENCES

Alcohol and aging. (October, 1998) *Alcohol Alert, (40).* National Institute on Alcohol Abuse & Alcoholism.

Allen, J.P. & Columbus, M. (1995). Assessing alcohol problems: A guide for clinicians and researchers. *The National Institute on Alcohol Abuse and Alcoholism,* 400–386.

As we grow older: Alcohol and medications. Pamphlet by Community Drug and Alcohol Commission, Pensacola, Florida.

Atkinson, R.M. (1991). Alcohol and drug abuse in the elderly. In R. Jacoby & C. Oppenheimer (Eds.), *Psychiatry in the elderly.* Oxford: Oxford University Press, 819–851.

Beechem, M. (1997). Beechem risk inventory for late-onset alcoholism. *Journal of Drug Education, 27*(4), 397–410.

Bienenfeld, D. (Aug. 1987). Alcoholism in the elderly. *American Family Physician, 36*(2), 163–169.

Blake, R. (July 1990). Mental health counseling and older problem drinkers, *Journal of Mental Health Counseling, 12*(3), 354–367.

Blow, F.C., Brower, K. J., Schulenberg, J.E., Demo-Damanberg, L.M., Young, K.J., & Beresford, T.P. (1992). The Michigan alcoholism screening test: Geriatric version instrument (abstract) Alcoholism: *Clinical and Experimental Research, 165,* 172.

Brown, B.B. (1982). Professionals' perceptions of drug and alcohol abuse among the elderly, *The Gerontologist, 22*(6), 519–24

Burge, S.K. & Schneider, F.D. (January 15, 1999). Alcohol-related problems: Recognition and intervention. *American Family Physician.*

Council on Scientific Affairs (1996) (1990). The world-wide smoking epidemic. *Journal of the American Medical Association, 263,* 3312–3318

DeHart, S.S. & Hoffman, N.G. (1997). Screening and diagnosis: Alcohol use in older adults. In A. M. Gurnack (Ed.), *Older adults' misuse of alcohol, medicines, and other drugs: research and practice.* New York: Springer.

Finlayson, R., Hurt, R.D., Davis, L.J., & Morse, R.M. (1988). Alcoholism in elderly persons: A study of the psychiatric and psychosocial features of 216 inpatients. *Mayo Clinic Proceedings, 63*(8), 761–768.

Graham, K., Saunders, S.J., Flower, M.C., Timney, C.B., White-Campbell, M., & Pietropado, A.Z. (1995). *Addictions treatment for older adults.* New York: The Haworth Press, Inc.

Higgins, J.P.; Wright, S.W., & Wrenn, K.D. (1996). Alcohol, the elderly, and motor vehicle crashes. *American Journal of Emergency Medicine, 14,* 265–267.

How to talk to an older person who has a problem with alcohol or medications. *Alcohol and Aging* (April, 1999). Center City: MN: Hazelden.

Huntington, D.D. (1990). Home care of the elderly alcoholic. *Home Healthcare Nurse, 8*(5), 76.

Alcohol and aging. (October, 1988). *Alcohol Alert, (2).* National Institute on Alcohol Abuse and Alcoholism report (Al. Alert p. 3)

Raschko, R. (1990). Gatekeepers: Do the case findings in Spokane. *Aging,* 361.

Schonfeld, L. & Dupree, L.W. (1990). Older problem drinkers–long-term and late-life onset abusers: What triggers their drinking? *Aging, (361),* 38–40.

Shipman, A. (1990). "Communities aren't helpless: Outreach to older workers works." *Aging* (2nd quarter), 18–32.

Willenbring, M. L., Christensen, K.J., Spring, Jr., W.D., & Rasmussen, R. (1987). Alcoholism screening in the elderly. *Journal of Geriatrics Society, 35*(9).

Chapter VI

SPECIAL POPULATIONS

Wisdom comes from the bad times, not the good times.
An elderly Cherokee Indian Medicine Man

This chapter will examine the impact that the stress associated with losses in the aging process has on special populations with extensive histories of discrimination and adversity. Chapter II identified and addressed the myriad of "stressors" to which an elderly population is subjected. "Stressors" mostly in the form of unresolved loss-grief issues were found to precipitate and/or exacerbate alcohol abuse and alcoholism.

The history of African-American slaves, Native Indians forced to flee their land in the forced march from North Carolina (Trail of Tears), Latinos subjected to anti-immigration policies and years of sub-par pay and dangerous working conditions as migrant workers, and, finally, the extreme discrimination directed toward Asian Americans and specifically the incarceration of Japanese-Americans in the infamous internment camps during World War II is well documented.

By examining special populations within historical and cultural context we are able to understand the interplay between unresolved loss-grief issues and the increased potential for elderly alcoholism and alcohol abuse. Also included in this chapter will be a discussion on the impact of gender-specific socialization on elderly men and women in American society and its influence in precipitating alcoholism, homophobic discrimination directed toward gay and lesbian persons, and the plight of the homeless elderly alcoholic.

PEOPLE OF COLOR

The term "people of color" will refer to African, Asian, Latino, and Native Americans. It is the author's intent to provide the necessary content to enhance the readers' knowledge base that will, in turn, facilitate competency in a culturally diverse practice with an elderly alcohol-dependent population.

Devore and Schlesinger (1996) suggest that people of color are especially vulnerable to "alcohol problems" by asserting that:

> With some exceptions, minority communities are at a disadvantage in respect to alcohol problems. Researchers are attempting to understand the dynamics by which factors such as the nature of the original encounter with American society, cultural dispositions, and experiences with the host society converge to minimize or exacerbate the likelihood of drinking problems. (p. 303)

By virtue of sheer numbers, elderly people of color are at a disadvantage in the distribution of power. According to the U. S. Census Bureau (1995) in 1994 one of ten nonwhites was sixty-five years or older; whereas, compared with the overall U. S. population, one of eight was sixty-five or older. It is projected that in 2050 the nonwhite elderly population will be two of ten. The white-dominant population makes the rules and therefore holds the power. Helms and Cook (1999) point out the implications when unequal distributions of power exist by asserting that "generally members of the socioracial group in the majority within the group have the most power." The authors further assert that "Whites frequently have more power because they are members of the group that define appropriate behavior; and men often have more power than women for similar reasons" (Helms, Cook, 1999, p. 244).

CULTURAL-SPECIFIC PRACTICE

African-Americans

To understand alcohol abuse among African-Americans, it is necessary to study it within a historical context. That African-Americans were encouraged by slaveholders to get drunk, especially on holidays, was a form of control in "keeping down the spirit of insurrection" (Joyner, 1991, p. 82). Frederick Douglas, the noted African-American leader principally responsible for assisting slaves to escape by way of the notorious "Underground Railroad," countered the slaveholders' strategy to pacify slaves by encouraging alcohol abuse by, instead, advocating sobriety, because being in possession of their full faculties was essential to attain freedom (Joyner, 1991, p. 82). By historical accounts most slaves were able to abstain from abusing alcohol. Gray (1995) writes that "this phenomenon was so pervasive that African Americans were thought to be physiologically immune to alcoholism" (Gray, 1995, p. 73). After the Emancipation, the "Negro problem" of alcohol abuse was blamed for White women being raped by Blacks and the intensification of racial strife. According to Gilbert (1991, p. 76) and Vega, Gill, and Zimmerman (1993), there seems to be a correlation between Black acculturation into the "majority culture" and substantially increased alcohol abuse. According to the National Urban League, the increase in alcohol abuse is attributable to stresses associated with unemployment, poverty, economic instability, and discrimination (Jacobs, 1993, p. 79). Goddard (1993, p. 11–18) insists that alcohol abuse is a coping strategy to medicate "racial pain."

Bell and Evans (1981) formulated a model that may have applicability in alcohol treatment by identifying interpersonal styles that correspond with differing world views embraced by African-Americans to optimally cope with racism:

Acculturate,

Biculture,

Culturally immersed, and

Traditional. (38, p. 81)

The model postulates that the interpersonal style must be identified in order to understand the various ways the person responds as an African-American in a "White society." The researchers insist that only after a precise identification of the person's interpersonal style is established can the practitioner intervene in a "culturally appropriate way." That is, to provide optimally effective alcoholism treatment, it is essential to understand how "the worldview of African Americans represents their general design for living and patterns for interpreting reality. It is how they make sense of their world and their experiences. . . and provides the process by which those events are made harmonious with their lives" (Butler, 1992, p. 29).

Seemingly, without either an understanding or an appreciation of cultural-specific differences in behavioral expression, an "excessive celebration" rule was enacted by the National Association of Collegiate Athletics (NCAA) that curiously affects mostly African-American collegiate football players whose expressive behaviors differ dramatically from the dominant culture that has been primarily influenced by staid Anglo-European culture. Because of unsuccessful efforts to obtain a copy of the specific ruling from various NCAA institutions, I phoned the Interactions Committee of the NCAA. Having received the "bureaucratic runaround" from the NCAA, who persisted on putting me on hold and transferring me from office to office, I opted, instead, to rely on the interpretation of "excessive celebration" from my alma mater's athletic director who thought that the ruling was enacted to discourage individual athletes from directing attention to themselves, rather than to the team.

Butler (1992) insightfully broaches this dissimilar behavioral expression:

> African Americans are a highly expressive people. Because of their sense of oneness with life and harmony with nature, they respond naturally and spontaneously to experiences. Their rhythmic sense of balance characterizes their physical movements as well as interpersonal understandings and interactions. Versatility and flexibility are two of their most positive assets. These two attributes have contributed greatly to their ability to adjust and adapt to the many pernicious experiences they have had to face. Because of these two primary attributes, as well as the many others who [sic that] are part of their emotional composition, African-Americans have been able to protect, preserve and maintain their deepest sentiments and traditional responses to people and things. As with all aspects of their culture, the emotional nature of African Americans is characteristic of their cultural heritage. (p. 23)

To prevent complete submission of people of color to the oppressive, dominant value system of White America, it is incumbent on non-White elders to preserve and transmit their ethnic culture, thus assuring cultural survival. Gelfaud (1994) offers a strategy for cultural survival:

> In order to survive, ethnic culture must be transmitted from one generation to another. One important method of transmitting ethnic values is through defining allowable and acceptable behavior for children, such as appropriate terms of respect for grandparents and obligations that the children have to the family as a whole. A second method of transmission is through setting an example, and in behavioral terms, serving as a role model. (p. 24)

One needs to transcend the American experience to understand the respect and reverence bestowed on elders by African-Americans. Butler (1995) writes that

> In African societies the ancestors are the most respected strata of the family. The elderly are the closest to the ancestors; therefore, they are accorded a great deal of respect. Consequently, African Americans of the diaspora have been observed to accord great respect to the elderly. (p. 36)

Devore and Schlesinger (1996) write that

> Traditionally, the elderly grandmother will then assume the "stabilizing role" and in her familiar caregiving role to her daughter's children will anguish over substance-abuse related matters. (p. 193)

Increasingly, researchers of African-American culture acknowledge the influences of West African culture. Because first-generation West African slaves to the United States were mostly "strong, mature individuals," with few children, most slaves were influenced by the tribal culture of West Africa that valued the role of the elderly (Riley, 1972, p. 22).

To provide optimally effective alcoholism treatment to west African-Americans, it is essential to understand a value system that has its roots primarily in West-African tribal cultures. A case in point is the African-American value system that is expressed by the core elements of African-American culture:

Self-identity: Each person is regarded as an extension of the cultural group as to "who we are."

Emotions: Because African-Americans are highly expressive, their emotions are based on "what we feel," which has its roots in their African cultural heritage.

Behavior: African-American behavior is a composite of who they are, what they know, and what they feel. But a key to understanding the essence of their behavior is that it is "an abstracted form as opposed to a concentration on concrete rules and standards" (Butler, J., 1995 in CSAP1, p. 33).

Knowledge: That "what we know" is derived through the senses, and that opposites can exist in harmony because they are interconnected. The interrelatedness of life experiences epitomizes the ability for opposites to co-exist in harmony.

Butler (1992) stresses the importance that these core values be culturally transmitted by the elders to preserve and facilitate intergenerational relationships when he asserts that:

> Traditionally, intergenerational relationships provided the fundamental process for transmitting cultural values and expectations, and they were sustained by the proximity of the young to the old. More recently, however, the socioeconomic and political stressors of society have complicated the ability of the extended units to remain in intimate contact. As a consequence, the character development of younger generations has been severely impaired, particularly around values pertaining to religion, discipline, education, work, sex, marriage, mutual aid, race, identity, and death. (CSAP1, p. 46)

For the counselor to achieve successful treatment outcomes in working with elderly African-Americans, it is essential to be knowledgeable of stressful life events associated with the aging process and the discrimination to which African-Americans have been subjected. Chapter X will address Nguzo Saba, also known as The Seven Principles, which is included in the annual Kwanzaa Celebration.

AMERICAN INDIANS

Although recognizable cultural differences exist among the myriad Indian tribes in the United States, there are nonetheless certain cultural values generally shared among tribes. Respect and reverence for the elders is demonstrated by the official and symbolic leadership positions assumed by Indian elders. In child-rearing grandparents have an official voice (Lum, 2000, p. 66). American Indians stress the importance of land, animals, and nature, and they strive to establish a harmonious relationship between themselves and nature (Barrow, 1992, p. 295). Of foremost importance, interrelationships between family members are intact as demonstrated by an "extended" family structure.

With the advent of industrialization after the turn of the 20th century, there emerged an individualistic spirit and a strong sense of competition, both valued traits in an increasingly capitalistic industrial society that conflicted with Indians' culturally laden sense of cooperation and sharing. "Rugged individualism" has its roots in Colonial America where survival in a sparsely-populated vast continent was contingent on an individualistic spirit of resourcefulness. With a value system diametrically opposed to that of the dominant White society, American Indians have traditionally stressed cooperation in group endeavors, with the individual subordinate to the group. Working interdependently with others in the problem-solving process is preferable to working independently of others. Cooperation takes precedence over competition. Although both American Indians and "mainstream Americans" may embrace a time orientation, there are vast differences. Although one time orientation accounts for precise time units (e.g. hours, minutes, seconds), the American Indian is oriented to seasons within the context of nature. Curiously, the Indian value system is more akin to eastern than western values. Corey (1993) delineates these differences in his analogy between "Western" and "Eastern" cultural values:

> Western culture places prime value on choice, the uniqueness of the individual, self-assertion, and the strengthening of the ego. By contrast, the Eastern view stresses interdependence, underplays individuality, and emphasizes the losing of oneself in the totality of the cosmos. From the Western perspective the primary values are the primacy of the individual, youth, independence, nonconformity, competition, conflict, and freedom. The guiding principles for action are found in the fulfillment of individual needs and individual responsibility. From the Eastern perspective, the primary values are the primacy of relationships, maturity, compliance, conformity, cooperation, harmony, and security. The guiding principles for action are found in the achievement of collective goals and collective responsibility. (pp. 113–114)

Largely because the value system embraced by American Indians is more suitable to agrarian societies, wherein sharing and cooperation are emphasized, American Indians have suffered greatly in a mainstream society whose cultural values encourage intense, individual competition. Sadly, withdrawal has generally been the response to an all-powerful value system that has influenced high unemployment, especially on reservations where it ranges from 30 to 70 percent, a low educational attainment, which averages 9.6 years of formal education, and an illiteracy rate that affects one of three adults (Brod & McQuiston, 1983). It is, therefore, not surprising that Lum (2000, p. 118) asserts that "Native Americans have the greatest needs in the areas of income, education, health, and mental health. Rates of arrest, drinking and unemployment are higher among Native Americans than among other ethnic groups."

Despite pervasive evidence that adverse social conditions influence alcoholism, it is a commonly held belief, even among alcoholism counselors, that American Indians are biologically predisposed to alcoholism. Unfortunately, many Indians have internally embraced the stereotypical notion of the "drunken Indian" who cannot hold his liquor despite the lack of scientific evidence to support this biologically based theory (Philleo,1995).

Mancall (1995) discusses this myth in his scholarly book, *Deadly Medicine: Indians and Alcohol in Early America:*

> Clinical studies have found no identifiable genetic trait that leads American Indians to abusive drinking. No measurable differences of any significant degree have been found to indicate that Indians metabolize alcohol more slowly than non-Indians. Further, Indians in North America have enough aldehyde dehydrogenase isozyme (ALDHI) to prevent the so-called flushing mechanism that occurs in individuals, notably Asians, whose livers normally contain less ALDHI. Thus American Indians' sensitivity to alcohol resembles that of the general population and cannot be explained on the basis of a simple inborn enzyme deficiency. (p. 7)

In 1997 at an alcoholism conference, I discussed the high rate of Indian alcoholism with an elderly Indian who held a departmental chair at a northwestern university. When I suggested that most current research findings do not support the once widely held biologically based theory on Indian alcoholics, he quickly retorted "You're correct but don't say that too loudly because Indians are the beneficiaries of substantial Federal money even though it's a myth."

Anxiety Drinking

According to Moran and May (1995), "anxiety drinkers," unlike "recreational drinkers," represent a drinking style developed as a reaction to environmentally based "stressors." The researchers write that:

> Anxiety drinkers tend to be older, and they drink chronically, are more solitary, and are generally physically addicted to alcohol. They generally drink cheap wine and beer and supplement with hard liquor, but they will consume almost any alcoholic beverage available. (Moran & May, 1995, p. 8)

The "anxiety drinker" is generally ostracized by Indian society, yet this drinking style is prevalent because of the adverse environmental conditions to which American Indians are subjected. Considering the American Indian's unique value system and the stress associated with having to survive within a majority culture, it is not surprising that the alcoholism rate is high.

Hispanics

Hispanics comprise a population of approximately 22 million and are considered by demographers to be the fastest growing ethnic group in the United States (U.S. Bureau of the Census, 1991, p. 45). The generic term, Hispanic, includes ethnic groups with cultural roots from Mexico, Cuba, Puerto Rico, Dominican Republic, and other Spanish-speaking countries. Mexican-Americans constitute the most populated U. S. Hispanic group with 13,421,000. Puerto Ricans are the next most populated with 2,382,100, followed by Cubans with 1,055,000, and 2,951,000 representing the remaining U. S. Hispanics (U.S. Bureau of the Census, 1991, p. 45).

Generally, U. S. Hispanics have an extensive history of economic problems, low educational levels, difficulty with the English language, high crime levels, and racism. Addictionologists generally attribute the high incidence of alcoholism among Hispanics to the unmanaged stress associated with social problems. For optimally effective intervention strategies to be included in treatment plans for alcoholism, it is essential for practitioners to be both knowledgeable and sensitive of the basic cultural milieu of the people receiving treatment, as well as their history. Although many Hispanics share cultural characteristics, including the "Spanish language, reliance on the family as the significant social structure, and the Catholic church, there are also many differences among the groups" (Padilla & de Snyder, 1995, p. 128).

MEXICAN-AMERICANS. Many elderly Mexican-Americans originally settled in the United States during World War II as part of the Bracero Program to import cheap "stoop" labor from Mexico to work as seasonal agricultural laborers. Many have established permanent residence in the Southwest, especially New Mexico, Arizona, Texas, and several Midwestern states. California and Washington also have sizeable Mexican-American populations, mostly because of the Bracero Program. Typically, these people were granted considerable cultural autonomy, but they were not encouraged to assimilate into "mainstream institutions" (McWilliams, 1968, p. 123).

As a precautionary practice, the counselor may want to refrain from using such designations as "Chicano," or "Mexican-American" until their preference is established. I have observed "Anglo" (White, English-speaking) professionals refer to Mexican-Americans as Chicanos only to be met with scorn by the elders who generally prefer the Mexican-American reference. Even with some younger persons the term, Chicano, is rejected; yet many young persons consider the Mexican-American reference a conservative, reactionary designation that is synonymous with keeping them down. The culturally sensitive alcoholism counselor needs to identify the acceptable designation for use, perhaps by eliciting the preferred reference.

CUBANS. The exodus of Cubans into the United States began on a large scale in 1959 during the Cuban revolution as a strong reaction to the expropriation of businesses and the large-scale implementation of agrarian land reform. According to Padilla and Salgado de Snyder (1995), Cuban immigration can be divided into several specific phases (Padilla & de Snyder, 1995, pp. 125–126). The first four phases involved mostly upper and middle-class Cubans, whereas the fifth, sixth, and seventh phases included mostly blue-collar, working-class Cubans. The seventh phase was probably the most controversial, the "Marielitos," because it included mental patients and prison inmates, but "no more than 20 percent" of this phase included social misfits, insists Padilla (1995, p. 126).

PUERTO RICANS. The history of Puerto Rico is characterized by political domination beginning with the Spaniards who systematically annihilated the entire Taino Indian population. As a former resident of Puerto Rico on two occasions (in 1961 for four months and from 1981 to 1982), I was reminded that the Taino Indians may have been exterminated physically by the Spaniards, but their spirit prevails—unlike the British, who rigidly enforced the segregation of African slaves of those Caribbean islands under their control, the Spaniards allowed racial intermingling. Because of the blood mixture mostly of African-Spanish, there has developed a strikingly handsome racial gumbo. The domination continued, even though political domination was transferred from the Spaniards to the United States as a result of the Spanish-American War of 1898 (Padilla & Salgado de Snyder, 1995, p. 124).

Under U. S. domination, in 1917 Puerto Rico became a Commonwealth territory of the United States, a vague status, that denied statehood status because, as some contend, Puerto Ricans were regarded as "racially inferior" (Longres, 1974, p. 124). With dual citizenship (Puerto Rico and United States) Puertorriquenos are able to travel freely between their mother country and the United States, and, as a consequence, there are large Puerto Rican populations in several large U.S. cities. Commonly, Puerto Ricans migrate to New York, hence the coined term "Nuyorican," where they may likely live for several years, only to return to their roots in Puerto Rico. It is common for elderly Nuyoricans to return to their beloved mother country to die on Puerto Rican soil.

Gender Roles in Latino Families

Researchers generally concur that men have traditionally assumed the dominant role, whereas the female family members are relegated to a survival, passive role in Latino families. The Hispanic family structure has undergone gender role changes, especially the Mexican-American family structure. Padilla and Salgado de Snyder (1995, p. 118) write "that gender roles have become more flexible in the past two decades in Latin America as a consequence of the spreading feminist movement worldwide." In describing gender roles in the Mexican-American family, Beechem (1995, p. 25) asserts that gender roles are "misunderstood by the casual observer, because wives will often give the pretense of subservience and then openly defy male authority by assuming major decision-making roles." Clark (1970, p. 150) writes that "the change toward a more equal relationship between spouses is not always apparent to Anglo observers, however." Falicov (1982, p. 134) explains that "Although in most Mexican marriages, there is outward compliance with the cultural ideal of male dominance and female submission, this is often a social fiction." Beechem (1995, p. 25) describes the relationship between el Senor and Senora Garcia in his case study when he writes that, "Even though Senor Garcia outwardly portrayed the authoritarian patriarchal leader, he looked to Maria (his daughter) and her mother for emotional strength." Matriarchal dominance has its origin in Mexico, where the elderly woman is known as "una torre," a tower; that is, a tower of strength.

Oscar Lewis (1959) in his well-known ethnographic novel, Five Families, describes the activities of an elderly Mexican woman who:

> . . . visited her son's home daily, usually arriving before noon, criticized the daughter-in-law's housekeeping, re-arranged furniture, supervised grandchildren, berated her son for his infidelity to his wife, and gave advice liberally. (p. 88)

There seems to be an interesting division of labor based on gender with some semblance of egalitarianism. For example, Cowgill (1986, p. 118) describes the elderly women who commonly assumes a dominant role within the confines of the household and "the elderly male is more likely to reach a plateau in activity and esteem."

Asian-Americans

Only a very small number of people in the United States react to the "flushing" response. The alcohol-flush reaction is characterized by headaches, nausea, heart palpitations, dizziness, and facial flushing. It is estimated that 50 percent of Asians experience this adverse reaction to alcohol, caused by a genetic mutation that prevents the liver from manufacturing sufficient amounts of aldehyde dehydrogenase (ADH), which serves to metabolize acetaldehyde, resulting in large buildups of acetaldehyde that causes discomfort and an adverse reaction to alcohol (Doweiko, 1999; Fishbein & Pease, 1996). The extreme toxic features of acetaldehyde along with significant accumulations in the blood system will cause the person to experience extreme physical discomfort. Researchers commonly report that alcohol use and abuse by Asians are at a lower level than among all major ethnic groups in the United States. The flushing response is considered to be an effective deterrent to alcohol abuse and alcoholism among Asian Americans. To avoid the physical discomfort that many Asians experience from this flushing, they purportedly avoid or abstain from alcohol use (Agarwal, Eckey, Harada, & Goedde, 1984, p. 113).

The Yamamoto, Lee, Lin, and Cho study, one of the few studies addressing elderly Asian and Pacific Islander men, reports that elderly Filipino men have the highest level of alcoholism among U. S. Asians (11 percent), and Japanese-Americans have the second highest at 6 percent, and the Chinese-Americans are at 4 percent (Yamamota Lee, Lin, & Cho, 1987, p. 115).

Value Orientation

The concept, "groupism," is generally practiced among Asians. "Groupism" as both a concept and a practice requires individual subjugation to the group to support the group's sense of well-being. Lum (2000, p. 75) asserts that "The individual has an obligation to the family and to others in the extended family and ethnic community." Asian cultures embrace harmony, confidentiality, and family obligations as essential values that require adherence. These values clearly have implications for treatment. To maintain a sense of harmony, for example, the Asian client will likely withhold information germane for assessment and treatment purposes for fear of jeopardizing harmony between himself or herself and the worker (Lum, 2000, p. 75). Information disclosed about family members is generally regarded as a serious breach of confidentiality.

To lessen the sense of shame in receiving alcoholism treatment, and to encourage disclosures that are germane to treatment a bicultural counselor, ideally of Asian descent, should be considered in providing alcoholism treatment to elderly Asians. Elderly Asians, especially the Japanese, are reluctant to use social services because of the profound sense of shame in disclosing disharmony outside the family unit. Hirayama (1987, p. 47) reports that "Many Japanese still consider that asking for help outside the family circle is not desirable because it is shameful to expose family problems to strangers."

LESBIANS AND GAYS

According to research, it is estimated that approximately 10 percent of the elderly U.S. population represents gay and lesbian couples (Berger, 1982, p. 305). Coupled with negative attitudes toward older people, a practice commonly referred to as "ageism," elderly lesbians and gay persons must also endure homophobic reactions. Van Wormer (1997) describes this "problem" in the following passage:

> A universal occurrence, homosexuality is a characteristic of all cultures and social groups. Its manifestations would be of no more than passing interest were it not for the heated response it engenders. To the extent that there is a problem, it is a heterosexual, not a homosexual, problem. This problem is rooted in society's intolerance for non-normative, gender-specific behavior—the name for this problem is homophobia. (p. 523)

Homophobia is an attitude directed toward not only gay men, but also lesbian women. The homophobic stress reactions experienced by both groups underlie social problems, namely alcoholism. The alcoholism rate for gays and lesbians is high, whereas one study of Los Angeles gays and lesbians reported that "31 percent of gays and lesbians" were alcoholic (Kus, 1988, p. 527).

Homosexuality has traditionally been considered to be a psychopathic (aka sociopathic) mental disorder, and it wasn't until the 1970s that the American Psychiatric Association's *Diagnostic and Statistical Manual of Mental Disorders* (DSM) declassified homosexuality; hence, the term no longer appears in the DSM. The National Association of Social Workers (NASW) belatedly announced in 1977 that it is "the right of all persons to define and express their own sexuality" (Hidalgo, Peterson, & Woodman, 1985, p.1). Despite these notable policy changes, there persists unrelenting, mean-spirited discrimination directed toward gay men and lesbian women that serves to precipitate elderly alcoholism. The disproportionately high rate of alcoholism among gay men and lesbian women is highlighted by Holmes and Hodge (1995):

In general, it is believed that some 10 percent of the total U.S. population suffers from alcohol dependency or alcoholism. The early research on alcohol abuse among gay and lesbian persons suggests much higher percentages for these groups. (p. 200)

Saghir and Robins (1973) reported that 35 percent of lesbian women and 30 percent of gay men were alcoholics. A major obstacle toward achieving successful treatment outcomes is the bar setting, from which much of the social life and activity is derived for gay and lesbian persons. Holmes and Hodge (1995) expresses the importance that the bar holds in the following description:

> . . . while racial and ethnic minorities have historically found a safe haven within their respective communities, gay and lesbian persons have not typically been accepted, even by their own families. It was necessary to create a sense of community. The bars provided this. Both in the past and now, the bars have often served as the location for community-based fund raising activities, for political rallies, and for events of special significance to the community. (pp. 202–203)

Although the bar provides for gay and lesbian persons a needed sense of community, it also perpetuates alcoholism and serves as an obstacle for successful alcoholism recovery. Holmes and Hodge (1995) assert, "the gay bar may be the only place to find connection with others, a sense of belonging, and a feeling of being with others who are like them" (p. 203).

GENDER-SPECIFIC SOCIALIZATION AND THE PROPENSITY FOR ALCOHOLISM

A keen observer of children at play will note that young boys will typically engage in so-called masculine games such as "war" and "cowboys and Indians," whereas young girls play "dolls" and "house." Although young boys learn to "brave it" and to repress their feelings as they play so-called boys games, young girls learn to express feelings; that is, they learn to communicate affectively. It is, therefore, not surprising that young girls grow up to be the nurturers in a marital relationship, typically an awkward role for men who had not been the beneficiary of such socialization. Although numerous factors have been cited as causes of alcoholism, there is increasing gender-specific socialization that should also be included. Silverstein and Rashbaum (1994) insist that biology alone does not explain gender differences and that our "differing capacity for intimacy" is not attributable to biology when they assert that:

Only the developmental paths we obediently tread can explain that distinction. It's time to question those paths, to alter the socialization process that sends boys and girls down such different ones. (p. 231)

Goldberg (1976) describes the disproportionate female influences in the early years of development, from the "mother, grandmother, and teacher, who is more often than not a woman." Whereas, the father is typically a "background figure, who is often away from home." Yet by age five or six, the male is expected to magically become "all boy—societal expectations for the male to exemplify maleness continues as he matures into adolescence, then into adulthood; and, finally, into late adulthood." He insists that for the male to attain appropriate gender behavioral expectations and to survive emotionally, he must disown his affective, inner feelings, which are associated with feminine influences, and transcend into the "macho male," so that he will not be labeled a "sissy" or a "fag." Goldberg (1976, p. 103) attributes the phenomenon of "reaction formation," a psychological defense mechanism that directs one's behavior to opposite extremes, to gender transformation.

Jerome Levin (1997) purports that there is an interrelationship between a sense of "machismo" and alcohol abuse and offers fresh insight into the interrelationship between alcohol abuse and gender-specific socialization:

> . . . there is something gender-specific about the way men drink and drug that is worth elucidating. The emergence of a literature on female addiction during the past decade has sharpened our awareness of this gender specificity and made us realize that there is a connection between maleness and the way that men use and abuse drugs. (p. 287)

THE HOMELESS ELDERLY ALCOHOLIC

There is some irony in the words of the Waterfront Rescue Mission chaplain (Pensacola, Florida) when he greeted the 2001 New Year by articulating his agency's policy on accepting the alcohol-smelling homeless person. "The only way we would turn someone away is if they [sic, he] didn't have a picture identification, or if their breath smelled of alcohol" (*Pensacola News Journal,* January 1, 2001). On New Years Eve 2000, the temperature dipped to a chilling 21 degrees in stereotypically warm, sunny Florida.

Kinney (2000) reports that there are more than 600,000 homeless people in the United States and that nearly half of them are alcoholics and characteristically "male, white, and elderly." In the following passage, the author describes a strikingly bleak scenario of the homeless alcoholic with a multiplicity of problems:

> The homeless alcohol abuser has been shown to be multiple disadvantaged with higher rates of physical, mental, and societal problems than the non alcohol-abusing homeless person. The homeless alcohol abuser tends to be male, white, and elderly. They often have troubled marital family histories and poor employment records, and they often are more transient and socially isolated. They are frequently incarcerated for petty crimes and often are victims of violent attacks. As many as one-half of alcohol-abusing homeless persons have an additional psychiatric diagnosis. Homeless alcohol abusers are at high risk for neurologic impairment, heart disease and hypertension, chronic lung disease, liver disease, and trauma. (pp. 452–453)

Considering the aforementioned description of homeless alcoholics who tend to be elderly men, it is not surprising that most neither seek nor are offered alcoholism treatment services. Miller (1999, p. 202) points out that many homeless alcoholics do not seek alcoholism treatment because of their distrust of "helping agencies," and the few who do request treatment are put on "waiting lists" because they either lack insurance or sufficient funds.

A series of studies based on fourteen treatment programs for homeless clients funded by the National Institute of Alcohol Abuse and Alcoholism (NIAAA) and the National Institute on Drug Abuse (NIDA) concluded that treatment that emphasized harm-reduction was more effective than those that were abstinence-based (Stahler & Stimmel, 1955). Even though abstinence-based treatment programs are seemingly less effective, at least it demonstrates an interest in the plight of the elderly homeless, something sadly lacking in the punitive attitude of the Waterfront Rescue Mission chaplain in Pensacola, Florida.

SUMMARY

Special populations, including people of color, lesbians and gay persons, and the homeless, experience stressful situations associated with the discrimination to which they are subjected. Unmanaged stress and discrimination as precipitating factors in the onset of alcoholism were explored. Also included in the special population category are men because of the nature of their "machismo" socialization, which lends itself to alcohol abuse for a disproportionate number.

Emphasis was placed on the need for counselors to acquire knowledge of their clients' cultural backgrounds to better understand the cause-and-effect relationship of alcohol abuse. This chapter, in effect, identified influential factors that cause elderly special populations to be vulnerable to alcoholism.

GLOSSARY OF TERMS

Acculturation: The process of adopting the cultural characteristics of the dominant, host culture. Acculturation is generally considered to be a less invasive process than assimilation, whereby few, if any, cultural characteristics are retained.

Bracero program: A program instituted by the United States government to allow Mexican agricultural laborers to enter the United States to fill unskilled jobs at low wages.

Diaspora: Its original meaning refers to the dispersion or displacement of Jews living outside of Palestine. In more recent years, it has taken on a more generic meaning to include any once homogenous people who became victims of dispersion.

Extended family structure: Unlike the "nuclear family," which consists of only immediate family members such as father, mother, and children, the extended family includes grandparents, aunts, uncles, and cousins.

"Groupism": Can be considered the antithesis of individualism and is commonly practiced in Asian countries, where group-related activities, especially in problem-solving pursuits, are preferred.

Homophobia: Refers to negative feelings and attitudes directed toward gay and lesbian persons.

Isozyme (ALDHI): Refers to an enzyme causing the chemical process of metabolizing alcohol.

"Marielitos": Those people included in the boatloads of Cubans who arrived in the United States in the latter 1970s. The "Marielitos" were mostly controversial people; they comprised about 20 percent of convicts.

Nguzo Saba: Black (African-American) value system

People of color: Racial and/or ethnic persons represented in the broad categories including African, Asian, Latino, and Native Americans.

"Rugged individualism":   A term describing the essential character required to survive the challenge inherent in Colonial America (i.e., individualism, competition, independence, and a sense of "hardiness").

Underground Railroad: Refers to a network of people in the mid-1800s (1830–1860) to assist slaves to gain their freedom through relocation in the North, notably southern Ontario, Canada. Many Quakers and white abolitionists were instrumental in this movement.

STUDY QUESTIONS

1. Why is an understanding of the elderly client's cultural history helpful in alcoholism treatment?

2. What is your understanding of a client's "world view?"

3. Compare and contrast "Eastern" vs. "Western" thinking.

4. What is meant by the "alcohol-flush reaction" and how does it affect most American-Asians differently?

5. Of what special significance does the bar setting have for lesbian and gay persons, and how does it influence alcoholism recovery?

6. How do you explain that the manner in which men are socialized in our society may contribute to future alcoholism?

7. Explain the myth that most American-Indians "cannot hold their liquor."

REFERENCES

Agarwal, D., Eckey, R., Harada, S., & Goedde, H. (1984). Basis of adelhyde dehydrogenase deficiency in Orientals. *Alcohol, 1*, CSAP (4), 111–118.

Barrow, G.M. (1992). *Aging, the individual, and society* (5th ed.) St. Paul, MN: West Publishing Company.

Beechem, M. (1995). Developing a culturally-sensitive treatment plan in pre-hospice south Texas. *The Hospice Journal, 10*(2), 25.

Bell, P., & Evans, J. (1981). *Counseling the Black client: Alcohol use and abuse in Black America.* City Center, MN: Hazelden Foundation, CSAP 4.

Berger, R.M. (1982). Gay and gray: The older homosexual man. Urbana: IL: University of Illinois Press. In Hooymonn, N.R. & Kiyak, H.A. (1988). *Social gerontology: A multidisciplinary perspective.* Boston: Allyn & Bacon, Inc.

Brod, R.L., & McQuiston, J.M. (1983). American Indian adult education and literacy: The first national survey. *Journal of American Indian Education, (1)*, 1–16.

Butler, J.P. (1992). Of kindred minds: The ties that bind. In: Orlandi, M.; Weston, R., & Epstein, L. (Eds.), *CSAP1: Cultural competence for evaluators.* Rockville, MD: U.S. Department of Health and Human Services.

Clark, M. (1970). *Health in the Mexican-American culture.* Los Angeles: University of California Press.

Corey, M., Schneider, J., & Corey, G. (1993). *Becoming a helper* (2nd ed.). Pacific Grove, CA: Brooks/Cole Publishing Company.

Cowgill, D.O. (1986). *Aging around the world.* Belmont, CA: Wadsworth Publishing Company.

Devore, W., & Schlesinger, E G. (1996). *Ethnic-sensitive social work practice.* Needham Heights, MA: Allyn & Bacon.

Doweiko, H.E. (1999). *Concepts of chemical dependency* (4th ed.). Pacific Grove, CA: Brooks/Cole Publishing Company.

Falicov, C.J. (1982). Mexican families. In M. McGoldrick, J. K. Pearce, & J. Giordano (Eds.), *Ethnicity and family therapy.* New York: Gilford Press.

Fishbein, D.H., & Pease, S.E. (1996). *The dynamics of drug abuse.* Needham Heights, MA: Allyn & Bacon.

Gelfaud, D.E. (1994). *Aging and ethnicity.* New York: Springer Publishing Company.

Goddard, L. (1993). Background and scope of the alcohol and other drug problems. In Goddard, L. (Ed.), *CSAP Technical Report, 6.* Rockville, MD: U.S. Department of Health and Human Services, CSAP 4, 11–18, 81.

Goldberg, H. (1976). The hazards of being male. In Staudacher, C., *Of men and grief.* New York: New American Library.

Gray, M. (1995). African Americans. In Philleo, J. (Ed.), *Cultural competence for social workers: A guide for alcohol and other drug abuse prevention professionals working with ethnic/racial communities* SAMHSA 4. National Clearinghouse for Alcohol and Drug Information 73 of CSAP 4, 73.

Helms, J.E., & Cook, D. A. (1999). *Using race and culture in counseling and psychotherapy.* Needham Heights, MA: Allyn & Bacon.

Hidalgo, H., Peterson. T.L., & Woodman, N.J. (Eds.), *Lesbian and gay issues: A resource manual for social workers.* Silver Springs, MD: NASW Press, 1985.

Hirayama, H. (1987). Public policies and services for the aged in Japan. In Dobrof, R. (Ed.), *Ethnicity and gerontological social work.* New York: Haworth Press, Inc.

Holmes, K.A., & Hodge, R.H. (1995). Gay and lesbian persons. In Philleo, J. (Ed.), *Cultural competence for social workers: A guide for alcohol and other drug abuse prevention professionals working with ethnic/racial communities.* SAMHSA 4. National Clearinghouse for Alcohol and Drug Information, CSAP4, 200.

Jacobs, J. (1993). Black America, 1992: An overview. In Tidwell, B. (Ed.), *The state of Black America. New York: National Urban League,* CSAP 4, 1–10.

Joyner, C. (1991). The world of the plantation slaves. In Campbell, E., & Rice, K. (Eds.), *Before freedom came: African-American life in the antebellum South.* Richmond, VA: The Museum of the Confederacy, CASP(4), 51–99.

Kinney, J. (2000). *Loosening the grip* (6th Ed.), Boston, MA: McGraw-Hill Higher Education, 452.

Kus, R. (1988). Alcoholism and non-acceptance of gay self: The critical link. *Journal of Homosexuality, 15:L,* 24–41.

Levin, J. (1997). Psychodynamic perspectives on substance abuse men. In Straussner, S.L.A., & Zelin, E. (Eds.), *Gender and addictions.* Northvale, NJ: Jason Aronson Inc.

Lewis, O. (1959). *Five families.* New York: Basic Books, 25-26.

Longres, J. F. (1974). Racism and its effects on Puerto Rican continentals. *Social Casework: 55:* 67–75. CSAP 1, 124.

Lum, D. (2000). Social work practice and people of color: A process-stage approach. Pacific Grove, CA: Brooks/Cole.

Mancall, P.C. (1995). *Deadly medicine: Indians and alcohol in early America.* Ithaca, NY: Cornell University Press.

McPerson, B. (December 8, 1999). *Vigil remembers homeless who did not survive.* Pensacola, FL: Pensacola News Journal.

McWilliams, C. (1968). North from Mexico: The spanish-speaking people of the United States. New York: Greenwood Press, CSAP, No. 1, 123

Miller, G.A. (1999). *Learning the language of addiction counseling.* Boston, MA: Allyn and Bacon.

Moran, J.R., & May, P.A. (1995) American Indians. In J. Philleo (Ed.), *Cultural competence for social workers: A guide for alcohol and other drug abuse prevention professionals working with ethnic/racial communities.* SAMHSA 4. National Clearinghouse for Alcohol and Drug Information, 8.

Padilla, A.M., & Salgado de Snyder, V.N. (1995). Hispanics: What the Culturally Informed Evaluator Needs to Know. In Orlandi, M.A. (Ed.), *Cultural competence for evaluators: A guide for alcohol and other drug abuse prevention practitioners working with ethnic/racial communities.* SAMHSA 1, U. S. Department of Health and Human Services.

Philleo, J. (Ed.) (1995). Introduction. *Cultural competence for evaluators: A guide for alcohol and other drug abuse prevention practitioners working with ethnic/racial communities.* SAMHSA 4. National Clearinghouse for Alcohol and Drug Information, XIV.

Riley, H. (1972). Attitudes toward aging and the aged among black Americans: Some historical perspectives. *Aging and Human Development, (3),* 66–70.

Saghir, M. & Robins, E. (1973). *Male and female homosexuality.* Baltimore: Williams & Wilkins. CSAP, 200.

Silverstein, O. & Rashbaum, B. (1994). *The courage to raise good men.* New York: Penguin Books, 231.

Stahler, G.L., & Stimmel, B. (1955). *The effectiveness of social interventions for homeless substance abusers.* Binghamton, NY: Haworth.

U.S. Bureau of the Census. (1991). The Hispanic population in the United States: March 1990. *Current Population Reports,* Series P-20, No. 449, Washington, DC: U.S. Government Printing Office, CSAP 4, 45.

U.S. Bureau of the Census. (1995). *Sixty-five plus in the United States.* http://www.census.gov/socdemo/agebrief.html

van Wormer, K. (1997). *Social welfare: A world view.* Chicago: Nelson-Hall Publishers.

Vega, W., Gil, A., & Zimmerman, R. (1993). Patterns of drug use among Cuban-American, African-American, and White Non-Hispanic boys. *American Journal of Public Health, 83*(2) 257–259.

Yamamoto, J., Lee, C., Lin, K., & Cho, K. (1987). Alcohol abuse in Koreans. *American Journal of Social Psychiatry, 4*(210–214). CSAP 4, 116.

Chapter VII

INTERVENTION

Older persons who are retired may not be regarded by society or their families as requiring treatment for alcohol problems
since their jobs are not jeopardized. Even when family members are embarrassed by their excessive drinking, they may
find it more convenient to deny or cover up the problem.
Thus, the criterion of what constitutes an alcohol problem
may vary.

Jung, 1994

CRISIS INTERVENTION

This chapter will focus on intervention strategies to successfully influence
the elderly alcoholic to seek treatment, which is the primary goal.
Before a discussion on specific intervention strategies ensues, a prevailing
belief shared by many, even some in the substance-abuse treatment community, will be explored: that before treatment can commence, the alcoholic must first "hit rock bottom," because it's only then that the alcoholic
will be motivated to recover.

"Rock Bottom"

The traditional approach used since the infancy of formalized alcoholism
treatment has been to wait until the alcoholic hits so-called rock bottom and
experiences major economic, social, emotional, spiritual losses, and major
crises. Conventional wisdom has traditionally embraced the belief that the
alcoholic will not be receptive to treatment until "rock bottom" has been
indelibly reached. Doweiko states that "the 'bottom' is the point where substance abusers have to admit utter, and total, defeat" (Doweiko, 1999, p.

369). But for many elderly alcoholics that may be too late for the ravaging effects of alcohol to take their toll with perhaps the onset of Wernike-Korsoff's syndrome or, worse, death. Wegscheider-Cruse (1989) insightfully addresses the pitfalls in delaying intervention:

> There was a time when it was thought that an alcoholic could not accept help until his disease had run its full course to the chronic phase–until he had "struck bottom". This pessimistic view seemed logical enough. How could anyone reach him earlier? By the time he was willing to admit psychologically that drinking was causing more pain than it relieved, he was really hooked physically. But, the cost of the long delay was high, nothing less than total bankruptcy of the person. For that reason alcoholism counselors and others have tried to find ways to stop the destruction sooner. (p. 75)

According to Beaver and Miller (1985, p. 81), "The aim of crisis intervention is to intervene with and on behalf of the client before maladaptation sets in." Schlaadt and Shannon (1994) write that intervention:

> is a process where an attempt is made by family, friends, and an alcohol-and-drug treatment counselor to stop substance abuse before a person bottoms out with the illness. It is a carefully executed process wherein friends, in a loving and caring manner, express their concern about the dependent's problem and cite specific examples of behavior they have observed while the dependent was under the influence of alcohol or other drugs. It is the goal of the intervention to get the dependent into a treatment center for help. (p. 230)

LEVELS OF INTERVENTION

Three levels of intervention and/or prevention have been identified that can serve as guides for addiction counselors: The primary, secondary, and tertiary levels of intervention.

Intervention at the Primary Level

The goal at this level is to forestall alcohol and/or prevent alcohol abuse for the person who, at this point, is neither an alcoholic nor abusing alcohol (Levinthal, 1996, p. 396). An example of intervention at the primary level would be a workshop for employees who will soon retire. As part of a pre-retirement counseling program, employees would receive alcoholism education within the context that retirement-related losses may lead to late-onset alcoholism. That is, intervention has begun before alcohol abuse occurs

(Carroll, 2000, p. 380). Intervention at the primary level for an elderly person is primarily directed toward the prevention of late-onset alcoholism. Unfortunately, our mental health community tends to intervene only when physical dysfunctioning is evident; that is, there must be concrete and, ideally, visible proof alcoholism is in fact a problem. At this stage of development, Western medical thinking lacks the sophistication so commonplace in Eastern medicine, where there is conceptualized an interdependent relationship between various components of human functioning. The interplay between the mind and the body requires meticulous scrutiny by the alcoholism counselor, especially in assessing the influence alcohol abuse has on the aging process as was suggested in Chapter III. The interplay between the mind and the body are significant components in the overall functioning rather than as separate, unrelated parts. Ideally, primary intervention should become an integral part of preretirement counseling, but realistically few organizations are inclined to implement programs to prepare retired employees to make successful life transitions.

Intervention at the Secondary Level

Intervention at the secondary level is designed to prevent development of serious alcohol-related problems such as the onset of alcoholism. Intervention at this level may also serve to curtail or eliminate alcohol-related problems from further development. An example is the elderly person who discovers that what had previously been considered safe, moderate, or even light drinking is suddenly causing such problems as prescription drugs interacting with even light to moderate levels of alcohol consumption. A goal for some elderly may be sobriety and, in other cases, reduction of alcohol consumption, sometimes referred to as a harm reduction strategy. Alcoholism at this early stage may not be evident without a comprehensive examination by health professionals trained in alcoholism symptoms. An example of appropriate intervention at the secondary level would be a physician advising his patient to reduce or to stop alcohol consumption, because alcohol is interacting with medications. Intervention, ideally, takes place during early stages of alcoholism (Carroll, 2000, p. 388).

Intervention at the Tertiary Level

Intervention at this level occurs when the seriousness of the problem has reached major crisis proportions, when alcoholism is in the advanced stages (Carroll, 2000, p. 394). A classic case scenario of intervention at the tertiary level is the client with Wernicke-Korsakoff's syndrome, also known as "wet brain, and Korsakoff's psychosis." Katherine Van Wormer (1997), a noted writer and expert on alcoholism, whose father had Wernicke-Korsakoff's syndrome, describes one of the most salient feature of the disease, confabulation:

> Confabulation is a unique characteristic that involves fantasizing to fill in the gaps of memory. Although the "tall tales" seem to be ridiculous fabrications or downright lies, there appears to be no "method in this madness" other than an inability to distinguish fact from fiction. Although individuals of this affliction can become paranoid on occasion, generally, they have a carefree unconcern about the present or future. (p. 95)

Although intervention with a person with Wernicke-Karsakoff syndrome is considered an extreme case of intervention at the tertiary level, the least severe case scenario at this level would be intervention with an elderly person who meets the standard criteria for alcoholism, either the late-onset or early-onset alcoholic. Clearly, the optimal level to intervene is not the tertiary level, wherein the elderly person has become essentially dysfunctional and has "hit rock bottom."

There are differing opinions among addictionologists about what constitutes intervention at the tertiary level; for some tertiary level intervention is when the disease has progressed to advanced stages (Carroll, 2000), whereas others identify tertiary level intervention at the point where there is regular use of the substance but the person "has not become a habitual user" (Fields, 1998, p. 299). Because of the wide range of definitions of the three levels of intervention, there exists an inevitable overlap.

Involuntary Client

Rivers (1994) has discerned differences between mental health clients and alcoholic clients regarding the extent to which they are motivated to seek professional treatment and their receptivity to behavioral changes. Typically, the mental health client has sufficient insight into his or her condition and, consequently, is often "self-referred"; it is, therefore, assumed that the desire to change is internally motivated. Conversely the alcoholic client has likely been referred by significant others and has reluctantly accepted treatment with strong feelings of anger and hostility (Rivers, 1994, p. 188). Without internally based self-motivation to influence the alcoholic to accept treat-ment, there is an immense challenge that once in treatment, while lacking the internal motivation to become sober, the prognosis for successful recovery is poor. With intense feelings of anger and hostility, and fiercely defensive in having been coerced into treatment, a major challenge is faced to encourage the alcoholic to accept and to remain in treatment.

Hepworth and Larsen (1990) describe the "involuntary or captive clients" who "come to agencies in acquiescence to ultimatums issued by spouses, par-ents, employees, or other significant persons." At this stage, they typically do not acknowledge alcohol-related problems, notwithstanding a physical dependency. The practitioner must therefore be successful in performing the following tasks:

> To neutralize negative feelings,
>
> To attempt to penetrate the client's refusal to acknowledge ownership of a problem, and
>
> To create an incentive to work on acknowledged problems. (p. 32)

Brief Intervention

Brief intervention, an intervention strategy used with increased frequency with alcohol-dependent clients, can appropriately take place at all levels of intervention. Fleming and Manwell (1999) recommend use of this five-step strategy by physicians during routine office visits. Brief intervention for alco-holic clients consists of five essential steps:

1. Provide an assessment and feedback to the patient concerning his or her alcohol use and related problems. The health care provider, typically a physician, describes the relationship between medical/physical problems and alcohol use.
2. Negotiate and set goals for establishing a reasonable plan to reduce alco-hol intake.
3. Identify triggers causing alcohol abuse and provide the patient with behavioral modification techniques to cope with these triggers, including the establishment of a support system.
4. Provide the patient with additional reading materials that reinforce the preceding steps.
5. Establish a follow-up support system that may include telephone contacts and additional office visits.

Fleming and Manwell (1999) report that their Guiding Older Adult Lifestyles project to implement brief intervention was successful in reducing alcohol consumption by 20 percent based on a sampling population of 158 elderly adults.

Societal Attitudes: Obstacle to Treatment

As an industrial society dependent on the strength of its workers to run the factories' machines, there is a strong tendency to be more concerned about the general welfare of our youth than the plight of the elderly, especially the frail elderly. Whenever alcoholism is identified in our youth, we are outraged and desperately, if not aimlessly, search for fast solutions; whereas for our elderly, we use avoidance and denial strategies or rationalize that "so what harm is there if they drink? After all, they've earned the right." The obvious question is raised: Do society's patronizing, condescending attitudes encourage elderly alcoholism? Jung (1994) astutely recognizes this attitude when he asserts that:

> Older persons who are retired may not be regarded by society or their family as requiring treatment for alcohol problems since their jobs are not jeopardized. Even when family members are embarrassed by their excessive drinking, they may find it more convenient to deny or cover up the problem. Thus, the criterion of what constitutes an alcohol problem may vary. (p. 260)

Coupled with the prevailing attitude that treating elderly alcoholics is inappropriate, there is also the likelihood that family members will feel shame and embarrassment that a family member is an alcoholic. The alcoholism counselor needs to be aware of these attitudes when either concerned relatives or friends request assistance from mental health professionals. Unfortunately, there is also a wide-spread belief that the elderly alcoholic cannot benefit from treatment, that he or she is far too set in his or her ways. Blake (1990) writes that:

> Family members, friends, service providers, uninformed professionals, and even the older client may share unduly negative expectations about the value of treatment. This may be the most important obstacle of all, but it is a belief that is contradicted by available evidence. (p. 260)

There is generally only minimal encouragement for the elderly to seek alcoholism treatment. Our society is eager to provide treatment to our younger population for whom the workforce is so dependent, whereas the elderly dependent's family suffers from embarrassment that one of their own is alcohol dependent. It is not surprising that the elderly are unmotivated to seek treatment, perhaps influenced by the attitude that they are unworthy of treatment and will only waste valuable resources that could be better used for a promising youthful working population. It should not appear as a shocking revelation that our fast-paced industrious society glorifies youth at the expense of its elderly members; unfortunately, there are implications insofar as discouraging the elderly to seek alcoholism treatment.

More than twenty years ago, Kola et al. (1980) identified the elderly as underutilizing alcoholism treatment services, to which he attributed "problems with ambulation or utilizing transportation" and negative attitudes toward the elderly. To counteract the underutilization of alcoholism services by an elderly population, Kola recommends increased use of outreach services and home visits (Jung, 1994).

It is apparent that the key to enhance successful treatment outcomes is to devise intervention strategies that will motivate people to accept treatment, with an intense, genuine desire for sobriety. The following discussion is an adaptation of the Johnson Intervention Model for an elderly alcoholic.

JOHNSON INTERVENTION MODEL

Vernon Johnson, a former pastor, departed from the approach of waiting until the alcoholic hits "rock bottom." In the 1960s he developed an intervention model that is now used by many alcoholism treatment programs in the United States (Fields, 1998, p. 267). Johnson's pioneering efforts have resulted in a very methodical step-by-step approach that uses a series of strategies to encourage the person to accept treatment. The typical scenario begins when a close relative of the alcoholic seeks help from an alcoholism counselor. The relative, for example the daughter, phones a substance abuse center to make an appointment to see an alcoholism counselor. At the meeting, the daughter explains that her widowed father continues to grieve his deceased wife very intensely since her death three years earlier. For about the last 1 1/2 years he has drunk heavily and had not experienced a drinking problem before his wife died. On receiving sufficient information about the dependent, especially his drinking behavior, the interventionist begins gathering the intervention team.

Gathering the Intervention Team

Step 1. The interventionist will direct the daughter to compile a list of persons who are especially close to her father. This list might include a few close friends, siblings, or a member of the clergy. Even though the intervention team includes only one or two family members, ideally the family should be involved in some capacity because, as Schlaadt and Shannon (1994) correctly point out, it's a family disease, and, therefore, a "family problem" (p. 230). Of potentially equal benefit is the inclusion of a friend who is an age cohort and sensitive to the aging process.

Step 2. The intervention team is formed. The Johnson Institute recommends three to five members as the most effective, but the optimal number depends on the specific nature of the intervention. Too many persons may be perceived by the alcoholic as intimidating and threatening. Members are then brought together and educated about alcoholism as a disease. As part of the educational component, it is stressed that alcoholism was not caused by a character defect, that alcoholism is indeed a disease with a number of possible causes. Predictably, members may express reluctance to be part of the intervention for fear of offending the dependent. An appropriate rebuttal might be that the alternative is inevitably a continuation of a low quality of life and premature death.

With the intervention team formed and educated on the basics of alcoholism, the group is ready to gather data concerning the dependent's drinking behavior and treatment options.

Gathering the Data

Step 1: The members are instructed to prepare written lists of the dependent's specific drinking behavior with detailed descriptions of specific incidents.

Step 2: Identify and then discuss treatment options in your area. After adequate discussion, determine the most viable. The Johnson Institute recommends making an advanced reservation in a treatment program so that the alcoholic can start treatment as soon as possible.

A formal treatment program with a staff physician to administer needed medications is preferred, because the dependent may experience severe physical withdrawal and die without medications to alleviate the physical withdrawal symptoms. For example, anticonvulsion medications may be needed. Alcoholics Anonymous (AA), Although a viable support group for many recovering alcoholics, provides neither treatment nor detoxification services and should be used primarily as an adjunct to formal professional treatment.

Rehearsing the Intervention
(One or Two Rehearsing/Practice Sessions)

Step 1: Designate a chairperson to direct the rehearsals and the actual intervention. With the potential for intense emotions and feelings by the intervention team members, the chairperson may need to prevent the intervention from becoming an arguing session.

Step 2: Go over each item on the written lists that team members have prepared. Team members' approval is required and revisions, may need to be made.

Step 3: Determine the order in which team members will read their lists during the intervention. With a specific order, you are able to avoid long pauses and, too, the most influential persons can lead off to break through inevitable barriers and defenses.

Step 4: Choose someone to role play the chemically dependent person during the rehearsals. Ideally, each team member needs to role play the dependent to gain a sense of how the dependent will react. The role playing serves as a strategy to gain an understanding of the dependent's inner world, a prerequisite to needed empathy.

Step 5: Determine the responses that team members will make to the chemically dependent person. If a team member gives the dependent person an ultimatum, then he or she will need to be consistent and not equivocate. "Each action on the part of the chemically dependent person must be met with a reaction that is in keeping with the tone and purpose of the intervention."

Step 6: Conduct the rehearsal: Both the rehearsal and the intervention itself begins with an "empathic introductory statement from the chairperson."

_____ (the name of the chemically dependent person), we're all here because we care about you and want to help. This is going to be difficult for you and for us, but one of the requests I have to start out with is that you give us the chance to talk and promise to listen, however hard that may be. We know that it's not going to be easy for the next little while. . .Would you help us by just listening?

It is important that the intervention be conducted in a setting that is not too anxiety provoking and is free of interruptions. Also, the intervention should not be conducted until the dependent is sober. It is essential that the dependent's role be established as that of a listener, and the group should maintain that role. As the complaints are read, there should be an attempt to precede each complaint with a positive statement, e.g., "You've always been a good father and grandfather, but I'm concerned about your heavy drinking." During the intervention, it is possible that the reality of the situation has occurred for the dependent and that he or she will now be receptive to treatment.

The Johnson Model has proven to be an enormously successfully intervention strategy for many alcoholics, but the individualized nature of the aging process necessitates the development of specific strategies that will be optimally effective in getting older people into treatment. The following strategies should be considered when conducting an intervention.

FIELDS' INTERVENTION MODEL

Richard Fields (1998) has formulated an intervention model that includes four stages: assessment, preintervention, intervention, and postintervention.

ASSESSMENT STAGE. After the trained interventist is contacted by the alcoholic's family member, an assessment is made to "determine if an intervention is appropriate" (Fields, 1998, p. 269). If an intervention is considered appropriate, they progress to the preintervention stage.

PREINTERVENTION STAGE. Included in this stage is the formulation of a group of significant others who will comprise the intervention team. Members are then educated about how alcohol affects the alcoholic and how the disease affects the family members behaviorally (Fields, 1998, p. 271). The members develop individual scripts and rehearse for the intervention.

INTERVENTION STAGE. Fields (1998, p. 274) emphasizes that each intervention "is different and unique," but there are essential commonalties for the successful interventions (the intervention team members need to be nonjudgmental and caring).

POSTINTERVENTION STAGE. After a successful intervention, there is a shared sense of relief and hope that the alcoholic will successfully recover, but this is only the beginning. The next step is for the family to meet with the interventionist "within a month" to discuss how their behavior may enable the alcoholic and to recommit themselves to successful recovery (Fields, 1998, 274). Alcoholism is a family disease that causes family dysfunctioning attributed to closed communication channels.

EDINBERG'S INTERVENTION GUIDELINES

Edinberg (1985) has identified intervention guidelines to encourage the elderly client to accept and to remain in alcoholism treatment. He stresses the importance of establishing a "strong relationship" with the elderly alcoholic, which requires "patience," because there is a high probability that the alcoholic will "progress and then go on a binge." Edinberg also includes in his intervention guidelines the need "to attend to both the stress placed on the family and the ways family members inadvertently reinforce the elderly alcoholic's behavior." The family members reinforce the drinking by accepting the alcoholic's rationalization for drinking. Too, the family will typically resort to denial and ignore problem behavior, largely because of the stigma associated with the disease (Edinberg, 1985).

Edinberg's insightful advice for the counselor to "attend to the family's reactions" to the disease process is well placed. Too frequently in alcoholism treatment the family is not included in the treatment plan, and therefore relapse is likely. Alcoholism is frequently described as a "family disease," because all family members are affected either positively or negatively. If, for example, the client begins treatment with only a tenuous acceptance of the disease and some of the family members are in denial of the disease, then relapse is likely. Using a family systems approach to successful treatment, a treatment strategy developed by the late Virginia Satir will be introduced in Chapter IX.

TARGET INTERVENTION SETTINGS

In Chapter I several factors were identified that influence the elderly to not seek treatment, which included:
- Job settings were typically targeted while most elderly are retired;
- Most elderly drink at home and are therefore infrequently arrested for drunk driving, a common basis for referral for treatment;
- The elderly are often misdiagnosed for acute dementia and not alcoholism;
- Enabling attitudes that condone and encourage elderly alcoholism; and
- Ineffective screening instruments to identify elderly alcoholism.

It is of utmost importance to intervene in settings frequented by the elderly alcoholic, including senior community centers, hospitals, and primary care physician offices. Dunlop (1990) recommends that intervention efforts include home visits and that few team members, not more than two, comprise the intervention treatment team so as to not deal "a heavy blow" to the self-image. He writes that,

> The classic-style intervention, which involves many close family members and others confronting the alcoholic with his problem, has been found to have a profoundly negative impact on the older patient's sense of self worth, even though done with sensitivity, caring and love. Often the wounded pride of the patient never quite heals and family relationships remain painful. (p. 28-32)

It is further recommended that the elderly person be urged to enter treatment for the purpose of gaining pertinent information concerning alcoholism so that he/she can make a more informed decision. With this nonconfronting approach, the elderly person is involved in the planning and decision-making processes and a sense of dignity, self-worth, and self-respect remain fully intact. By use of a supportive approach there is enhanced probability that the person will be sufficiently motivated to enter treatment and complete those tasks needed to achieve successful treatment outcomes, which is usually sobriety. Kola et al. (1980) predicted more than twenty years ago that elderly alcoholism "will increase in the next decades," and this development will require more effective strategies to identify, diagnose, and treat the elderly alcoholic. Twenty plus years henceforth and we have sadly not met that challenge (Edinberg, 1985).

IDENTIFYING VIABLE INTERVENTION STRATEGIES

Empathy rather than coerciveness should be of paramount consideration in seeking intervention strategies to encourage elderly alcoholics to receive treatment. As previously noted, alcoholics, unlike mental health clients, generally agree to treatment only after intense, persuasive pressure from significant others. In effect, when they enter treatment as involuntary clients, they frequently harbor pent-up rage and anger. Ideally, the elderly person needs to enter treatment voluntarily and to be highly motivated to successful recovery from alcoholism. The likelihood of successful treatment outcomes is enhanced when the elderly alcoholic is not coerced but, instead, volunteers, even if reluctantly, to accept treatment. A firm commitment from the dependent is, of course, the ideal.

SELF-ESTEEM ENHANCEMENT. For the elderly person to become sufficiently motivated to recover successfully, he or she must have a fairly good sense of self-worth or self-esteem, which are characteristically absent from alcoholics, especially the elderly alcoholic. Through years of alcohol abuse and attendant maladaptive behaviors, there is usually a profound sense of shame from years of alcoholic behaviors. One of the strategies of recovery is to restore the dependent's ego strengths. Chapter IX will introduce practice strategies to develop ego strengths.

INVOLVEMENT IN THE PLANNING AND DECISION-MAKING PROCESSES. The dependent should be encouraged to become part of the decision-making process concerning treatment so that a sense of dignity and self-respect will be restored. Too, if the dependent becomes part of the planning and decision-making processes, he or she will be more likely to become sufficiently motivated to successfully recover. Possible treatment options include hospitalization, inpatient treatment, and outpatient treatment. Alcoholics Anonymous should be considered a viable support group but not an alternative to treatment.

The dependent may stop drinking, but recovery has not begun, because he or she exhibits "dry drunk" behaviors. That is, the dependent may have physically stopped drinking but continues to exhibit drinking behaviors, including those behaviors characterized by irritability, anxiety, nervousness, resentment, and self-pity.

EMPATHIC SUPPORT. Although it is essential to impress on the dependent the seriousness of his or her alcoholism, it is important to not be punitive by using a "tough love" approach. The "tough love" approach to intervention may be moderately effective with some clients, but it is likely to cause the elderly alcoholic to assume a defensive, unapproachable position. Support in the form of empathy involves communicating to the dependent your understanding of the alcoholic situation and how it adversely affects his life. Empathy, unlike sympathy, which tends to promote feelings of self pity, is a process that leads to the elderly alcoholic client's sense that there is a genuine support for entering treatment. Further discussion on empathy and its major components along with ways to practice empathic behaviors will be discussed in Chapter IX.

UNCONDITIONAL ACCEPTANCE AND LOVE FOR THE DEPENDENT. Regardless of how the dependent's behaviors have caused problems in his or her life, as well as with those with whom the dependent has come into contact, it is now important to communicate unconditional love and support of the dependent in the recovery process.

SUMMARY

This chapter described the primary, secondary, and tertiary levels of intervention within an alcoholism context. The traditional "rock bottom" approach to intervention at the tertiary level was compared with the preferred approach of intervening before the onset of alcoholism. The Fields and the Johnson Intervention Models were adapted to an elderly alcoholic population with the various steps described. Some of the challenges to treating an elderly alcoholic population were explored, including society's attitude that the elderly cannot benefit from treatment because of the lack of ambulation, transportation, and age. It was proposed that improved strategies be developed and implemented to identify, diagnose, and treat the elderly alcoholic whose numbers will inevitably increase.

GLOSSARY OF TERMS

Ambulatory: Not bedridden and with the ability to walk. A broad definition includes those persons who through the use of wheelchairs and/or walkers are also considered to be ambulatory.

Assessment: Refers to the information-gathering process of the client that continues throughout treatment, beginning at intake into the termination stages, and for many clients, assessment continues into aftercare treatment.

Brief intervention: A methodical straightforward approach to educate alcoholics about their physical dependency on alcohol. With increased frequency, this strategy has been successfully implemented by physicians.

Confabulation: A condition commonly exhibited by the Wernike-Korsakoff's patients, whereby they believe that certain events occurred as they fill in memory lapses with fictitious events.

Harm reduction: This approach attempts to reduce the harm and danger associated with alcohol abuse, and sobriety may not be the primary goal.

Involuntary client: Refers to clients who are required to receive services, especially therapeutic in nature, against their will. The term frequently refers to court-ordered drunk drivers who must seek alcoholism treatment.

Primary level of intervention: Intervention before onset of the program, e.g., educational services provided before alcohol becomes a problem.

"Rock bottom": A term used in alcohol treatment where intervention does not occur until the alcoholic is in a desperate situation and is optimally receptive to treatment intervention.

Secondary level of intervention: Intervention before dependency on alcohol (alcoholism).

Tertiary level of intervention: Intervention at the stage of chronic alcoholism.

STUDY QUESTIONS

1. What was the rationale in traditional alcoholism treatment in waiting until the alcoholic hits "rock bottom" before intervening? What are the pitfalls and/or problems in forestalling intervention until the alcoholic has hit "rock bottom?"

2. Within the context of alcoholism, describe the three levels of intervention.

3. Compare Fields' intervention model with the Johnson intervention model.

4. What is the basis for society's reluctance to encourage elderly alcoholics to seek treatment?

REFERENCES

Beaver, M.L. & Miller, D. (1985). *Clinical social work practice with the elderly: Primary, secondary, and tertiary Intervention.* Homewood, IL: The Dorsey Press.

Blake, R. (July 1990). Mental health counseling and older problem drinkers, *Journal of Mental Health Counseling, 12*(3), 354–367.

Carroll, C.R. (2000). *Drugs in modern society* (5th ed.). New York: McGraw-Hill.

Doweiko, H.E. (1999). *Concepts of chemical dependency* (4th ed.). Pacific Grove, CA: Brooks/Cole Publishing Company.

Dunlop, M.A. (1990). Peer groups support seniors fighting alcohol and drugs. *Aging, 361,* 28–32.

Edinberg, M.A. (1985). *Mental health practice with the elderly.* Englewood Cliffs, NJ: Prentice Hall, Inc.

Fields, R. (1998). *Drugs in perspective: A personalized look at substance abuse and use* (3rd ed.). The McGraw-Hill Companies, Inc.

Fleming, M. & Manwell, L.B. (1999). Brief intervention in primary care settings: a primary treatment method for at-risk, problem, and dependent drinkers. *Alcohol Research and Health, 23,* 128–137. Retrieved at April 16, 2000 from FirstSearch database (WilsonSelect) Number BSSI00002888.

Hepworth, D.H. & Larsen, J. (1990). *Direct social work practice: Theory and skills,* (3rd ed.). Belmont, CA: The Dorsey Press.

Johnson, V.E., (1986). *Intervention: How to help someone who doesn't want help.* Minneapolis: MN: Johnson Institute QVS, Inc.

Jung, J. (1994). *Under the influence: alcohol and human behaviors.* Belmont, CA: Brooks/Cole Publishing Company.

Kola, L.A., Kosberg, J.I., & Wegner-Burch, K. (Winter, 1980). Perceptions of the treatment responsibilities for the elderly client. *Social Work in Health Care, 6*(2), 69–76.

Levinthal, C.F. (1996). *Drugs, behavior, and modern society.* Needham Heights, MA: Allyn & Bacon.

Rivers, P.C. (1994). *Alcohol and human behavior: Theory, research, & practice.* Englewood Cliffs, NJ: Prentice-Hall.

Schlaadt, R.G. & Shannon, P.T. (1994). *Drugs: Use, misuse, and abuse* (4th ed.). Englewood Cliffs, NJ: Prentice-Hall.

van Wormer, K. (1997). *Alcoholism Treatment: A social work perspective.* Chicago: Nelson-Hall Publishers.

Wegscheider-Cruise, S. (1989). *Another chance: Hope and health for the alcoholic family* (2nd ed.). Palo Alto, CA: Science and Behavior Books, Inc.

Chapter VIII

PRACTICE VALUES/ATTITUDES

> Thinking of all difficulties as opportunities for creating something new instead of the beginning of the toll of funeral bells. Each person can learn and grow from each creative handling of a difficulty. This may include dropping a burden as well as creating a new possibility.
>
> Satir, 1976

PROFESSIONAL VALUES FOR ALCOHOLISM COUNSELORS

Because alcoholism counseling for an elderly clientele is a relatively new field of practice, a specific value system with which to guide the practitioner remains undeveloped. Practitioners represent numerous professional disciplines from which they most likely derive their guiding professional values, but a professional value system that succinctly represents the counseling needs of an elderly alcoholic clientele needs development. Foremost, a strong nonageist value system is needed for counselors working with an elderly population, so that society's negative perceptions of the elderly will not influence effectiveness. There exists a strong societal belief that the elderly should not be included in alcoholism treatment services because they are incapable of learning new behaviors and that our youths' addictions should receive first priority for treatment. Robert Butler (1975), who coined the term "ageism," describes the ageist society that exists in the United States:

> A process of systematic stereotyping of and discrimination against people because they are old, just as racism and sexism accomplished this with skin color and gender. Old people are categorized as senile, rigid in thought and manner, old-fashioned in morality and skills. . . . Ageism allows the younger generations to see older people as different from themselves; thus they subtly cease to identify with their elders as human beings. (p. 12)

Largely because of stereotypical beliefs concerning the elderly, many individuals will continue to be excluded from alcoholism treatment based on the notion that treatment will benefit neither the elderly nor society and that the elderly are incapable of learning new behaviors. As a guide for the practitioner, a professional value system would provide the needed legitimacy to serving an elderly clientele. The first section in this chapter will introduce values used by other human services professionals that may be adapted to a standard value system to guide the practice of the elderly alcoholism counselor. The remainder of the chapter will focus on common pitfalls to which counselors are frequently subjected. Hepworth and Larsen (1990) have developed a set of values commonly referred to as "The Cardinal Values of Social Work;" their adaptation to an elderly alcoholism clientele follows:

- Developing and utilizing resources
- Affirming the worth and dignity of clients
- Affirming uniqueness and individuality
- Affirming problem-solving capabilities and self-determination
- Safeguarding confidentiality

1. DEVELOPING AND UTILIZING RESOURCES. The counselor must be knowledgeable of all community agency resources for possible referrals that would enhance alcoholism treatment outcomes. Typically, this age-specific clientele will face aging-related problems that will need attention. Resources include public welfare departments, Councils on Aging, Area Agencies on Aging, health services, social security administration offices, senior community centers, and a host of other resources. Also, an excellent resource to assist families to identify appropriate treatment facilities is the Addiction Resource Guide that identifies age-specific treatment programs. To promote use of resources for an elderly population there is a growing trend that services need to be advertised and made accessible as a right as opposed to a privilege.

2. AFFIRMING THE WORTH AND DIGNITY OF CLIENTS. Elderly alcoholics commonly have low self-esteem and a profound sense of shame in a society that stigmatizes them with having character defects. Practitioners need to instill in their clientele a sense of self-worth; instead of treating the elderly client in a patronizing childlike fashion, they must be treated as dignified, mature adults.

3. AFFIRMING UNIQUENESS AND INDIVIDUALITY. Rather than stereotyping all elderly clients as senile, weak, and incapable of benefiting from alcoholism treatment, the counselor must identify strengths and weaknesses so that individualized treatment plans are formulated that address clients' unique needs.

4. AFFIRMING PROBLEM-SOLVING CAPABILITIES AND SELF-DETERMINATION. The elderly client must be involved in the planning and decision-making

processes, especially with respect to the formulation of the treatment plan, so that needs and outcome measures are determined in consultation with the client. Incumbent on successful treatment outcomes, elderly clients need to be fully engaged in the formulation of the treatment plan so that they will be in agreement with the treatment plan's goals and objectives, and, therefore, be sufficiently motivated to recover successfully. Through involvement in the planning and decision-making processes, the client becomes invested, a managerial principle that has application to alcoholism treatment. Inherent in this value is the belief that the elderly client has the innate capabilities to become fully engaged in the problem-solving process and that the role of the counselor is essentially of a facilitative nature to provide support and direction. The ageist attitude that the elderly alcoholic is incapable of self-direction is archaic and an obstacle to successful treatment outcomes. The self-determination component of this value advocates clients' rights to determine treatment goals as opposed to formulating the treatment plan independently of the client. Arrogantly superimposing counselors' values can only lead to unsuccessful treatment outcomes.

5. SAFEGUARDING CONFIDENTIALITY. Clients in general and elderly clients in particular do not avail themselves of alcoholism treatment largely because of the commonly held perception that confidentiality is frequently breached. It is not uncommon for human service workers to casually discuss clients' problems during informal work breaks. When there is a need for a counselor to confer with colleagues regarding treatment-related concerns, counselors should be duty bound to seek client authorization. Any departure from this practice should be construed as a blatant breach of clients' rights to the safeguarding of confidentiality.

There is a scarcity of available research literature to address essential values to work effectively with a geriatric population. A value and attitude-based study conducted by Parette, Hourcade, and Parette (1990) asked 220 providers of geriatric services to rank order in importance those values/attitudes in providing services to an elderly clientele. The respondents rank ordered them as follows:

- Right of self-determination
- Respect for human differences
- Confidentiality for clients
- Dignity of persons
- Uniqueness of persons
- Maximum independence possible
- Patience

PATIENCE. Ironically, patience was ranked last. As the Director of the Aging Studies Program at my University, I have found that patience is the most difficult to teach. It's not surprising that our students' practicum supervisors in gerontology-based settings identify patience as the most challenging value to acquire.

When elderly people express criticism of the services they receive, they will commonly bemoan the lack of patience of their professional service providers. I impress on my students the need to acquire active listening skills. Carl Rogers, whose passionate plea for counselors to be client-focused and develop active listening skills, continues to have relevance.

Ranked number 6 (allow and encourage) "maximum independence possible," was not considered to be of high priority, which may explain why the elderly are subjected to the highly structured medical regimen of institutional settings whose dependency relationships are the norm. One elderly person after a brief convalescence in a nursing home sadly disclosed that she felt "stripped" of her personality; her very autonomy, sense of self-worth and dignity, and her self-esteem and independence had undergone a "stripping out process." It leaves little to the imagination what impact this process has on one's overall sense of well-being.

Father Felix Biestek (1954) has identified what many consider the most salient principles (values) required by professional caregivers. His classic casework principles have been applied to virtually every social service setting.

- Individualization
- Purposeful expression of feelings
- Controlled emotional involvement
- Acceptance
- Nonjudgmental attitude
- Client self-determination
- Confidentiality

Although some of Biestek's principles duplicate values already identified, a few deserve discussion.

INDIVIDUALIZATION. "It is the recognition and understanding of each client's unique qualities." Individualization is an especially valued principle in working with an elderly person, because there is the tendency to presume that all elderly are alike without an appreciation for individual, unique differences. Treatment plans therefore must be formulated to meet individual client needs.

PURPOSEFUL EXPRESSION OF FEELINGS. Biestek writes that the "purposeful expression of feelings is the recognition of the client's need to express his feelings freely, especially his negative feelings." He stresses that the counselor should control his or her emotional involvement, especially when reacting to client disclosures. Reacting with shock to a client's assertion that "I like to get as drunk as I can just to get the courage to let my wife know how angry she makes me," could serve to discourage further disclosures. A shocked or scolding reaction by the counselor would effectively discourage further disclosure. A precondition to encourage the purposeful expression of feelings is the counselor's patient attitude.

As a precautionary measure, it should be noted that although client expressions of feelings are generally a healthy catharsis, overdisclosures can lead to undue embarrassment if a counselor-client trust relationship has not been established. Before a full cathartic expression of feelings is encouraged, the client must have trust in the counselor that the disclosure is appropriate. Without a trusting relationship, the client likely will later feel embarrassed in having disclosed so much of his or her feelings and therefore elect not to return for further treatment. Premature client termination can be avoided by a sensitive, experienced counselor who knows when to appropriately discourage further disclosures of feelings.

ACCEPTANCE. This principle relates to the counselor's acceptance of the client "regardless of his individual qualities arising from heredity, environment, behavior, or any other source." Biestek stresses that acceptance of behaviors, attitudes, and standards does not suggest approval (Biestek, 1954).

NONJUDGMENTAL ATTITUDE. Although the counselor does not assign "guilt or innocence," his or her role appropriately makes evaluative judgments "about the attitudes, standards, or actions of a client." The judgmental counselor will likely encourage a defensive posture by the recovering alcoholic.

Whereas the first part of this chapter stressed the ethical prudence for professional elderly alcoholism counselors to embrace a uniform value system to guide their practice, the second part will identify counterproductive attitudes that will neither enhance an effective counselor-client relationship nor promote successful treatment outcomes.

Attitudes Toward Client

Carl Rogers (1975) stresses the therapeutic value for the therapist to convey a supportive, genuine interest in the client's welfare. Countless studies purport that successful treatment outcomes are attributable largely to a healthy, warm, trusting worker-client relationship. Alfred Benjamin (1981), author of *The Helping Interview*, a classic text for the professional counselor, also stresses the importance for the counselor to embrace a genuinely good feeling for the client:

> A genuine liking for people is a gift from heaven. We are either born with it or we are not. Those upon whom the gift was not bestowed are neither better nor worse than other men but they lack a trait indispensable in the helping professions. If our preferences lead us to machines, plants, animals, abstractions, or whatever, but not people, we should indulge and foster such preferences. Many professions do not demand–some even exclude–a genuine liking for people. However, for those who use the helping interview as one of their tools, it is essential. (p. 43)

Largely because of society's prevailing ageist influences, many young, aspiring counselors prefer to not provide services to an elderly clientele, especially an alcoholic elderly clientele seeking alcoholism treatment; instead, they tend to choose client populations and settings that are socially sanctioned and supported. Parette, Hourcade, and Parette (1990) explored and probed the nursing profession's attitudes toward the elderly and generally found nurses' attitudes toward the elderly alcoholic to be negative, to which they attribute society's perception of elderly alcoholism as a "moral problem" rather than as a disease. Nurses' attitudes toward this client population are strikingly similar to society's attitudes, which likely influence nurses' attitudes toward their elderly patients. Nurses' educational levels were found to be an influential factor. The authors noted that masters-level nurses were not as prone to view elderly alcoholism as negatively as B.S.–level nurses. The need for graduate education was the authors' recommendation to improve attitudes. The authors conclude in their attitudinal study that:

> Additional educational experiences, especially those emphasizing information about alcoholism and alcohol-related problems, can provide nurses with effective treatment strategies. A large proportion of nurses report having limited classroom training in alcoholism and express a need for additional education in this area. Nurses who see themselves as competent and able to provide effective treatment to patients with alcoholism are less likely to possess negative attitudes toward that condition. (pp. 26–30)

It would behoove alcoholism counselors who provide alcoholism treatment to an elderly clientele to conduct an honest, genuine inventory of their personal attitudes toward the elderly alcoholic. Negative attitudes will adversely influence the assessment, the overall treatment plan, and ultimately treatment outcomes.

SIX COMMON PITFALLS FOR THE COUNSELOR-THERAPIST

Ageism

Ageism, like racism, sexism, and other forms of discrimination, is exemplified by prejudice directed toward a particular group based on a common characteristic, such as age. Moreover, ageism is a negative stereotypical depiction of the elderly. The gerontologist Robert Butler (1991), who coined the term ageism, describes its effects:

> Older people are often stereotyped as slow thinkers, forgetful, rigid, mean-tempered, irritable, dependent, and querulous. Certainly they do suffer, from anxiety, grief, depression, and paranoid states that may be experi-

enced at any age. But one must separate out the personality traits demonstrated in earlier life, realistic responses to actual loss of friends and loved ones, personal reactions to the idea of one's own aging and death, and the predictable emotional responses of human beings at any age to physical illness or social loss. (p. 69)

Older people are stereotyped to exhibit many behavioral characteristics presumed to be shared by their age cohorts. Ageism is rampant in literature, humor, letters to "Dear Abby," periodicals, advertising, poetry, newspapers, and television programs (Kart, 1990). The elderly alcoholism counselor needs to work through issues associated with an ageist society that embraces negative perceptions of the elderly. Because successful alcoholism treatment outcomes require clients to feel good about themselves, treatment must be geared toward developing positive self-concepts; hence, clinicians must be free of ageist attitudes that will predictably have a negative impact upon their elderly clientele.

Countertransferences

Related to ageism is the concept of countertransference. Unlike negative and positive transferences, which refer to clients' feelings toward their counselors, countertransferences refer to feelings by counselors toward clients. The strict, clinical definition of countertransferences suggests an unconscious process that arouses counselors' "unresolved conflicts and problems" (Freud, 1959, pp. 285–286). In our fast-paced society that glorifies strength and youth at the expense of the elderly person's sense of dignity and respect, especially the weak elderly, the tendency, whether on conscious or unconscious levels, is to use avoidance behaviors. As helping professionals, rather than be reminded of negative features associated with the elderly, we may choose a younger client population that suggests a favorable prognosis.

Corey, Schneider, and Corey (1993) describe how countertransference can influence the younger professional:

One area of difference in helping relationships with older people is the increased potential for countertransference on the helper's part. Elderly clients can activate the helper's recollections of parents and grandparents. At times, helpers avoid dealing with the elderly because of the stark reminders of their own inevitable aging and death. If helpers are unaware of the reactions that are being stimulated within them as they work with elderly clients, their efforts at helping will be twarted. (p. 123)

The definition of countertransference has evolved considerably from the early history of psychoanalysis when countertransferences were perceived as solely an unconscious process. Katz (1990) reflects on the contemporary conception of this process as "the totality of feelings experienced by the therapist toward the client–whether conscious or unconscious, whether prompted by the client or by events in the therapist's own life" (p. 18).

A common countertransference relates to the stereotypes of the elderly alcoholic. Amodeo (1990) asserts that "often this stereotype is of a male, suffering obvious physical and social deteriation, who is perhaps disheveled and homeless. Such a narrow definition interferes with the caregiver's ability to engage in early identification and intervention with alcoholics seen regularly in medical, social services, and mental health settings" (Amodeo, 1990, pp. 93–105).

Avoidance and Denial Coping Strategies

Robinson (1990) calls attention to professional caregivers who use avoidance and denial coping strategies when assessing their elderly clients. Even when alcoholism is clearly present, they fail to recognize the alcoholism symptoms. Denial of their clients' alcoholism may have its antecedents as members of alcoholic families. Professionals who have not worked through their transferences are apt to deny alcoholism in their clients as a defense of the "shame" felt as a child in an alcoholic family (Genevay & Katz, 1990, p. 97). Adult children of alcoholics, a population that has received considerable attention in recent years, frequently exhibit many behaviors associated with alcoholism, even though they may have chosen sobriety as a reaction to their parents' alcoholism. The apt term "the family disease" helps to understand how even the nondrinking members of an alcoholic family will continue to exhibit alcoholism-related behaviors well into adulthood, unless they, too, enter therapy to work through the insidious entrappings of membership in an alcoholic family. Because alcoholism is rampant and affects numerous families, the alcoholism counselor must fully reflect on his personal family experiences to identify possible influences that may adversely affect the ways in which clients are perceived, thus influencing the quality of services provided to an elderly clientele.

Professional Co-dependent Enabling

This discussion will make interchangeable use of co-dependency and enabling behaviors, terms commonly associated with alcoholics and their family members; but, to a large extent enabling co-dependent behaviors potentially describe counselors who enter the helping profession because of an excessive need to serve themselves under the presumptive need to help others. Melody Beattie (1987), who coined the term, describes the co-dependents in her pre-alcoholism recovery days as:

> . . . hostile, controlling, manipulative, indirect, guilt producing, difficult to communicate with, generally disagreeable, sometimes downright hateful, and a hindrance to any compulsion to get high. They hollered at me, hid my pills, made nasty faces at me, poured my alcohol down the sink, tried to keep me from getting more drugs, wanted to know why I was doing this to them, and asked what was wrong with me. But they were always there, ready to rescue me from self-created disasters. (p. 1)

The destructive nature of co-dependency enabling behaviors creates dependency relationships, clearly undesirable behaviors for counselors who need to foster independent client behaviors. Doweiko (1990) describes the co-dependent person as someone attempting to relate to the addict to gain a sense of strength (Doweiko, 1990). Although there does not seem to be empirical research to support this behavior, it is a term used extensively in the alcoholism counseling field that cannot be ignored. Although co-dependency is excluded from the DSM-IV-TR, the term is used extensively by alcoholism counselors to describe a specific dysfunctional relationship within the alcoholic family. Brown, Beletsis, and Cermak (1989), long-time advocates for the inclusion of co-dependency in the DSM-IV-TR as a psychiatric disorder, have recommended various criteria for the diagnosis:

1. Continued investment of one's self-esteem in the ability to control oneself and others in the face of serious adverse consequences.

2. Assumption of responsibility for meeting others' needs to the exclusion of one's own.

3. Anxiety and boundary distortions with respect to intimacy and separation.

4. Emmeshment in relationships with personality disordered, chemically dependent, other co-dependent, and/or impulse disordered individuals.

5. Three or more of the following: excessive reliance on denial; restriction of the emotions; repression; hypervigilence; compulsions anxiety; substance abuse; being the victim of past or current physical or sexual abuse; stress-related illnesses; remaining in primary relationships with an active substance abuser for at least 2 years without seeking help.

Taking Sides

One of the counselor's objectives is to work effectively with all family members, because, as the preceding discussion points out, alcoholism is a family disease that affects all family members. The inexperienced counselor is vulnerable to manipulation when taking sides. However persuasive the family member's argument may be concerning a particular issue, the counselor must not take sides, because it further intensifies and aligns the opposing sides, and the counselor's actions will be perceived as lacking objectivity and credibility as a family counselor. Herr and Weakland (1979) insist that in working with older persons "if anything, taking sides within a family tends to tear it further apart rather than to heal it" (Herr & Weakland, 1979, p. 21).

Sympathy vs. Empathy

Sympathy has the effect of reinforcing feelings of self-pity. The person who expresses sympathy is attempting to do the impossible, which is to feel the feelings of the person to whom he expresses sympathy. Not only is it infeasible to feel the other person's feelings but it jeopardizes the counselor's objectivity in the problem-solving process. As the counselor assumes a sympathetic posture, he or she becomes less effective. The client begins feeling pity and sorrow for himself or herself, and successful resolution in the problem-solving process is doomed. Empathy, unlike sympathy, is essentially an understanding of clients' feelings. While caring for the person, the counselor does not want to become part of the problem, and, therefore, become ineffective in assisting the client to reach a satisfactory closure with the problems faced. Lewis, Dana, and Blevins (1994) describe why the substance-abuse counselor needs to be empathic (empathetic) and not sympathetic:

> A counselor may listen to a client explain how hopeless and useless, how unable to go on, he or she feels. An empathetic response would be direct and comforting. The response does not indicate that the counselor is experiencing what the client is experiencing but, rather, that the counselor is beginning to develop a clear picture of what the client is experiencing. An empathic response to the above situation might be: 'I hear you saying that you're useless and that you don't feel hopeful about the future. It's as if you're very sad, very depressed—just feeling overwhelmed. Am I reading the situation correctly?' Thus empathy is caring, but it is not sympathy. (p. 18)

Burn out

Moreover, the effective elderly alcoholism counselor must use appropriate coping strategies to prevent job burnout. A common definition suggests that job burnout is characterized by complete physical and emotional exhaustion. A typical burnout scenario involves the counselor who does not want to face clients and their problems and has difficulty coming to work. In effect, the counselor has become as dysfunctional as his clients. Maslach and Leiter (1997) have identified six factors that contribute to burnout: (1) work overload, (2) lack of control, (3) insufficient reward, (4) breakdown in community, (5) absence of fairness, and (6) conflicting values. Although factors (1), (2), and (3) are straightforward, factors (4), (5), and (6) require discussion.

4. BREAKDOWN IN COMMUNITY. Refers to the fragmentation of personal relationships and an undermining of teamwork caused by a disproportionate focus on short-term profits (Maslack & Leiter, 1997, p. 49). Increasingly in recent years, especially beginning in the latter 1970s, United States organizations tended to follow Japan's use of task groups, or quality circles, to attain goals. Through the use of quality circles, there is generated a sense of cohesive bonding with fellow workers, which in turn promotes a higher quality of services to the clients. Alcoholism treatment programs would benefit by adopting some form of peer support through which counselors could work through the stress associated with their jobs.

5. ABSENCE OF FAIRNESS. Maslach and Leiter have identified three components that constitute fairness: trust, openness, and respect. The authors write that:

> When an organization achieves community, people trust one another to fulfill their roles in shared projects, to communicate openly about their intentions, and to show mutual respect. When an organization acts fairly, it values every person who contributes to its success, it indicates that every individual is important. All three elements of fairness are essential to maintain a person's engagement with work. In contrast, their absence contributes directly to burnout. (p. 52)

6. CONFLICTING VALUES. The authors argue convincingly that too frequently work organizations subvert the esteemed values of excellence to service while undermining quality with a short-term profit motivation.

7. BURNOUT. As a former counselor in varied client settings, I have observed countless numbers of once productive professionals fall victim to job burnout. My first job after graduation with a BSW degree (social work) was as a coordinator of migrant workers' social services in a three-county catchment area. Because I worked closely with each of the county's social services departments, I became well acquainted with their staff. In one county I worked closely with a counselor who was responsible for providing

emergency financial services to migrant families in need. I learned from family members who had applied for assistance through his office that no action had been taken. When I questioned the counselor about this discrepancy, he was quick to attribute the problem to someone losing the paperwork. With a cursory glance at the piles on piles of paperwork scattered about his office, it became abundantly obvious that he was the source of lost paperwork. I then impressed on him the critical nature of the migrant family with seven children that was in dire need of emergency assistance to purchase food. I persuaded him to drive us to the migrant camp to complete the necessary paperwork for the family's application for services. Finalized, we returned to his car for the drive to his office; instead, he began driving around the countryside aimlessly. "I do this every day before I come to work, and again, after lunch. It's my coping strategy in dealing with stress."

8. CLIENT OVERIDENTIFICATION, UNSUCCESSFUL TREATMENT OUTCOMES/BURNOUT. I've known several counselors who belatedly discovered that their overidentification with clients contributed to noncompliance of treatment plan's objectives/tasks. These counselors established essentially "buddy" worker-client relations, rather than the more businesslike professional worker-client relationships. It is more difficult to enforce specific due dates for task completions if your client is a buddy. In a more professionally based worker-client relationship, the counselor maintains the needed leverage to encourage compliance of treatment plan tasks and objectives. It's not uncommon for the "buddy-based" worker-client relationship to consistently suffer from unmet tasks. Successful treatment outcomes are contingent on completion of tasks and objectives in a timely fashion. For example, if the due date to begin attending AA group meetings has been ignored by the client, there is the likelihood that the goal of sobriety will remain unmet. If the client has successfully manipulated his "buddy-counselor" into not going to AA, then relapse is inevitable. Appropriately there can and should exist a warm, nurturing relationship based on clearly defined professional goals and objectives, but problems occur when the counselor and client develop a personal relationship, whereby the counselor is vulnerable to manipulation. Eventually, the counselor will recognize that treatment goals were unmet at the specified date for completion and will then feel inadequate in having not met the treatment plan's goals. Burnout is the final outcome and not problem resolution.

SUMMARY

Elderly alcoholism counseling, still in the infancy stage of development, is in need of a value system to guide its practitioners. Various value systems were explored to identify those features most germane to counseling the elderly alcoholic. Research studies indicate that there is a close relationship between counselors' attitudes and successful treatment outcomes.

Common pitfalls frequently experienced by counselors were explored, including ageism, countertransferences, professional co-dependent enabling behaviors, taking sides, sympathizing, and burnout. For the counselor to provide optimally effective services for the elderly alcoholic, he or she must work toward becoming free of these common issues facing the professional counselor.

GLOSSARY

Burnout: A term coined to refer to employees who become physically and psychologically exhausted from stressful jobs.

Countertransference: Feelings and/or thoughts toward the client based on events that occurred in the counselor's personal life.

Empathy: Empathy is an understanding of one's feelings.

Individualism: An important counseling principle whereby each client is perceived foremost by the counselor as an individual. The individualization principle is essential in working with an elderly clientele because aging is an individualized process.

STUDY QUESTIONS

1. Explain how noncompliance with the counseling principles identified in Chapter VIII can adversely influence treatment outcomes.
2. As a counselor, what can you do to prevent or counteract the "six common pitfalls" to successful counseling?
3. The definition of countertransferences has evolved from a more clinical to a broader definition. Explain.
4. What are the behavioral characteristics of the "burned out" counselor?
5. Under what specific situation is the counselor most vulnerable to job "burnout"?

REFERENCES

Amodeo, M.A. (1990). Treating the late life alcoholic: Guidelines for working through denial, integrating individual, family, and group approaches. *Journal of Geriatric Psychiatry, 23*(2), 91–105.

Atkinson, R.M., Tolson, R.L., & Turner, J.A. (January, 1993). Factors affecting treatment compliance of older male problem drinkers. *Journal of Studies on Alochol,* 102–105.

Beattie, M. (1987). *Co-dependent no more.* New York: Fiat Harper & Row.

Beechem, M. & Comstock, J. (1997). Teaching empathy skills to undergraduate social work students. *The Journal of Baccalaureate Social Work, 2*(2), 87–96.

Benjamin, A. (1981). *The helping interview,* (3rd ed.). Boston: The Houghton Miffin Company.

Beresford, T.P. (1995). Alcoholic elderly: Prevalence, screening, diagnosis, and prognosis. In Bresesband, T. & Gomberg, A. (Eds.), *Alcohol and aging: Looking ahead.* New York: Oxford University Press.

Biestek, F.P. (Feb. 1954). An analysis of the casework relationship. *Social Casework,* p. 183.

Brown, S., Beletsis, S.G., & Cermak, T.L. (1989). *Adult children of alcoholics in treatment.* Deerfield Beach, FL: Health Comunications.

Butler, R.N. (1975). *Why survive?* New York: Harper & Row.

Butler, R.N., Lewis, M., & Sunderland, T. (1991). *Aging and mental health: Positive psychosocial and biomedical approaches,* (4th ed.), New York: MacMillan Publishing Company, 209.

Corey, M., Schneider, J., & Corey, G. (1993). *Becoming a helper,* (2nd ed.). Pacific Grove, CA: Brooks/Cole Publishing Company.

Doweiko, H.E. (1999). *Concepts of chemical dependency,* (4th ed.). Pacific Grove, CA: Brooks/Cole Publishing Company.

Freud, S. (1959). *The future prospects of psychoanalytic therapy.* In E. Jones (Ed.) Collected papers of Sigmund Freud Vol. 2, pp. 285–286, New York: Basic Books.

Genevay, B. & Katz, R.S. (1990). *Countertransference and older clients.* Newbury Park, CA: Sage Publications, Inc.

Hartford, J.T. & Thienhaus, O.J. (1984). Psychiatric aspects of alcoholism in geriatric patients. In J. T. Hartford & T. Samorajski (Eds.), *Alcoholism in the elderly,* New York: Raven Press.

Hepworth, D.H. & Larsen, J. (1990). *Direct social work practice: Theory and skills,* (3rd ed.). Belmont, CA: The Dorsey Press.

Herr, J.J. & Weakland, J. H. (1979). Counseling elders and their families: Practical techniques for applied gerontology. New York: Springer Publishing Company.

Kart, C.S. (1990). *The realities of aging: An introduction to gerontology,* (3rd ed.). Needham Heights, MA: Allyn & Bacon.

Katz, R.J. (1990). Using our emotional reactions to older clients: A working theory. In Genevay, B. & Katz, R.J. (Eds.), *Countertransference and older clients.* Newbury Park, CA: Sage Publications, Inc.

Lang, R. (1983). Therapists' reactions to the patient. *The Technique of Psychoanalytic Psychology, 2,* 139.

Lewis, J.A., Dana, R.Q., & Blevins, G.A. (1994). *Substance abuse counseling* (2nd ed.). Pacific Grove, CA: Brooks/Cole Publishing Company.

Maslach, C., Leiter, M.P. (1997). *The truth about burnout.* San Francisco, CA: Jossey-Bass Publishers.

Parette, H.P., Hourcade, J.I., & Parette, P.C. (1990). Nursing attitudes toward geriatric alcoholism. *Journal of Gerontological Nursing, 16*(1), 26–30.

Robinson, J. (1990). Monograph. In Genevay, B., & Katz, R.S. (Eds.), *Countertransference and older adults.* Newbury Park, CA: Sage Publications, Inc.

Rogers, C. (1975). The necessary and sufficient condition of therapeutic personality change. *Journal of Consulting Psychology, 22*, 95–103.

Chapter IX

PRACTICE STRATEGIES:
AN ECLECTIC APPROACH

> It is common knowledge, of course, that the mind influences
> the body and vice verse, but there needs to be more scientific
> experimentation of this interplay. . . . Modern medicine will
> become really scientific only when physicians and their
> patients have learned to manage the forces of the body and the
> mind that operate in *vis medicatrix* naturae.
>
> Cousins, 1986

The prudent counselor will likely select appropriate intervention strategies that fit the specific client situation rather than selecting a strategy
based on a strict theoretical orientation; that is, the counselor's repertoir of
intervention strategies will likely include those from among a variety of varied theoretical orientations. Hepworth and Larsen (1990) refer to the "sys-
tematic eclectic practitioner" who:

> Adheres exclusively to no single theory but rather selects models and theo-
> ries that best match a given problem situation and accords highest priority
> to techniques that have been empirically demonstrated to be effective and
> efficient. (p. 18)

THE ASSESSMENT

The assessment is frequently used interchangeably with the "diagnosis" or
the "psychosocial diagnosis," terms that suggest a "negative association with
symptoms, disease, and dysfunction" (Hepworth & Larsen, 1990, p. 193).
Instead, the clinician should treat the assessment as an ongoing information-
gathering process that seeks to identify not only client weaknesses but also
strengths that are germane to providing a comprehensive picture of the situ-

ation. Lum (2000) proposes that the counselor depart "from the language of pathology and deficit" and embrace a strength perspective (p. 199).

Typically, at the beginning of treatment, the client undergoes a grueling "drinking history," where disclosure about everything from specific alcoholic beverages to drinking companions is required. Understandably, drinking-related behaviors are essential information for the counselor to formulate an individualized treatment plan. There is, however, a risk that the elderly alcoholic will assume a defensive stance and perceive the counselor's role as intrusive. Katherine Graham (2000) asserts that questions concerning drinking history may be perceived as intrusive if broached before developing a trusting worker-client relationship.

Asking about substance use, particularly alcohol use, may seem intrusive and may be better left until you have developed a relationship with the older client and an appropriate opportunity presents itself rather than during a single structured interview.

The cliché "you take your client where she/he is," has applicability insofar as establishing a counselor-client relationship based on trust. When the elderly client is forced into disclosing his or her drinking history, it is obvious that the principle of "taking your client where he is," has been violated as the client's defensive posture intensifies. As an alternative to requiring client disclosure of his or her drinking history, conducting a life review would likely serve as a needed "ice breaker" and trust builder while also enhancing client self-esteem in identifying positive life events. The identification of negative life events would be an opportunity to do the needed grief work.

Life Review as a Part of the Assessment

The life review, a strategy first introduced by the noted gerontologist Robert Butler, has its roots in twelfth century Europe where

> . . . strong individualism was emerging. For one facing an impeding death it was considered a personal responsibility to prepare a "written will" or a "personal testament," which, in effect, was a moral balance sheet of a person's life because it dealt with how one's life was lived and not the disposition of personal wealth. That is, an individual had the moral responsibility to conduct oneself properly through his/her life. Also in the twelfth century, inscriptions began appearing on grave markers, such as "Here lies so and so. . . ." (Barrow, 1992, p. 295)

Much like the life review, the written will was a reflection of positive and negative features of an individual's life as it enhanced his life's meaning and importance. Butler (1975) defines the life review as a "type of reminiscence that covers the whole life span" (Corey, Schneider, & Corey, 1993, pp.

113–114). Contrary to the prevailing belief, Butler insists that reminiscing is not an "aimless wandering of mind or living in the past." He adds that "the value of reminiscence is seen in the great memories in old age. Not only has reminiscing provided fascinating accounts of unusual and gifted people but it is of great historic value" (Brod & McQuiston, 1983, p. 413).

Baum (1980–1981), an oral historian, defines the life review as "the process of evaluating one's life—one's goals, accomplishments, failures." He explains that the life review process is prompted by a change in one's life caused by experiencing a loss (Lum, 2000, p. 118). Merrian (1989) makes an effort to distinguish the differences between the life review and reminiscing by looking at reminiscing as, first, "simple reminiscing," which is a recounting of life events through story telling that is essentially recreational; whereas "therapeutic reminiscing" is evaluative and akin to the life review process. In effect, "simple reminiscing" recalls "past experiences," whereas "life-review reminiscing" is more comprehensive, because it includes analysis and evaluation (Philleo, 1995, p. 27). Haight (1991) insists that "future research must reflect the differences between life review and reminiscing and must contribute to a uniform and best way of conducting any reminiscing process" (Moran & May, 1995, p. 8).

Because I assign service-learning projects for my students that frequently involve interviewing older people, students invariably express a sense of awkwardness and discomfort in arriving at appropriate issues and questions to broach. I therefore developed a structured life review guide as the following describes:

> . . . a guide to provide the interviewer with a methodological systems approach for information gathering in the life review process. The guide is structured in such a way as to elicit positive events for the purpose of enhancing a sense of well-being as well as to elicit negative life events to encourage the client to address unresolved loss-grief issues. In effect, the Life Review Interview Guide serves to promote high self-esteem and to assist the interviewee through the grieving process. In addition, the guide assisted the student-interviewer in formulating and selecting a wide range of questions. (Beechem, Anthony, & Kurtz, 1998)

Students soon discover that the life review guide serves basically two important purposes: (1) It provides an assessment whereby the practitioner concisely identifies positive and negative features in the elderly person's life. The positive features enhance a sense of well-being. (2) The negative features tend to identify unresolved loss-grief issues that provide a frame of reference to begin the grief work.

Although the original goal in developing a life review guide was to provide for students an orderly, methodical instrument or guide to interview elderly persons, its unintended goal inadvertently provided an effective assessment tool to readily identify positive and negative life events. By emphasizing positive events, self-esteem building is promoted, and by focusing on negative events, which inevitably identifies unresolved loss-grief issues, the practitioner can begin the grief work to assist the elderly person through the grieving process. Since the article was published in an international journal, countless mental health professionals worldwide have reported that the life review guide has served effectively in providing therapy to an elderly clientele, especially grief therapy. My students report that the guide assists them to readily establish rapport with their interviewees and in a more meaningful way. The guide additionally serves to promote intergenerational communication.

Some of my graduate students involved in a project to develop a training video that included interviews with recovering elderly alcoholics also found the life review guide to be a straightforward instrument to obtain essential client information in a nonintrusive manner. Commonly, the elderly interviewees proudly signed their names in the designated right-hand corner as having completed their personal life reviews.

Unlike elderly clients who typically become defensive and resentful when coerced into answering a barrage of seemingly intrusive questions, the interviewees reported that they felt that they had completed an important process; quite unlike the feelings associated with completing an oral drinking history. It is suggested that practitioners experiment by using the Guide in different ways in the recovery process. It is suggested in this discussion that the Guide be used as an "ice breaker" before conducting the drinking history. The following review guide has served not only as a needed "ice breaker" to establish trusting counselor-client relationships but also as an effective assessment tool to identify strengths and weaknesses in the elderly client. The idea was derived from the well-known eco-map influenced from the family systems approach introduced by Virginia Satir, and the lifeline is Maggie Kuhn's (the founder of the Grey Panthers) contribution, whereas the life review concept was developed by Robert Butler. The following is an adaptation for students' use in conducting interviews with elderly persons.

LIFE REVIEW

SOCIAL

SPIRITUAL

HEALTH

ACTIVITIES
RECREATION

FAMILY

ECONOMIC

RECOGNITION

EDUCATION

Key:
Strength: ——————
Conflict: ++++++++++++
Tenuous: - - - - - - - -

Life Review
Author: _____

LIFE REVIEW

SOCIAL

SPIRITUAL

HEALTH

ACTIVITIES
RECREATION

FAMILY

ECONOMIC

RECOGNITION

EDUCATION

Key:
Strength: ————————
Conflict: ++++++++++++
Tenuous: - - - - - - - -

Life Review
Author: _____

Client-Centered Approach to Counseling

There is clearly a need for elder-specific alcoholism treatment. As noted in Chapter VII, the elderly alcoholic tends to become defensive in treatment settings that are confrontational. The elderly alcoholic is as resilient as younger clients in alcoholism treatment but nonetheless tends to become defensive when confronted. Furthermore, the elderly deserve to be treated respectfully rather than to be badgered with a rapid succession of personal questions concerning their drinking history.

Carl Rogers, the late psychotherapist whose therapeutic principles continue to influence students and counselors, is internationally renown for his approach that places the client at the center of importance. As a proponent and practitioner of the humanistic school of counseling, he stressed the therapeutic value of recognizing the dignity and worth of clients and their capacity for self-realization through reason (Zastrow, 1992, p. 408). To counter the ageist attitude that the elderly, especially the elderly alcoholic, is "over the hill" and incapable to learning new behaviors, Rogers' principles have obvious applicability. Client-centered therapy is further characterized by the practitioner exemplifying "realness, caring and a nonjudgmental attitude" to the client. Humanistic psychology has its philosophical roots in existentialist philosophy that postulates that every person regardless of circumstances has the innate ability to draw on his or her inner strengths to endure and survive severely adverse conditions. Despite the strong influences from existential humanistic philosophy, Rogerian psychology has assumed its own distinctive uniqueness with its emphasis on "unconditional positive regard," "non-passive warmth," and "authenticity" or "genuineness" to facilitate the optimal client relationship (Padilla & Salgado de Snyder, 1995, p. 128).

Empathy as an Essential Counseling Skill

Valle concluded that counselors with high levels of genuine empathy skills were better able to affect improved treatment outcomes with their alcoholism clients as demonstrated by fewer relapses (MacKay et al., 1990, Chap. 9, p. 123). In providing counseling to elderly alcoholics, empathy skills will prove to be far more effective than confrontational skills.

Empathy Defined

Redmond (1985) describes empathy as an "understanding of the other's emotional state" (p. 337). As early as 1946, empathy was identified by Charlotte Towle as essential in fostering warmth in the counselor-client relationship. She described that relationship as "a warm relationship in which the worker feels into and with the client without feeling like him" (Perlman, 1969, p. 104). Rogers maintained that the practitioner needs to gain a sense of the "client's private world" by entering the world to gain an understanding "without getting bound up in it" (Keefe, 1976, p. 11). Kalisch (1973) asserts that "empathy is the ability to enter into the life of another person, to accurately perceive his current feelings and their meanings" (p. 1548). He also stresses the importance of the practitioner in retaining his or her personal identity and writes that

> In empathy the helper borrows his patient's feelings in order to further understand them, but he is always aware of his own separateness. He realizes that the feelings of the patient are not his own. (p. 1548)

Coupled with the affective (feeling) and cognitive (understanding) components, there is support for the inclusion of a behavioral component in defining empathy. Stiff, Dillard, Somera, Kim, and Sleight (1988) assert that an altruistic interest in helping someone in distress is precipitated by an empathic response. That is, empathy precipitates "helping and other forms of prosocial behavior" (p. 448). Adding support to the behavioral component of empathy, Daley, Vangelisti, and Daughton stress the need for conversational sensitivity to "pick up hidden meanings in conversations." They insist that "people with high levels of conversational sensitivity are more adept at making more high-level inferences when listening to social exchanges" (Petronio, Alberts, Hecht, & Buley, 1993, p. 240). They further conclude in their study's findings that conversational sensitivity is positively related to empathy.

Beechem and Comstock (1997), in their study of empathy, arrived at a three-part definition that encompasses the affective (feelings), the cognitive (understanding), and the behavioral (communicating empathy) components. The affective component is used momentarily as the counselor enters into the client's world to experience his or her feelings. The cognitive component's role is to understand the client's feelings as they relate to the presenting problem to engage the client in the problem-solving process. The third component, the behavior component, is "the vehicle used to put the affective and cognitive components into action to facilitate the problem-solving process" (p. 88). A case in point is the counselor who provides warmth and empathy to the recovering elderly alcoholic who feels a deep sense of shame and guilt from many years of alcoholism.

EMPATHY VS. SYMPATHY. Rogers stresses the need for the practitioner to "sense the client's private world" to gain an understanding of his or her problem, while also advising the practitioner to know when to leave that world to avoid becoming part of the client's problem, and losing objectivity (Kalisch, 1973, p. 1543). Lacking objectivity, the practitioner is limited to sharing feelings; that is, rather than providing empathy to the troubled client, the practitioner is reduced to providing sympathy in the problem-solving process. Ehmann (1971) cautions that there are dissimilarities in meanings between empathy and sympathy, yet it is common for practitioners to use empathy synonymously with sympathy, whereas empathy "does not contain elements of condolence, agreement, or pity" (p. 76). Miller, Stiff, and Ellis (1988) write that "Unfortunately, this sympathy can turn to apathy and the desire to help can turn to a desire to escape if the process which has come to be known as burnout sets in" (p. 250). The authors argue that the emotional contagion associated with sympathy is a precipitating cause of burnout for "people who choose to work in human service occupations such as health care, social work, and teaching" (p. 250). They further add that "burnout is a reaction to constant, emotional, communicative contact with individuals in need of help" (p. 250).

Although feeling sympathetic for the client can be a precursor to professional burnout, providing empathy can prevent burnout, because, as Miller et al. (1988) insist, the professional worker who develops empathy skills enhances his or her "communicative responsiveness" and overall effectiveness in the worker-client relationship (p. 262). In brief, they conclude that there is a correlation between improved practitioner effectiveness and the client/patient's mental health improvement. With improved treatment outcomes, practitioners feel better about themselves as professionals and are, therefore, less likely to become victimized by job burnout. Gazda and Evans also argue that worker-client relationships based on empathy enhance the likelihood of positive treatment outcomes. They write that "empathic relationships lead to significant improvement in client functioning. . ." (MacKay et al., 1990, p. 69).

Family Systems Therapy

The late Virginia Satir, generally credited with the formulation of the family systems approach to therapy, stressed the need for the counselor-therapist to look at all factors (systems) when assessing and seeking problem resolution to a crisis. The therapist-counselor must be able to identify the interrelatedness of all systems and subsystems. To simply conclude that an elderly recovering alcoholic's depression is symptomatic of neurological changes may be at the exclusion of significant multifacted factors in the client system. Conceivably, drug medication would be administered when other factors (systems) remain unexamined.

Practitioners of family systems therapy consider the potential influences of virtually all systems and subsystems in the assessment process. Predictably, a comprehensive client assessment will disclose that the dysfunctioning of one system, say the health system, will inevitably cause dysfunctioning in other systems, such as the psychosocial systems. Satir (1976) explains the implications of change when she writes that "You can start anywhere and something will change. Each change affects the other parts. Sometimes it works a little like a mobile, change one part and another one or two go out of balance. Sometimes, people feel afraid when it happens. All that it means is that you have disturbed the old balance and you have new balancing to do" (Lum, 2000, p. 66). In Chapter XIII, through the use of case studies, family systems theory will be applied to real-life situations.

Health Intervention Strategies

The need for good physical health must be included in the overall recovery. It is prudent for the counselor to insist on a comprehensive medical examination at the outset of treatment, because it is common for a neurological disorder to be misdiagnosed as depression and treated accordingly. With a complete medical history at the counselor's disposal, certain diagnoses can be reasonably ruled out.

As previously indicated, there is an interplay between the mind and the body as demonstrated by stress theory. The inability to manage stress will predictably have physical health implications. Likewise, when an alcoholic is subjected to the stress associated with recovery the immune system will not work at full capacity and, therefore, deemed ineffective in defending against diseases. The immune system is especially limited in its ability to defend against diseases, when its function has been diverted during stressful times. Cousins (1986) insists that "during periods when the natural immune system is overworked that one's mental state must be called upon. Cousins claims that the body's defense against infection depends in large part on the mechanisms of humoral and cellular immunity, but these mechanisms themselves are influenced by the mental state." Cousins further elaborates on how one's mental state becomes impaired when the natural operation of the immune system is impaired:

The therapeutic successes of nonmedical healers throughout the ages must be evaluated in the light of the capacity of self-healing that exists in all living forms and particularly in human beings. Although the mechanisms of spontaneous recovery from organic and mental disease are not completely understood, it can be assumed that they all operate through a few common organic pathways and that the organism has only a limited repertoire of responses to healing agencies as diverse as ataractic drugs, the laying on hands of hands, transcendental meditation, the use of biofeedback techniques, Zen and yoga practices, faith in a Saint, a person or a drug–and of course the proper patient-doctor relationship. (Padilla & Salgado de Snyder, 1995, pp. 125–126)

With the depletion of the organism's natural defenses against diseases, it is of course prudent for the counselor to integrate into the treatment plan such health objectives as good nutrition, appropriate sleeping habits, and adequate exercise. With Cousin's insistence that with the optimal mental state one can defend against disease, it makes practical sense for counselors to integrate into the recovery regimen such strategies as yoga, transcendental meditation, biofeedback, Zen, relaxation exercises, and other medication techniques. Of particular significance is the increasing use of seemingly unconventional strategies by a myriad of alcoholism treatment programs. Relaxation therapy, in particular, has become a standard strategy for many programs. Counselors report the positive features of relaxation therapy, including enhanced focus and concentration, lower anxiety levels, improved problem-solving capacity, less hypertension, more assertive and less aggressive behaviors, and an overall improved sense of well-being.

Raines Life Transition Model

Raines formulated a methodical, step-by-step model to assist people through major life transitions. The Model includes five specific phases of a transition and tasks to be completed at each phase by the person undergoing the life transition. Raines' Model is designed for virtually any life transition, but it has particular applicability for recovering alcoholics, primarily because its structure allows for the recovering alcoholic and the counselor to readily assess the effectiveness of the transition in each phase. The Model's high level of structure affords the needed security for a person who is discarding a repertoire of familiar, secure behaviors for new ones. Although the discarded behaviors are dysfunctional and an obstacle to successful recovery, they, nonetheless, suggest familiarity and security. The following is an adaptation of Raines Life Transitions Model for elderly persons in alcoholism recovery.

ACTIVATING COMMITMENT. Typically, the alcoholic begins this phase during a successful intervention after the team members' urging that he or she make a commitment to enter a treatment program. During this phase, the alcoholic begins to assume some responsibility for behaviors related to alcoholism. This phase of the transition continues as the person enters treatment and engages in some risk taking as he or she tries new behaviors while committing to new relationships. This is a very challenging phase of the life transition for the recovering alcoholic as commitments to new behaviors and friends take place while, simultaneously, discarding old, dysfunctional behaviors and very likely former drinking companions. An added challenge is the potential resentment from family members and friends whose enabling behaviors, to which they have become accustomed, are now in jeopardy as the recovering alcoholic's emotional needs are beginning to change.

DEVELOPING SUPPORT. The recovering alcoholic is in treatment where he must develop needed support to enhance the recovery. Educational materials will be available to learn about aspects of the disease and how he or she is affected. In this phase he or she will be encouraged to form relationships with those who are also working to recover successfully. The mutual support derived from meaningful relationships is considered by alcoholism counselors as essential in successful recovery. Although it is beneficial to receive emotional support from recovering cohorts, it is during this phase, typically in early treatment, that the recovering person learns how to be mutually supportive as he or she learns to listen and provide needed empathy. As self-esteem and self concept are enhanced, there is observed a certain sense of confidence that one needs to continue successful recovery. Along with an improved self-concept, self-esteem, and confidence he or she becomes more assertive and less in need to resort to nonassertive behaviors, including passivity, aggression, and passive aggression. The recovering alcoholic must also continue to be encouraged to socialize with his recovering cohorts to learn and practice these new behaviors that will in turn support successful recovery.

ADJUSTING EXPECTATIONS. In this phase, there is the likelihood that discrepancies between what was expected in the recovery and what in fact occurred will be recognized; expectations, therefore, may need to be adjusted. For example, the numerous losses experienced by the elderly recovering alcoholic may not have been expected. It is therefore essential that the counselor explain to the recovering person what has happened and why it is necessary to grieve these losses. Such losses as familiar surroundings, friends, and a drinking and social lifestyle will need to be addressed and grieved by the elderly alcoholic or the predictable outcome is depression. This phase is challenging and can cause the recovering person to become discouraged in not having met expectations. In this phase the recovering person may revert to more familiar, secure behaviors such as lashing out at others and withdrawing from his socializing. He may stop participating in group and individualized counseling sessions and, instead, seek the security of his room. In the AA vernacular, these composite behaviors are what constitute a "dry drunk." The alcoholic at this juncture of recovery may have exhibited many behaviors that suggest relapse is eminent.

PRIORITIZING GOALS. In this phase with relapse posing a real threat to continued sobriety, the counselor needs to impress on his client that sacrificing short-term satisfactions (return to drinking) for longer term gains (successful recovery) is at stake and that the recovering alcoholic must value clarify his goals, which may include a return to a drinking lifestyle or a continuation of successful recovery. It is in this phase in which the person has an enormous opportunity to grow, because he or she is encouraged to look at the larger picture and determine what the future holds. With stress and anxiety levels high, the counselor will be able to support the client in teaching strategies to manage the stress and anxiety effectively.

TRANSPOSING IDENTITY. In this phase the recovering alcoholic's self-perception begins to change, when identity as a new person who is successfully recovering emerges. Although there is a markedly improved, healthier self-concept, there is always the lingering fear that relapse can occur at any time and that continued caution and safeguards must always be in place to protect oneself from this insidious disease of alcoholism. The need to continue with a support group such as AA should be encouraged, as well as other viable support groups. Successful recovery may be a major milestone in the once practicing alcoholic's life, but he or she knows that the "one day at a time" slogan must serve as a reminder of how tenuous recovery is and that euphoria is counterproductive.

GRIEF WORK

As noted in Chapter II, the elderly experience disproportionately more losses than any age group, and, therefore, need to fully grieve their losses or the inevitable, predictable outcome is depression. Unfortunately, the alcoholism counselor is at a disadvantage in belatedly providing intervention services for elderly clients after the onset of alcoholism and depression. Therefore, rather than intervening at the ideal primary or even secondary levels, the alcoholism counselor is challenged with intervening at the tertiary level when alcohol dependency is clearly evident. With onset of alcoholism and a clear pattern of repressing ("stuffing") feelings associated with losses, the alcoholism counselor must begin at once to assist the client through the needed grief work or successful alcoholism treatment outcomes are unlikely.

Recovering alcoholics can be heard at any number of AA group meetings or treatment facilities around the country convincingly identifying with their addiction by disclosing "My name is _____, I'm a recovering alcoholic." Despite convincing fellow AA members and themselves that they are successful "recovering alcoholics," questions are raised: Have they fully internalized on an affective, feeling level that they are recovering alcoholics? Will an inability to accept alcoholism on simply a cognitive, intellectual level facilitate relapse? (Chapter XI will specifically address relapse issues and relapse prevention strategies.) Relapse prevention models tend to use behavioral approaches to teach the recovering alcoholic to identify those high-risk situations to avoid. Although lacking empirical research data to support the success rates of the various behaviorally based relapse prevention models, it seems that they can justifiably claim relative success. Surprisingly, there do not seem to exist relapse prevention models that include strategies to address and grieve unresolved loss-grief issues.

As part of the journal-writing activity that I undertook as a former "inpatient" in an alcoholism treatment facility in 1989, I contacted by phone thirty-five of my fellow patients after discharge. At intervals of about two to three months, and then again at five to six months, I discussed with either themselves, or close relatives, their progress, or lack thereof. To my dismay, I identified nine persons who had relapsed during the first two- to three-month period after discharge, and learned that at least fourteen persons had relapsed within the first five to six months after discharge. Altogether, at least twenty-three of thirty-five persons relapsed within five to six months after treatment after twenty-eight to thirty days of inpatient treatment. One of the callers who had insisted that he was "clean and sober" seemed overly eager to convince me of his successful recovery. That very day he phoned me to apologize for being less than truthful and that he was unable to withstand the guilt he had felt in having been less than honest about his lack of successful recovery.

I vividly recall each of these people in treatment announce to their fellow patients, "My name is _____, and I am a recovering alcoholic." Because bonding was so indelibly complete, I felt personal defeat with each of the twenty-three relapses. But what was there about these proclamations that lacked genuineness and sincerity? I considered loss-grief theory that I had used successfully with the terminally ill persons with whom I had worked as a grief counselor for so many years. It occurred to me that successful recovery would also require one to evolve through the grieving process, much like the terminally ill persons who were trying to come to terms with impending death to accept its finality. Although able to locate the scarce literature in applying loss-grief theory in alcoholism counseling, I was struck with its generally superficial application. In retrospect, I questioned whether my relapsed fellow patients had accepted their addictions on an affective, feeling level, or on a cognitive, thinking level. It was obvious that what I had presumed to be a full acceptance of the addiction was instead a mechanical expression of wanting to successfully recover; but to successfully recover, the addict must internalize on a feeling, affective level that he or she is an alcoholic.

Loss-Grief Inventory

Dismayed in seeing so many of my fellow patients relapse, I developed a loss-grief inventory to identify unresolved loss-grief issues to assist the counselor in the assessment and treatment. This inventory was initially administered to court-ordered persons arrested for drunk driving who were required to receive three hours of counseling per week for twelve weeks.

The loss-grief inventory lists twenty-four items, each with time categories (preaddiction losses, losses associated with the addiction, and losses associated with entering treatment) with a Likert scale indicating the extent to which the client experiences the loss. Also included is the "Does not apply" category. Both time and extent categories can be used more than once. For example, when coping with the death of a friend, a client could have been affected to a different extent by the loss during preaddiction, during association with the addiction, and during treatment.

Sample	1	2	3	4	5
	<Least			Most>	
1. Loss of freedom of choice(s)		does not apply			
(A) Preaddiction losses					
(B) Losses associated with addiction					
(C) Losses asscociated with entering treatment					

Loss items were worded in concrete, and not abstract, terms to enhance comprehension. Three open-ended "Other Losses" items were included for those losses not identified in the inventory. The loss-grief inventory items were derived from clients' direct reporting in counseling sessions that occurred before the study began.

LOSS-GRIEF RANKING SCALE

The following sample demonstrates how a total loss-grief weighted ranking can be computed. A general range will indicate the respondent's overall loss-grief rating score.

Sample	1	2	3	4	5
		<Least		Most>	
1. Loss of freedom of choice(s)		does not apply			
(A) Preaddiction losses					
(B) Losses associated with addiction			X		
(C) Losses asscociated with entering treatment					X

0 times 0=	0	Preaddiction
1 times 3=	3	Losses associated with addiction
1 times 5=	5	Losses associated with entering treatment

The twenty-four-item scores are then totaled, with the total overall score yielding the respondent's loss-grief rating. As a result of this survey of ninty-eight respondents, the following ranges were established:

	Low	Medium	High
Item Score	0–49	50–99	100
% Inventories within each category	6%	38%	56%

Beechem, Prewitt, & Scholar, 1996, p. 191

BEECHEM UNRESOLVED LOSS-GRIEF ADDICTION INVENTORY

Check the appropriate categories for each of the losses. You may check off as many time period categories as are appropriate. Then for each of the losses, rate on the 1 to 5 scale the extent to which you are feeling each of the losses.

Categories of losses
(A) Pre-addiction (losses before addiction to substance)
(B) Losses associated with the addiction (losses resulting from either drinking and/or drugging)
(C) Losses associated with entering treatment (losses experienced as a result of entering treatment programs)

	1	2	3	4	5
	<Least			Most>	
Sample					
15. Loss of independence *does not apply*					
(A) Preaddiction losses					
(B) Losses associated with addiction					X
(C) Losses asscociated with entering treatment					
1. Loss of freedom of choice(s) *does not apply*					
(A) Preaddiction losses					
(B) Losses associated with addiction					
(C) Losses asscociated with entering treatment					
2. Loss of support (e.g. friends, relatives, church social services) *does not apply*					
(A) Preaddiction losses					
(B) Losses associated with addiction					
(C) Losses asscociated with entering treatment					
3. Loss of ability to remember details (e.g. blackouts) *does not apply*					
(A) Preaddiction losses					
(B) Losses associated with addictionX					
(C) Losses asscociated with entering treatment					
4. Loss of a driver's license (DUI) *does not apply*					
(A) Preaddiction losses					
(B) Losses associated with addiction					
(C) Losses asscociated with entering treatment					
5. Loss of a goal or a dream *does not apply*					
(A) Preaddiction losses					
(B) Losses associated with addiction					
(C) Losses asscociated with entering treatment					
6. Loss of security caused by sexual, physical or emotional abuse *does not apply*					
(A) Preaddiction losses					
(B) Losses associated with addiction					
(C) Losses asscociated with entering treatment					

	1	2	3	4	5
	<Least			Most>	
7. Loss of a social life	does not apply				
(A) Preaddiction losses					
(B) Losses associated with addiction					
(C) Losses asscociated with entering treatment					
8. Loss of financial stability	does not apply				
(A) Preaddiction losses					
(B) Losses associated with addiction					
(C) Losses asscociated with entering treatment					
9. Loss of self-respect (Negative feelings toward self)	does not apply				
(A) Preaddiction losses					
(B) Losses associated with addiction					
(C) Losses asscociated with entering treatment					
10. Loss of someone special through death	does not apply				
(A) Preaddiction losses					
(B) Losses associated with addiction					
(C) Losses asscociated with entering treatment					
11. Loss of marriage through devorce	does not apply				
(A) Preaddiction losses					
(B) Losses associated with addiction					
(C) Losses asscociated with entering treatment					
12. Loss of children through divorce or seperation	does not apply				
(A) Preaddiction losses					
(B) Losses associated with addiction					
(C) Losses asscociated with entering treatment					
13. Loss of good health	does not apply				
(A) Preaddiction losses					
(B) Losses associated with addiction					
(C) Losses asscociated with entering treatment					
14. Loss of self-trust	does not apply				
(A) Preaddiction losses					
(B) Losses associated with addiction					
(C) Losses asscociated with entering treatment					

	1	2	3	4	5
	<Least			Most>	
15. Loss of trust in others	does not apply				
(A) Preaddiction losses					
(B) Losses associated with addiction					
(C) Losses asscociated with entering treatment					
16. Loss of security due to self-inflicted abuse	does not apply				
(A) Preaddiction losses					
(B) Losses associated with addiction					
(C) Losses asscociated with entering treatment					
17. Loss of a romantic relationship	does not apply				
(A) Preaddiction losses					
(B) Losses associated with addiction					
(C) Losses asscociated with entering treatment					
18. Loss of a social relationship	does not apply				
(A) Preaddiction losses					
(B) Losses associated with addiction					
(C) Losses asscociated with entering treatment					
19. Loss of marital stability	does not apply				
(A) Preaddiction losses					
(B) Losses associated with addiction					
(C) Losses asscociated with entering treatment					
20. Loss of self-confidence	does not apply				
(A) Preaddiction losses					
(B) Losses associated with addiction					
(C) Losses asscociated with entering treatment					
21. Loss of confidence in others	does not apply				
(A) Preaddiction losses					
(B) Losses associated with addiction					
(C) Losses asscociated with entering treatment					
22. Loss of time (e.g. wasted time)	does not apply				
(A) Preaddiction losses					
(B) Losses associated with addiction					
(C) Losses asscociated with entering treatment					

	1	2	3	4	5
	<Least			Most>	
23. Loss of respect for others	does not apply				
(A) Preaddiction losses					
(B) Losses associated with addiction					
(C) Losses asscociated with entering treatment					
24. Loss of respect from others	does not apply				
(A) Preaddiction losses					
(B) Losses associated with addiction					
(C) Losses asscociated with entering treatment					
25a. Other losses (specify)	does not apply				
(A) Preaddiction losses					
(B) Losses associated with addiction					
(C) Losses asscociated with entering treatment					
25b. Other losses (specify)	does not apply				
(A) Preaddiction losses					
(B) Losses associated with addiction					
(C) Losses asscociated with entering treatment					
25c. Other losses (specify)	does not apply				
(A) Preaddiction losses					
(B) Losses associated with addiction					
(C) Losses asscociated with entering treatment					

SUMMARY

This chapter used an eclectic approach in identifying those practice strategies considered effective in working with an elderly alcoholic clientele. As an alternative to conducting the traditional "drinking history" that tends to make elderly alcoholics defensive, an "ice breaker" may be used as a substitute for the "drinking inventory," and the life review is recommended as an ice breaker.

A client-centered approach, as well as the use of empathy skills, was recommended as an effective strategy to enhance counselor-client relationships in working with the elderly alcoholic in need of self-concept development.

Family systems theory, integrated into the repertoire of practice strategies, provides for the counselor an understanding of the interplay between the client's systems. It was stressed that the maintenance of good health must include strategies that support and restore the functioning of the immune system.

Raines' Life Transitions Model provides for the counselor and client a step-by-step approach to affect a successful transition with an effective built-in mechanism to measure success at each phase of the transition.

Chapter IX concluded with a discussion on grief work and its importance as a strategy in working with elderly alcoholics, a client population that has experienced numerous losses, many of which remain unresolved. The key to this section is for the counselor to appreciate the need for the recovering alcoholic to accept his addiction on an affective (feeling) level that needs to transcend the cognitive (thinking) level.

GLOSSARY OF TERMS

Affective: Relates to feelings.

Assessment: A process of information gathering that identifies pertinent client information, including strengths and weaknesses.

"Authenticity": As used by Carl Rogers, the term suggests a warm, genuine counselor-client relationship, as opposed to one that is emotionally detached. Rogers uses authenticity and genuineness interchangeably.

Cognitive: Relates to thinking.

Drinking history: Part of the assessment that seeks to obtain information related to the client's drinking behavior and alcoholic beverages of choice.

Eclectic approach: An approach that borrows the most applicable and positive features from any number of psychological theories and strategies; e.g., combining behavioral and psychodynamic practice strategies.

Eco-map: Made popular by Virginia Satir and used as a practitioner's tool to apply the systems approach in counseling/therapy.

Empathy: Although there exist varying definitions, empathy is generally regarded by mental health professionals as an understanding of the feelings.

Family systems approach: A counseling/therapeutic approach that seeks to understand and analyze the interrelationship between client's systems, including economic, and spiritual, and psychological systems.

Genuineness/authenticity: Terms used sometimes interchangeably to describe the counselor's open, honest relationship with the client.

"Ice breaker": A low-keyed strategy to lower client resistance and defensiveness (e.g., life review).

Life review therapy: A low-keyed counseling strategy used to gain a broad understanding of the client's life history from birth to the present.

Raines' life transition model: Designed by Dr. Max Raines to assist a person through a major life transition.

Reminiscing therapy: Used interchangeably with life review therapy.

Sympathy: As opposed to empathy, sympathizing is a reinforcement of pity.

"Unconditional positive regard": A term coined by Carl Rogers that refers to the counselor's attitude toward the client.

STUDY QUESTIONS

1. It is recommended that the counselor embrace a strength perspective in the assessment process. Explain.

2. In which ways do you feel that the Life Review Guide would serve an elderly clientele effectively?

3. Distinguish between empathy and sympathy.

4. A "three-part definition" of empathy was introduced. Identify and describe each of the three parts.

5. To what is Virginia Satir referring when she alludes to the "interrelatedness" of systems and subsystems? Give examples as it applies to alcoholism treatment of the elderly person.

6. Norman Counsins draws attention to the benefit of a strong immune system. What are the implications in treating an elderly alcoholic person if the immune system is either healthy or unhealthy?

7. Demonstrate through example of the applicability of Raines' five-step model in evolving through a life transition related to alcoholism recovery for an older person.

8. Why is it especially important to use grief work intervention strategies in treating elderly persons for alcoholism.

9. As an intervention tool, the loss-grief inventory is recommended. Identify the three "time categories" and provide an example of each.

REFERENCES

Barrow, G.M. (1992). *Aging, the individual, and society* (5th ed.). St. Paul, MN: West Publishing Company.

Beechem, M., Anthony, C., & Kurtz, J. (1998). A life review guide: A structured systems approach to information gathering. *The International Journal of Aging and Human Development, 46*(1), 25–44.

Beechem, M. & Comstock, J. (1997). Teaching empathy skills to undergraduate social work students. *The Journal of Baccalaureate Social Work, 2*(2), 87–96.

Beechem, M., Prewitt, J., & Scholar, J. (1996). Loss-grief Addiction Model. *Journal of Drug Education, 26*(2), 183–198.

Brod, R.L. & McQuiston, J.M. (1983). American Indian adult education and literacy: The first national survey. *Journal of American Indian Education, (1)*, 1–16.

Corey, M., Schneider, J., & Corey, G. (1993). *Becoming a helper* (2nd ed.). Pacific Grove, CA: Brooks/Cole Publishing Company.

Cousins, N. (1986). *Human options.* New York: Berkley Publishing Group.

Ehmann, V.E. (1971). Empathy: Its origin, characteristics, and process perspectives. *Psychiatric Care, IX*(2), 76.

Graham, K., Saunders, S.J., Flower, M.C., Timiney, C.B., White-Campbell, M., & Pietropado, A.Z. (1995). *Addictions treatment for older adults.* New York: The Haworth Press, Inc.

Hepworth, D.H. & Larsen, J. (1990). *Direct social work practice: Theory and skills* (3rd ed.), Belmont, CA: The Dorsey Press.

Kalish, B.J. (September, 1973). What is empathy? *American Journal of Nursing, 73*(9), 1548–1551.

Keefe, T. (1976). Empathy: The critical skill. *Social Work, 71*(1), 10–14.

Lum, D. (2000). Social work practice and people of color: A process-stage approach. Pacific Grove, CA: Brooks/Cole.

MacKay, R.C., Carver, E.J., & Hughes, J.R. (Eds.). (1990). *Empathy in the helping relationship.* New York: Springer Publishing Company.

Miller, K.I., Stiff, J.B., & Ellis, B.H. (September, 1988). Communication and empathy as precursors to burnout among human service workers. *Communication Monographs, 55*(4), 250–265.

Moran, J.R. & May, P.A. (1995) American Indians. In J. Philleo (Ed.), *Cultural competence for social workers: A guide for alcohol and other drug abuse prevention professionals working with ethnic/racial communities.* SAMHSA 4. National Clearinghouse for Alcohol and Drug Information, 8.

Padilla, A.M. & Salgado de Snyder, V.N. (1995). Hispanics: What the culturally informed evaluator needs to know. In Orlandi, M.A. (Ed.), *Cultural competence for social workers: A guide for alcohol and other drug abuse prevention professionals working with ethnic/racial communities.* SAMHSA 1, U. S. Department of Health and Human Services.

Perlman, H.H. (Ed.). (1969). *Helping: Charlotte Towle on social work.* Chicago, IL: Univerisity of Chicago Press.

Petronio, S., Alberts, J.K., Hecht, M.L., & Buley, J. (1993). *Contemporary perspectives on interpersonal communication.* Madison, WI: Brown & Benchmark.

Philleo, J. (Ed.) (1995). Introduction. *Cultural competence for social workers: A guide for alcohol and other drug abuse prevention professionals working with ethnic/racial communities.* SAMHSA 4. National Clearinghouse for Alcohol and Drug Information, XIV.

Raines, M. (1983). *Life transitions workshop* (unpublished). E. Lansing, MI: Michigan State University.

Redman, M.V. (December, 1985). The relationship between perceived communication competence and perceived empathy. *Communication Monographs, 52,* 337.

Stiff, J.B., Dillard, J.P., Somera, L., Kim, H., & Sleight, C. (1988). Empathy, communication, and prosocial behavior. *Communications Monographs, 55,* 198–213.

Zastrow, C. (1992). *Practice of social work,* (5th ed). Pacific Grove, CA: Brooks/Cabe Publishing Company.

Chapter X

THE SPIRITUAL COMPONENT OF TREATMENT

Every addiction is, in the final analysis, a disease of the spirit.
Doweiko, 1999

SPIRITUAL NEEDS AND THEIR VARIED MEANINGS

Well known among alcoholism counselors is their clients' lack of a deeper, fuller meaning of life and its purpose. Although few, if any, addictionologists concur on a precise definition of spirituality, there is apparent unanimity of agreement that spiritual needs must be addressed and met for successful recovery, because it serves as the vehicle to explore feelings, thoughts, desires, and the power to change from within. In effect, spiritual fulfillment frees the alcoholic as a slave to his or her addiction to make choices that lead to successful alcoholism recovery.

Van Wormer (1997) likens recovery to a journey of sorts that is intertwined with serenity and "spiritual health." The journey takes the recovering alcoholic from "isolation to intimacy, from alienation to meaning, and from running away to reaching toward" (p. 155). Wegscheider-Cruse (1989) draws attention to the confusion between "spiritual" and "religious" when she asserts that "every bona fide religion is strongly spiritual, but not all that is spiritual is religious." With the following examples, she broadens the definition of spirituality as she distinguishes between "religious" and "spiritual" by stating:

> In a fully developed person the spiritual potential can find expression in a wide variety of both inner and outer activities: Meditation, prayer, discipline, organized religion, development of the higher self, humanitarian service, commitment to causes fostering justice, health, human dignity, and respect for other parts of our plenary community–to name a few. The pos-

142

sibilities for joy and satisfaction in such pursuits transcend anything else that the human potentials can offer. (p. 40)

Bullis (1996) makes a distinction between religion and spirituality when he suggests that religion "refers to the outward form of belief including rituals, dogmas and creeds, and denominational identity," and that spirituality relates to the "inner feelings and experiences of the immediacy of a higher power." He further separates spirituality from religion, because the former requires a higher level of consciousness (i.e., alpha consciousness); that is, one transcends beyond beta, a lower level of consciousness, to alpha consciousness to experience spirituality. Bullis writes that "it is here that the beta consciousness characteristics of logic, analysis, and empiricism give way to the alpha consciousness of intuition, poetic thinking, and analogy." He adds that "Alpha is the key to spiritual consciousness" (p. 5). For the ultimate attainment of spirituality Bullis includes the delta and theta levels of consciousness in the following description:

> The two deepest states, designated delta and theta, can illustrate the most remarkable spiritual consequences. In this stage, adepts can undergo painless dentistry, surgery, and childbirth. These stages, thus, manifest perhaps the most dramatic example of how spiritual exercises can influence and control physiological activities. There is, currently, little research on these states. Science is just beginning to scratch the surface of understanding such phenomena. Delta and theta states are rarely even recognized—let along researched. (Bullis, 1996)

SUPPORT GROUPS AND SRATEGIES

The following discussion will briefly describe some of the support groups and strategies that purport to assist the recovering alcoholic in facilitating their spiritual needs. Included in this category are Alcoholics Anonymous (A.A.), the Twelve-Step Program, Rational Recovery (R.R.), Secular Organizations for Sobriety (S.O.S.), and Nguzo Saba .

Alcoholics Anonymous (A.A.)

Alcoholics Anonymous' founders Bill Wilson and Dr. Bob Smith began what has become a well-known support group that has gained both national and international reputations for its effectiveness in supporting thousands of alcoholics seeking sobriety.   From A.A.'s humble beginnings in 1935 in Akron, Ohio, the organization, with its highly developed spiritual orientation, has made optimal use of its Twelve-Step Program to meet the spiritual needs of its followers.

Twelve-Step Program

The classic Twelve Steps to Recovery are as follows:
1. We admitted we were powerless over alcohol–that our lives had become unmanageable.
2. Came to believe that a Power greater than ourselves could restore us to sanity.
3. Made a decision to turn our will and our lives over to the care of God *as we understood Him.*
4. Made a searching and fearless moral inventory of ourselves.
5. Admitted to God, to ourselves, and to another human being the exact nature of our wrongs.
6. Were entirely ready to have God remove all these defects of character.
7. Humbly asked Him to remove our shortcomings.
8. Made a list of all persons we had harmed, and became willing to make amends to them all.
9. Made direct amends to such people wherever possible, except when to do so would injure them or others.
10. Continued to take personal inventory and when we were wrong promptly admitted it.
11. Sought through prayer and meditation to improve our conscious contact with God as we understood Him, praying only for knowledge of His will for us and the power to carry that out.
12. Having had a spiritual awakening as the result of these steps, we tried to carry this message to alcoholics and to practice these principles in all our affairs. (Twelve Steps and Twelve Traditions, 1997)

In addition to Alcoholics Anonymous' Twelve-Step Program, which explains the organization and its principles, the spirituality component is supported by the Serenity Prayer, which A.A. considers as a nondenominational affirmation, and the Big Book which chronicles forty-four life histories of alcoholics representing a wide spectrum of socioeconomic groups. Despite A.A.'s broad acceptance as a viable support group for alcoholics in recovery, it is not without its critics. It has indisputably a strong religious orientation, specifically Christianity, as suggested by the wording of the Twelve Steps with the following religiosity-laden references:

"A power greater than ourselves" (Step Two)

"To turn our will and our lives over to the care of God" (Step Five)

"To have God remove all of these defects of character" (Step Six)

"Humbly ask Him" (Step Seven)

"Sought through prayer and meditation to improve our conscious contact with God as we understand Him" (Step Eleven)

"Praying only for knowledge of his will" (Step Eleven)

"A spiritual awakening" (Step Twelve)

Jung (1994) suggests that the Twelve Steps' religious overtones may present obstacles for agnostics, or nonbelievers of God, when he asserts that the Twelve Steps ". . . often represent major hurdles for those who do not believe in the concept of God, even though A.A. expands the definition of God to allow even nonreligious conceptions" (p. 181).

Wallace (2001) whose research study explored the existence of patriarchy in Alcoholics Anonymous meetings concluded that a pervasive male dominance exists with the covert and overt features. The covert evidence relates to female A.A. members rarely being called on to either speak or to lead meetings, and the tendency for women not to hold leadership positions. The overt existence of male patriarchy relates to the sexual harassment to which new female members are frequently subjected. Her study draws attention to the vulnerability of newly recovering women whose sobriety is threatened when sexually harassed. "Thirteen Stepping," A.A. jargon that refers to efforts to date new female members, is apparently quite common.

The Pueblo Indian Twelve-Step Approach

I was asked to conduct a training segment of a workshop at a substance abuse conference at Boston University. One of my fellow participants, an American Indian faculty member in a social work program at a southwestern university, also presented a workshop on the Pueblo Indian version of the Twelve Steps. I was struck by the creativity and resourcefulness in adapting the Twelve-Step Program to meet cultural needs. The counselor needs to be aware that the wording emphasizes nature, which reflects American Indians' close interrelationship with this theme. Because agnostics (nonbelievers), as well as non-Christian religions may regard some of the Twelve Step's wording as objectionable, they may wish to modify the wording to meet their cultural needs much as the Pueblo Indian Tribe has done in the following version of the Twelve-Step Program.

1. We surrendered, and admitted great defeat by the evil nature of alcohol—that it took great control of our life and made our life miserable and unbalanced.
2. We came back to believe in *THE WAY*; that a GREAT MYSTERY exists (in and about the universe), and in all things, seen and unseen that this GREAT MYSTERY can guide us from our crazy ways and most inner cravings.
3. Every day, we place down our tobacco/cornmeal in a sacred manner and called upon the GREAT MYSTERY, to take care of our will and our lives because we were unable to run it by ourselves.
4. In silence, we think deeply without fear of our own moral strengths and weaknesses; then placed them in good order with our past, at peace with ourselves and found what good it does for us;
5. We sat in council with that GREAT MYSTERY, a spiritual advisor admitted that exact nature of **ALL** our wrongs and weaknesses, making way to do good in our lives;
6. After laying down our tobacco/cornmeal in a sacred manner, with the help of the GREAT MYSTERY, we were ready to change and now walk the good road;
7. We humbly asked the GREAT MYSTERY and our friends to look at our shortcomings and help us change.
8. We counted all earth beings hurt by our drinking and then went out to make up for these hurts;
9. As we walked the good road, we make up for these hurts except when the hurts would cause further damage or injury to them or others. Then we forgave ourselves and work to put back goodness in the lives of them and others;
10. At sunrise and sunset, we placed down our sacred tobacco/cornmeal in a good way and think about our strengths and weaknesses, and when we were wrong, we say so;
11. We continue to ask through our spiritual gatherings, prayers and silence, a sacred togetherness with the GREAT MYSTERY and all beings; asking forgiveness and strength to do what is right;
12. Understanding a spiritual goodness in the Native Peoples' belief and values and way of life, we try to help others with addiction help themselves, and to show them how it is done by working all these shields and foundations in all our daily affairs. (Pueblo Indians, Jan. 1998)

I conducted a phone interview with Mr. James Williams, an acquaintance from Tahlequah, Oklahoma, who is employed as a substance abuse counselor for the Cherokee Nation. His fascinating description of how the Sweat Lodge is used spiritually as a viable alcoholism treatment modality follows:

The round, dome-shape of the Sweat Lodge symbolizes a return to Mother Nature and the womb. In a circular pit are placed the granite or lava rocks which are heated from the burning cedar, sage, or sweet grass sprinkled on top of the rocks. The swirling smoke ascends above in a waving motion as it moves from participant to participant. The terms "smoked me" or "smudging" refer to the effects of a participant's encounter with the smoke. As steam rises from the rocks prayers are directed to the Creator from the Sweat Lodge. The medicine man fans in a circular motion to ward off evil and to send prayers to heaven. That is, prayers go up with smoke. The rocks help people to focus on ourselves and what is important in the "here and now."

In the blessing, there are four rounds of prayers around the center. In the first round, going from left to right, water is slowly sprinkled onto the rocks. In round two, the open round, songs are sung, or you talk about anything that is on your mind or in your head. In the third round, you pray for others, and in the fourth round, prayers are for one's self.

If you have had feelings going into the lodge, it will make you ill because the spirituality is very powerful. Your bad thoughts will make you sick, so act the way you want to feel.

In reply to my question regarding whether the Pueblo Indians' revision of the Twelve-Step Program was helpful in generally reflecting Indian culture, Mr. Williams explained that "the revised version is more meaningful to Indian people because the power is within us, and not above, or higher than us."

The Serenity Prayer

The Serenity Prayer, which is faithfully recited at the conclusion of every A.A. meeting, is considered by many to be further evidence of the presence of religious and/or Christian thinking pervading A.A.'s philosophical orientation: "God grant me the Serenity to accept the things I cannot change, courage to change the things I can, and the wisdom to know the differences" (Wegscheidor-Cruse, 1989, p. 269).

The obvious question raised is whether the alcoholic who does not relate to the concept of God can benefit from A.A., to which A.A. responds in Chapter IV of the Big Book, "We Agnostics":

When, therefore, we speak to you of God, we mean your own conception of God. This implies, too, to other spiritual expressions which you find in this book. Do not let any prejudice you may have against spiritual terms deter you from honestly asking yourself what they mean to you. At the start, this was all we needed to commence spiritual growth, to effect our first conscious relation with God as we understood Him. Afterward, we found ourselves accepting many things which then seemed entirely out of reach. That was growth, but if we wished to grow we had to begin somewhere. So we used our own conception, however limited it was. (The Big Book, 1976)

In reply to a request for A.A. printed materials, I received a very gracious, personalized letter thanking me from "All of us here at the General Service Office." Enclosed in the packet were the 1998 Membership Survey, the Research Service piece that stated "We welcome additional information from researchers and from members of A.A. who have experience to share or comments to make," as well as a fact sheet titled "Information on Alcoholics Anonymous." Curiously, there was no inclusion of printed materials about their role in meeting spiritual needs of recovering alcoholics. The literature does, however, contain one reference in underscored, bold print about **"WHAT A.A. DOES NOT DO."** Following this emphatic assertion appear fourteen items that A.A. purports not to do, including "Offer religious services." Although the literature refers to the Big Book and Twelve Steps and Twelve Traditions, there is no reference to spirituality. Is the spirituality omission indicative of A.A.'s intention to disassociate with the claim that they have a strong Christian religious affiliation? Although the disclaimer concerning a religious affiliation is understandable considering the criticism to which it has been subjected, it is unfortunate that A.A. would omit spirituality references for fear that the public would perceive religion and spirituality to be one and the same. Because of the striking similarities between religion and spirituality, it might be prudent to educate the public about the dissimilarities.

Sharon Wegscheider-Cruse's prayer is intended to serve counselors and is absent of religious reference and should, therefore, not be construed as offensive regardless of one's belief system.

A PRAYER FOR GUIDES

Help me to create a setting for risk.

As each new person and family comes to visit me,
    help me to recognize and accept
    the fear and pain they bring with them.

Let me show them that I am not afraid.

Let me use my sensitivity and courage
    to mirror back to them all that I see and hear
    that keeps them in their bondage
    of pain and loneliness.

Give me the care and perception
    to show them their gifts and their power.

Let me reach out and touch—
    then let me leave them alone.

Let me trust in their strength and courage.

Let me let them make their own decisions and choices.

Help me to lead people to wholeness
   by being whole.

                                   Wegscheider-Cruse, 1989

Rational Recovery (R.R.)

In the late 1980s, Rational Recovery's founder Jack Trimpey created rational recovery (R.R.) as a support group for chemically addicted persons. Many of R.R.'s concepts are derived from rational emotive therapy (RET) developed by Albert Ellis. As an alternative to A.A., much of R.R.'s belief system is markedly dissimilar to A.A., although many similarities remain such as rejection of the disease concept of alcoholism, the need for a "higher power," and the development of a "moral inventory" to address moral shortcomings. Yet R.R. is similar to many of A.A.'s practices in that both organizations have abstinence as their goal, strict confidentiality at meetings, and a belief that lives are destroyed through the continued use of alcohol (Mooney, Eisenberg, & Eisenberg, 1992, p. 42).

Comparison of Rational Recovery to Alcoholics Anonymous characteristics	
• Rational Recovery (R.R.)	• Alcoholics Anonymous (A.A.)
• Goal of total abstinence	• Goal of total abstinence
• Sobriety is best defense against alcoholism	• Sobriety is best defense against Alcoholism
• Strict confidentiality	• Confidentiality at meetings
• Meetings once a week	• Meetings seven days a week
• Nonacceptance of disease concept of alcoholism (you're recovered)	• Acceptance of disease concept of alcoholism (you're recovering)
• People are free to make decision to stop drinking. Supports belief that individuals have power/free choice to stop drinking • "Think yourself sober" is a common expression; accept yourself as you are (i.e., love yourself). Regard of moral shortcomings. Commit self to sobriety forever	• Alcoholics are powerless to stop alcohol addiction • Embraces need to surrender to "higher power • Develop a "moral inventory" • "One day at a time"
• Recovered	• Recovering

• Emphasis on here and now	• Emphasis on history
• Professional coordinates run meetings	• Nonprofessionals ("old timers") run meetings
• Primary written material: small book	• Primary written material: Big Book
• Look within yourself for strength and direction	• Embrace "higher power" for strength/direction

Secular Organizations for Sobriety (S.O.S.)

Like Rational Recovery, S.O.S. was established as an alternative to Alcoholics Anonymous. Although it is considered "nonspiritual", S.O.S. is closer in its principles and practices to A.A. than is R.R.

S.O.S.'s guidelines follow:

- To break the cycle of denial and achieve sobriety, we first acknowledge that we are alcoholics.

- We reaffirm this truth daily and accept without reservation—one day at a time—the fact that, as clean and sober individuals, we cannot and do not drink or use, *no matter what.*

- Since drinking/using is not an option for us, we take whatever steps are necessary to continue our sobriety priority lifelong.

- A high quality of life—the good life—can be achieved. However, life is also filled with uncertainties; therefore, we do not drink/use regardless of feelings, circumstances, or conflicts.

- We share in confidence with each other our thoughts and feelings as sober, clean individuals.

- Sobriety is our priority, and we are each individually responsible for our lives and our sobriety. (p. 44)

To assist its members in the recovery process, the acronym BEAST was developed:

B is for Boozing Opportunities (weddings, parties, trips, and so on). R.R. says you need to be aware of the pitfalls but do not need to avoid such events. You are not powerless in the face of temptation, and can choose not to succumb.

E is for Enemy Recognition. You need to distinguish those thoughts coming from the Enemy (Beast) that are positive about booze or drugs.

A is for Accuse the Beast of Malice. You can be angry at the Beast for its evil deeds (trying to tempt you) or you can laugh at it. Either way you need to make clear to the Beast that you have the upper hand and you won't relinquish it.

S is for Self-Control and Self-Worth Reminders. You must find ways of showing the Beast that you have self-control (like moving your hands in front of your face and holding them there, totally in your control, until Beast backs down); you must also find ways of telling yourself that you are a worthwhile person. You then choose not to drink for the same reason you drank: to feel good about yourself.

T is for Treasuring Your Sobriety. This means focusing on the pleasures of life that are attainable only in sobriety (a concept similar to that in A.A.).

Mooney, Eisenberg, & Eisenberg, 1992, p. 44

Kwanzaa and Nguzo Saba (The Seven Principles)

Following the Watts Riots, Dr. Manlana Karenga, a philosopher in African Culture, created the Kwanzaa Celebration and the Nguzo Saba in 1966 in an effort to establish cultural ties between African-Americans and Africa, so that African-Americans would recognize and be proud of their rich African cultural heritage. He borrowed the Swahili word, Kwanzaa, which means "first fruits of the harvest" and created Nguzo Saba, the Seven Principles that are to be observed annually with one principle observed daily beginning from December 26 through January 1 (1998). There is also emphasized intergenerational communication, a cultural transmission from Africa, in which the highly revered elders pass on The Seven Principles to a younger generation.

Mrs. Julia Arnold, a leader in the Pensacola, Florida, African-American community, discussed with my cultural diversity students how the principles contained within Nguzo Sabo have also been used successfully in treating African-Americans for substance abuse addictions. Following is a brief description of the Seven Principles, or Nguzo Saba:

- Umoja (OO-MO-JAH) Unity stresses the importance of togetherness for the family and the community, which is reflected in the African saying, "I am We," or "I am because We are."

- Kujichagulia (KOO-GEE-CHA-GOO-LEE-YAH) Self-Determination requires that we define our common interests and make decisions that are in the best interest of our family and community.

- Ujima (OO-GEE-MAH) Collective Work and Responsibility reminds us of our obligation to the past, present and future, and that we have a role to play in the community, society, and world.

- UjamA.A. (OO-JAH-MAH) Cooperative economics emphasizes our collective economic strength and encourages us to meet common needs through mutual support.

- Nia (NEE-YAH) Purpose encourages us to look within ourselves and to set personal goals that are beneficial to the community.

- Kuumba (KOO-OOM-BAH) Creativity makes use of our creative ener-
gies to build and maintain a strong and vibrant community.
- Imani (EE-MAH-NEE) Faith focuses on honoring the best of our traditions, draws upon the best in ourselves, and helps us strive for a higher
level of life for humankind, by affirming our self-worth and confidence in
our ability to succeed and triumph in righteous struggle. (Everything about
Kwanzaa, 2001)

Existential Approach to Counseling

With numerous spiritually focused practice strategies, there is one that
deserves special attention, existential therapy. As so many accomplished
counselors will testify, there is in every person an inner strength that must be
ignited to become a catalyst in the recovery process. Existentialists such as
Carl Rogers and other like-minded mental health practitioners stress the lim-
itless innate client potentialities that are rarely, if ever, discovered, nurtured,
and fully realized. Perhaps influenced by an industrial society that recognizes only concrete entities that contribute to productivity, there exists the
tragedy of ignoring such intangibles as the inner strength to reach virtually
impossible goals. Although the main thrust in the early beginnings of alcoholism treatment is to "surrender to a higher power," are we not, in effect,
stifling the innate, untapped potential of the recovering alcoholic to play an
active role in the attainment of successful treatment goals, sobriety?
Katzenbaum (1998) describes existentialism as "a philosophical position that
emphasizes people's responsibility for their own lives" (p. 72). As counselors
engage their clients in the decision-making process regarding recovery, they
will, in effect, be taking responsibility for their recovery, or "their own lives,"
as Katzenbaum asserted. Of course, there is another position that seems diametrically opposed that insists that successful recovery is contingent on surrendering to a "higher power." Counselors are fully cognizant of the alcoholic's long history in arrogantly working independently of others' advice,
such as to recover, and work toward problem resolution independently,
rather than interdependently. Surrendering to a "higher power" was largely
designed to encourage the recovering alcoholic to defer to a "higher power"
that would in effect cause his arrogant behavior to be rendered ineffectual–
somewhere, a semblance of balance needs to be struck between untapping
the creative inner power of the client and the need to use strategies that deter
arrogant decision making.
Numerous definitions of existentialism abound, but there are common elements with which most theorists concur. Corey's (1986) definition, which
falls within the counseling/therapeutic context, includes the following elements:

. . . a respect for the client's subjective experience and a trust in the capacity of the client to make positive and constructive conscious choice so . . . an emphasis on the vocabulary of freedom, choice, values, personal responsibility, autonomy, purpose, and meaning. (p. 101)

SUMMARY

Several definitions of spirituality were examined that established its separateness from religiosity. Support groups, including Alcoholics Anonymous, Rational Recovery, and Secular Organizations for Sobriety, were identified that facilitated spirituality in elderly recovering alcoholics. The Twelve-Step Program, a strategy used in various types of treatment settings, was analyzed for its religious and spiritual content. Its religious content was primarily of a Christian orientation that may pose problems for non-Christian recovering alcoholics, including agnostics. Nguzo Saba (The Seven Principles) was discussed as a potentially viable culturally specific strategy for African-American recovering alcoholics. Also studied was an American Indian version of the Twelve Steps that contained culturally relevant content for the American-Indian elderly alcoholic.

Chapter X discussed the importance for the counselor to identify and nurture inner strengths to enhance the likelihood of successful alcoholism recovery for the elderly person. The concern was raised that the clients' submission or "surrendering to a higher power" may stifle the innate inner creative energy that exists in every person that can be activated to facilitate successful alcoholism recovery.

Existentialism was examined as a philosophy embraced by a growing number of professional counselors that emphasizes the inner powers and abilities of the individual. It further stresses the importance of assuming responsibility for one's behavior.

GLOSSARY OF TERMS

Alcoholics Anonymous: a support group for alcoholics founded in 1935.

Alpha: One level higher than beta consciousness and characterized by poetic thinking and analogy. Considered the key to spiritual consciousness.

Beta: Lowest level of consciousness characterized by logical and analytical thinking.

The Big Book: A compilation of stories representing virtually every socioeconomic station in life that depicts alcoholism.

Delta and Theta consciousness: In these levels of consciousness, painless dentistry and surgery can be performed, as well as childbirth.

Existentialism: A philosophy embraced by a growing number of counselors that emphasizes the inner power and ability of the individual. It further stresses the importance of assuming responsibility for one's behavior.

"Higher power": A power greater than one's self. The "Higher Power's" varied meanings range from God to one's A.A. group.

Kwanzaa: An annual celebration of African-American culture.

Nguzo Saba: A component of the Kwanzaa celebration to transmit the Seven Principles by the elders to the younger members.

Rational Recovery (R.R.): Support group for recovering alcoholics with a philosophy patterned after Albert Ellis' Rational Emotive Theory (RET).

Secular Organizations for Sobriety (S.O.S.): A support group for recovering alcoholics. Without a spiritual component it is considered an alternative to A.A.

Serenity prayer: Recited at each A.A. meeting to promote sobriety.

Spirituality: Numerous varied definitions exist; for some, it is an internal sense of serenity and peacefulness in having surrendered to a "higher power" to assist in the recovery process. A less religious and more existential meaning suggests that it is associated with the attainment of one's potential.

Twelve-Step Program: An intervention strategy that originated with A.A., consisting of twelve principles to follow for recovering alcoholics. It is currently embraced by numerous support groups.

STUDY QUESTIONS

1. Based on the definitions of religiousity and spirituality provided in Chapter X, distinguish differences between the two.

2. Having arrived at a definition of spirituality from the preceding question, of what benefit is it for recovering alcoholics to meet spiritual needs?

3. Do A.A.'s strategies, especially with its use of the Serenity Prayer, The Twelve Steps, and the Big Book, serve to support or hinder successful treatment goals in non-Christian elderly alcoholics? Support your position with concrete examples.

4. Identify the similarities and the dissimilarities between the following support groups: Alcoholics Anonymous, Rational Recovery and Secular Organizations for Sobriety.

5. As an intervention strategy in alcoholism treatment, do you feel that the Pueblo Indian version of the Twelve-Step Program has potential to be effective for the elderly American Indian seeking sobriety?

REFERENCES

The big book: The basic text for alcoholics anonymous (3rd ed.). (1976). New York: Alcoholics World Services, Inc.

Bullis, R.R. (1996). *Spirituality on social work practice.* Washington, DC: Taylor and Francis Publishers.

Corey, G. (1986). *Theory and practice of counseling and psychotherapy* (3rd ed.). Monterey, CA: Brooks/Cole Publishing Company.

Doweiko, H.E. (1999). *Concepts of chemical dependency* (4th ed.). Pacific Grove, CA: Brooks/Cole Publishing Company.

Everything About Kwanzaa. (March, 2001). http://www.tike.com/celeb-kw.htm

Indian Twelve Steps. June, 1996 paper presented at the Cirriculum Development and Educational Institute at Boston University's Alcohol and Drug Institute, Boston, MA.

Jung, J. (1994). *Under the influence: alcohol and human behaviors.* Belmont, CA: Brooks/Cole Publishing Company.

Katzenbaum, R.J. (1998). *Death, society and human experience* (6th ed.). Boston: Allyn & Bacon.

Mooney, A.J., Eisenberg, A., & Eisenberg, H. (1992). *The recovery book,* New York: Workman Publishing.

Twelve steps and twelve traditions. (1997). New York: Alcoholics Anonymous World Services.

van Wormer, K. (1997). *Alcoholism treatment: A social work perspective.* Chicago: Nelson-Hall Publishers.

Wallace, G. (2001). *Does patriarchy exist in alcoholics anonymous: The fight for social justice continues.* 18th Annual Baccaleaureate Program Directors Conference at Destin, Florida, 2001.

Wegscheider-Cruse, S. (1989). *Another chance: Hope and health for the alcoholic family* (2nd ed.). Palo Alto, CA: Science and Behavior Books, Inc.

Chapter XI

RELAPSE

There is evidence that approximately 90 percent of alcoholics
are likely to experience at least one relapse over the 4-year
period following treatment. Despite some promising leads, no
controlled studies definitively have shown any single or combined intervention that prevents relapse in a fairly predictable
manner. Thus relapse as a central issue of alcoholism treatment warrants further study

The National Institute on Alcohol Abuse and Alcoholism,
1989

RELAPSE RATE HIGH

Alcoholism researchers and counselors generally concur that the relapse
rate among recovering alcoholics is generally at unacceptable levels and
that successful treatment outcomes are frequently unmet. Bowman and
Jellinek (1941), pioneers in alcoholism research, reported in 1941 that the
composite success rate of seven case studies with use of traditional psychotherapy was 25 to 30 percent. The researchers defined success as two to
four years of abstinence after treatment termination (Bowman & Jellinek,
1941). A study conducted by Vaillant (1983) on 685 alcoholics who were surveyed two years after completing treatment showed that 67 percent continued to abuse alcohol, whereas only 20 percent were abstinent, a success rate
comparable to Bowman and Jellinek's pioneer study in 1941. After eight
years the subjects were again interviewed, and 95 percent had resumed
drinking (Vaillant, 1983). McNeece and DiNitto (1994) assert that the relapse
rate for alcoholic clients is at high levels, "perhaps two-thirds or more"
relapse despite the type of treatment (p. 127).

Persons seeking effective alcoholism treatment should be cautious of programs that advertise glowingly of high success rates but fail to support their

claims with substantiated data derived from reliable studies. Based on veri-
fied case studies, it seems that few, if any, reliable, valid instruments are
available to measure treatment outcomes.

Chiauzzi (1989), who trains professionals in relapse-prevention strategies
at the Adult Chemical Dependency Unit at Brookside Hospital in New
Hampshire, examined numerous treatment programs and their success rates.
He writes that:

> Our age of addictions boasts countless treatment programs and glowing tes-
> timonials from recovering alcoholics and addicts. Some programs report
> that as many as 90% of the "graduates" give up completely the substances
> that once governed their lives. But research disagrees. Roughly 60% of
> alcoholics relapse within three months after their treatment. (pp. 18–19)

Relapse Defined

Generally, alcoholism relapse is defined as a resumption of alcohol consumption after efforts to abstain. Wanigaratine (1990) defines relapse within
a medical context "as a recurrence of symptoms of a disease after a period of
improvement" (p. 9). Relapse definitions generally indicate that alcohol consumption has returned to previous levels. A useful composite definition for
the counselor would be to conceptualize relapse as a resumption of alcohol
use to previous consumption levels with evidence of continued addiction.

"Lapse"/"Slip"

A "lapse" or "slip" falls short of a full-blown relapse and is generally perceived as a discreet, one-time occurrence that may or may not develop into
a full-blown relapse. Crandell (1987) effectively identifies dissimilarities
between a full-blown relapse and a "lapse" or "slip":

> It helps to distinguish a lapse from a relapse. The former, colloquially
> known as a slip, can be countered. It can provide motivation for renewed
> efforts to maintain a recovery program and to build stable abstinence. A
> slip is a crisis and it provokes expectations of future failure, or if it is seen as
> the first step in an inevitable slide back into active addiction, full relapse is
> likely to follow. (p. 226)

Whenever a slip occurs with a recovering elderly alcoholic, the person
needs to be assured that slips are common and not necessarily a precursor to
a full-blown relapse, or the result of a character defect. Older persons, typically, are of the mistaken belief that alcoholism is symptomatic of a character defect. Without a sufficiently high level of efficacy or the confidence to
return to a successful recovery regimen, the slip will likely evolve into a full-
blown relapse.

"Slip"/"Slippers"/"Chippers"

One way of describing the "slipper" is one who has "slipped" away from the A.A. program and has purposely returned to drinking. In the early stages of recovery "slipping" is considered common, because the alcoholic has yet to learn the needed behaviors to remain sober. But once an alcoholic has successfully recovered for at least a year and then returns to drinking, his behavior is no longer considered acceptable by A.A. standards. Denzin (1987) distinguishes between the two situations when one loses sobriety.

> Once an alcoholic has recovered and maintained a year of sobriety, a slip is no longer explained solely in terms of the illness. Rather, it is interpreted as being a willful self-act. These are often called "planned" drunks in contrast to the perhaps unplanned slip of the newcomer. Thus, alcoholics who drink after a long period of sobriety are seen as using their illness as an excuse for drinking. On the other hand, newcomers are seen as drinking because their illness causes them to drink. This interpretive strategy locates alcoholism as the cause of slips at one point in the recovery career, while inverting its causal position in the later stages of recovery. (pp. 129–130)

"Chipping" is a rarely used term even among the "A.A." community to describe a recovering alcoholic who risks a few drinks without fear of a full-blown relapse. Alcoholics Anonymous (A.A.) does not distinguish a relapse from a slip or lapse; instead, they insist that all departures from sobriety constitute a relapse regardless of duration.

Unmanaged Stress

The slogan "one day at a time" is indelibly engrained into the psychic of virtually all recovering alcoholics. When they first heard the slogan at an A.A. meeting or in either outpatient or inpatient treatment, it was directed to the recovering alcoholic who will occasionally revert to a "dry drunk," whereby he or she can euphorically accomplish anything and will unrealistically attempt several projects simultaneously, only to fail and become discouraged. The "one day at a time" and "keep it simple" slogans serve to curtail grandiose, unrealistic undertakings that set the recovering alcoholic up for failure and relapse. Brown, Vik, Patterson, Grant, and Schuckit (1994) assert that: "Alcoholics experiencing highly threatening or chronic psychosocial stress following treatment are more likely to relapse than abstaining individuals not experiencing such stress" (p. 538).

Etiology of Relapse

Gorski (1986, 1990) maintains that the causes for relapse are either external or internal; whereas the external causes include stress and the pain associated with medical illness, the internal causes include irrational thinking and unresolved conflicts associated with past events. Gorski (1986) suggests that without effective coping skills to address the internal causes, the recovering person is vulnerable to relapse (Gorski, 1986; Gorski, 1990).

Stress-Vulnerability Model of Relapse

Brown, Vik, Patterson, Grant, and Schuckit (1995) conducted in-depth follow-up studies with sixty-seven male alcoholics after inpatient treatment to determine the effects of chronic psychosocial stress on relapse vulnerability. After one year, 56 percent of the sample population relapsed. The researchers concluded that those recovering alcoholics with the best chance of not relapsing were those who were best able to manage stress effectively. The researchers concluded:

> . . . that improvements in psychosocial domains (e.g. coping skills, social networks, perceived ability to tolerate relapse-risk situations) enhanced the ability of the men to remain abstinent despite severe stress. This study highlights the importance of cognitive and behavioral interventions for increasing improvements in these psychosocial domains. (pp. 538–545)

In Chapter II it was stressed that elderly alcoholics, especially late-onset alcoholics, typically are depressed and it's associated with the rapid succession of losses so common in the aging process. The depressed elderly are vulnerable to alcoholism, and the depressed elderly alcoholic is also vulnerable to suicide. Not surprisingly, there seems to be a correlation between depression and relapse (Mason & Kocsis, 1991).

Process➡ Losses associated with Aging	Alcoholism➡	Relapse➡	Suicide

Based on clients' self-reporting, those factors considered to significantly influence relapse include the following:

Stress: Stressful events associated with normal daily events and specific negative events.

Negative emotions: Those emotions associated with anger, rage, depression, frustration, and anxiety can contribute to relapse.

Positive emotions: Commonly, people will reward themselves through use of alcohol to celebrate.

Interpersonal conflict: Conflict with family members, friends, and others can contribute toward relapse.

Social pressure: In an alcohol-accepting society, social pressure to drink is likely to cause relapse.

Use of other substances: Prescription medications and other substances can cause a relapse.

Presence of drug-related cues: Craving for alcohol, frequently associated with being around those who drink alcohol or being in settings where alcohol is consumed, is likely to influence a relapse (Annis, 1990, pp. 117–124, Baer & Lichtenstein, 1988, pp. 104–110; Wallace, 1989, pp. 95–106; Weiner, Wallen & Zankowski, 1990).

Precipitating Events/"Triggers"

Marlatt and Gordon (1985) maintain alcoholism relapse relates to (1) negative emotions (e.g., frustration, anger, anxiety, depression, boredom); (2) interpersonal conflict (e.g., argumentation and confrontation); (3) social pressure (e.g., peer group influence to relapse). Marlatt and Gordon's theory on alcoholism relapse has received wide acceptance among alcoholism treatment professionals, but alcoholism relapse among the elderly, especially late-onset alcoholics, has a unique set of factors influencing relapse. Although "triggers" such as peer pressure and work-related problems are common among nonelderly alcoholics, the elderly alcoholic is more apt to be influenced by late-life situations, including a diminished social support system and unresolved loss-grief issues related to loneliness, retirement, widowhood, transportation and financial problems, and boredom.

Dupree, Broskowski, & Schonfeld (1984) developed a modified version of Marlatt's Drinking Profile designed to identify high-risk situations that cause relapse. Schonfeld, Dupree, and Rohrer (1995) compared two groups of pre-treatment alcoholics, one younger elderly and one nonelderly, with alcohol abuse antecedents. The nonelderly group's antecedents were consistent with Marlatt's research that identifies "triggers" in essentially two categories, the intrapersonal "triggers" that relate to negative emotional states, and the interpersonal "triggers" that relate to peer pressure and interpersonal conflicts

(Schonfeld, Dupree, Rohrer, & Glenn, 1995). Conversely, the antecedents that primarily contributed toward alcoholism in the elderly were depression, loneliness, and losses, especially loss of a spouse associated with either divorce or widowhood. Although the nonelderly group frequently experienced divorces, it was more traumatic for the elderly group because of their inadequate support networks. That is, the nonelderly group members who frequently had drinking companions were able to work through their losses associated with divorce, unlike the elderly alcoholics who tended to drink alone. It is especially noteworthy that the researchers recommended that group treatment be provided for elderly alcoholics as a relapse prevention strategy to develop and/or strengthen support systems to cope with losses.

The A-B-C's of Drinking Behavior

Despite Marlatt's success in his model to identify "triggers" that influence relapse for the general population, there was clearly a need to modify the model to individualize its use for elderly alcoholics. In effect, West, Dupree, and Schonfeld (1988) modified Marlatt's model to apply to the elderly alcoholic; hence, the development of *The A-B-C's of Drinking Behavior*. Like Marlatt, these researchers recognized that elderly alcohol abuse, much like alcoholism across the specter, is influenced by internal and external antecedents; that is, high-risk situations are identified so that the recovering alcoholic is made aware of those situations, emotions, and feelings that can cause alcoholism relapse. This approach to relapse prevention addresses not only the cognitive component of alcoholism that relates to negative thinking but also a frequently neglected influence, the affective component that relates to feelings and emotions. The urge to relapse is complex, and its antecedents are multifaceted, thus necessitating a major departure from the traditional, conventional wisdom: that one relapses solely because of the physical urge.

I interviewed Dr. Larry Schonfeld at his University of South Florida office to learn first hand about his unique behavioral approach in working with elderly alcoholics. The A-B-C approach to relapse prevention for an elderly alcoholic is a three-stage approach which follows:

Stage One: In this stage, through use of the Gerontology Alcohol Project (GAP) Drinking Profile, high-risk situations are identified for the individual. According to Dr. Schonfeld, "this highly structured interview focuses on the individual's antecedents and consequences of the first drink on a typical day of drinking."

Stage Two: Schonfeld stresses that in this stage, the individual learns "to recognize antecedents and the consequences." In stage two, the individual is a member of the A-B-C group, instructed to keep an alcohol "log" for continuous self-monitoring of the antecedents and consequences of drinking, the urge to drink, and behavior substitutes for drinking.

Stage Three: Schonfeld points out that in "Stage Three, clients are in self-management groups in which they are taught cognitive behavioral problem solving, and other skills necessary to deal with the antecedents and consequences. Schonfeld adds that "self-management is the key to successful relapse prevention."

The A-B-C's of Drinking Behavior is a relapse prevention strategy that answers the nagging question: Why does a person want to drink in certain situations? The reasons for drinking can also provide appropriate treatment strategies. For example, as Dr. Schonfeld explained to me, "If a person says I drink to relax, then you would want to use relaxation therapy."

Self-management is actually a series of groups in which clients focus on their personal antecedents to drinking and learn new skills to cope with those high-risk situations. These skills have the capacity to disrupt, terminate, or preclude the individual's drinking chain (Antecedents➡ Behavior➡ Consequences; or the "A-B-C's") (West, Dupree, & Schonfeld, 1988).

Desipramine Treatment as a Relapse Prevention Strategy

Alcoholism counselors commonly treat alcoholics who also are depressed. Because the concurrent existence of alcoholism and depression increases the suicidal potential, the counselor is faced with a major challenge to provide suicide prevention intervention strategies in conjunction with relapse prevention.

With alcoholism and depression existing concurrently, there is an increased probability of relapse and suicide. There is hope that treating secondary depressives with desipramine (DMI), an antidepressant, will reduce the depression in alcoholics and, as a consequence, prevent relapses. Mason and Kocsis (1991) conducted a study designed to administer DMI to depressed persons undergoing alcoholism treatment. Of the forty-two subjects (thirty-four men and eight women), twenty-one were depressed placebo subjects. All of the nonplecebo subjects were primary alcoholics and secondary depressives; the onset of alcoholism preceded the onset of depression. According to the researchers the DMI-administered subjects were substantially less depressed than the placebo subjects at the completion of the study. If DMI proves to be an effective treatment modality in reducing depressive reactions, it would be an encouraging development for elderly alcoholics who commonly are depressed.

A Self-efficacy Relapse Prevention Model

Annis and Davis (1989) developed a relapse prevention model based on "the client's self-efficacy or confidence across all drinking situations in the hierarchy." Clients are required to "perform homework assignments involving entry into progressively more risky drinking situations." The client is involved in the planning and decision-making processes in the development of the hierarchy and learns to evaluate his process or lack thereof so that dependency on the counselor is lessened.

It is noteworthy that the researchers have integrated many of the humanistic, professional counselor values and principles identified in Chapter VIII, including self-determination, client respect, and involvement in the planning and decision-making processes. Annis and Davis (1989) have also recognized the benefits of empowering clients to develop the necessary skills and confidence to implement the relapse prevention plan. They write that: "It is critical that homework assignments be designed so that the client experiences 'mastery' and begins to build confidence (self-efficacy) in his or her ability to cope in drinking-related situations" (p. 63).

Evolving from homework assignments is a clear sense of the client's strengths, supports, and coping responses. This relapse prevention model is based on the notion that the client is not a failure should relapse occur; rather, he or she learns to identify strengths and coping responses. This relapse prevention model has obvious applicability to an elderly alcoholism clientele, who tend to respond more favorably to positive than negative reinforcements.

Relapse as a Precursor to Suicide

William Leipold, the clinical director of the Valley Hope Association, a grouping of inpatient substance abuse treatment centers, describes the angry behavior of the alcoholic as self-destructive and suicidal because of his or her helplessness to cope with himself and his environment. Soon the anger transforms into rage, which he terms "externalized anger." Leipold (1995) insists that "the person who kills himself has to be angry at himself. Anger leads to destruction, and (an) inability to cope with oneself and/or one's environment (helplessness) leads to anger–anger at oneself and/or others" (p. 34).

Support Needed when Relapse Occurs

Characteristically, the recovering alcoholic who is on the verge of a relapse will revert to prerecovery behaviors, including compulsivity, grandiosity, and rationalization. He has yet to imbibe but is experiencing what is termed a "dry drunk." Fields (1998) describes one in a dry drunk as "either unaware of other behavioral, personality, and relationship problems, or are choosing not to address these maladaptive behaviors."

For relapsing alcoholics there is great despair, especially after expending so much hope on successful recovery only to lose control and return to drinking. Not only did they let themselves down, but friends and family members also had great expectations that the recovering alcoholic would remain sober. For the elderly alcoholic who relapses, a profound sense of hopelessness and helplessness is felt, typical conditions for high suicidal potential.

Vernan Johnson (1980), a pioneer in developing strategies for the intervention team, describes the emotional impact that alcoholism relapse has on the individual: "Normal self-esteem, as we saw, is replaced progressively by discomfort, twinges of remorse, severe and chronic remorse, self-hatred, and, at the last, by self-loathing that may even reach suicidal proportions" (p. 109).

Unfortunately, for the elderly alcoholic, relapse typically causes the support system to dissipate as frustrated family and friends withdraw from the struggling elderly alcoholic who has let them down. Relapse, instead, should be an opportune time to provide needed empathic support to reassure the despairing alcoholic that their love and support are unconditional and not contingent on remaining sober. Because the possibility exists that the relapsing elderly alcoholic is suicidal and ambivalent about living or dying, counselors need to reinforce the positive features of living. Strengths that may include various family roles, skills, and hobbies should all be emphasized. Efforts must be made to appeal to that part of the person who wants to live rather than to emphasize weaknesses that serve only to influence the part of the person who wants to die. Margaret Flower (1998) recommends that the relapsing alcoholic receive support by asserting that:

> If the client experiences a relapse, respond with empathy and help him or her to cope with feelings of guilt by focusing on strengths, past achievements and things that gives the client pleasure. If a person feels ashamed about relapsing, he or she is more likely to go back to the pre-contemplation phase. The client should be reminded that he or she has acquired new knowledge. Help the client to view a relapse as an opportunity for further learning rather than as a failure. (p. 55)

SUMMARY

Various causes of relapse were considered along with relapse prevention strategies that have proven effective with elderly recovering alcoholics. The model developed by Dupree and Schonfeld, in particular, was especially effective in relapse prevention with an elderly client population. The chapter concludes with a suggestion that there is an interrelationship between relapse when the client experiences a deep sense of helplessness and hopelessness and an increased likelihood of suicide.

GLOSSARY OF TERMS

Dry drunk: A term used to describe the recovering alcoholic who has maintained abstinence but continues to exhibit dysfunctional behaviors associated with alcoholism.

Lapse: Usually considered only one incident of a return to substance use.

Relapse: A full resumption of alcohol use on a frequent basis. (It should be noted that there is wide disagreement among counselors as to what constitutes a lapse, slip, or a relapse.)

Self-efficacy: A concept that one has the capacity (ability) to exhibit behaviors that will produce positive outcomes (e.g., successful alcoholism recovering).

"Slip": Used interchangeably with lapse.

Triggers: Events and/or situations that precipitate alcoholism relapse.

STUDY QUESTIONS

1. Distinguish between relapse, lapse, and slip.
2. Give examples of external and internal causes of relapse.
3. Identify the three factors that precipitate relapse according to Marlatt and Gordon. Give an example of each.
4. Schonfeld and Dupree identified two categories of "triggers" that lead to relapse. What are the two categories? Give examples of each.
5. Dupree and Schonfeld formulated a relapse prevention model appropriate for elderly recovery alcoholics. Describe each of the three parts of the model.
6. Describe the relapse prevention model developed by Annis and Davis.
7. What is the text author's rationale for suggesting that recovering alcoholics are especially vulnerable to commit suicide when they relapse?

REFERENCES

Annis, H.M. (1990). Relapse to substance abuse: Empirical findings within a cognitive-social learning approach. *Journal of Psychoactive Drugs, 22,* 117–124.

Annis, H.M., & Davis, C.S. (1989). *Relapse prevention: The handbook of alcoholism treatment approaches.* New York: The Plenum Press.

Baer J., & Lichtenstein, E. (1988). Classification and prediction of smoking relapse episodes: An exploration of individual differences. *Journal of Consulting and Clinical Psychology, 56,* 104–110.

Bowman, K.M., & Jellinek, E.M. (1941). Alcohol addiction and its treatment. In: E.M. Jellinek (Ed.), Effects of alcohol on the individual, Vol. 1, Ch. 1. New Haven, CT: Yale University Press. Also in Quart. *Journal of Studies of Alcohol, 56*(2): 98–176.

Brown, S.A., Vik, P.W., Patterson, T., Grant, I., & Schuckit, M.A. (Sept. 1994). Stress, vulnerability, and adult alcohol relapse. *Journal of Studies on Alcohol, 56*(5), 538.

Chiauzzi, E. (1989). Breaking the patterns that lead to relapse. *Psychology Today, 23*(12), 18–19.

Crandell, J.S. (1987). *Effective outpatient treatment for alcohol-abusers and drinking drivers,* Article 22. Lexington, MA: Lexington Books.

Denzin, N.K. (1987) *The recovering alcoholic,* Article 23. London: Sage Publications.

Dupree, L, Broskowski, H. & Schonfeld, L. (1984). The Gerontological alcohol project: A behavioral treatment program for elderly alcohol abusers. *The Gerontologist, 24*(5), 510–516.

Fields, R. (1998). *Drugs in perspective: A personalized look at substance abuse and use* (3rd ed.). New York: The McGraw-Hill Companies, Inc.

Flower, M. (1998). Choosing to change: A client-centered approach to alcohol and medication use by older adults. Toronto, Canada: Center for Addiction and Mental Health.

Gorski, T.A. (1986). Relapse prevention planning: A new recovery tool. *Alcohol Health and Research World II, 6,* 8–11, 63.

Gorski, T.A. (1990). The CE NAPS model of relapse prevention: Basic principles and procedures. *Journal of Proactive Drugs, 22,* 125–133.

Johnson, V.E. (1980). *I'll quit tomorrow: A Practical guide to alcoholism treatment.* New York: Harper & Row Publishers, Inc.

Leipold, W.D. (1995). *Walk through the valley.* Independence, MO: Independence Press.

Marlatt, A., & Gordon, J. (1985). *Relapse prevention.* New York: Guilford Press.

Mason, B.J., & Kocsis, J.H. (1991). Desipramine treatment of alcoholism. *Psychopharmacology Bulletin, 27*(2), 155–161.

McNeece, A.C., & DiNitte, D.M. (1994). *Chemical dependency: A systems approach.* Englewood Cliffs, NJ: Prentice-Hall.

Relapse and craving. *Alcohol Alert.* (October 1989). National Institute on Alcohol Abuse and Alcoholism, No. 6, PH 277.

Schonfeld, L., Dupree, L.W., Rohrer, G.L., & Glenn, F. (1995). Age-specific differences between younger and older alcohol abusers. *Journal of Clinical Geropsychology,* 1(3), 219–227.

Vaillant, G.E. (1983). *The natural history of alcoholism.* Cambridge, MA: Harvard University Press.

Wallace, B.C. (1989). Psychological and environmental determinants of relapse in crack cocaine smokers. *Journal of Substance Abuse Treatment, 6,* 95–106.

Wanigaratine, S. (1990). *Relapse and prevention.* London: Blackwater Scientific Publishers.

Weiner, H.D., Wallen, M.C., & Zankowski, G.L. (1990). Culture and social class as intervening variable sin relapse prevention with chemically dependent women *Journal of Psychoactive Drugs, 22,* 239–248.

West, H., Dupree, L., & Schonfeld, L. (1988). The A-B-C's of drinking behavior: Training elderly alcohol abusers in the analysis of drinking behavior. *FMHI Publication Series.* Gainesville, FL: Florida Mental Health Institute, The University of South Florida.

Chapter XII

ELDERLY SUICIDE: CAUSES AND PREVENTION STRATEGIES

Silence is the enemy of recovery.
Alcoholics Anonymous

SUICIDE RATE

According to Quinnett (1998), the suicide rate among alcoholics is substantially higher than in the general population, and they are 60 to 120 times more apt to successfully commit suicide (Fields, 1998, p. 352). Including all age groups the elderly have the highest suicide rates, about twice the rate of the general population. Although the elderly comprise 12 to 13 percent of the population, they successfully commit 20 percent of all suicides (Yesavage, 1992, p. 114). Among the elderly, the most vulnerable group to commit suicide are white men age 85 and older (Devons, 1996, p. 67(5)).

In 1986, there were 19.7 suicides per 100,000 persons between the ages sixty-five and seventy-five, compared with the national average of twelve to thirteen suicides per 100,000 persons. The numbers increase between the ages seventy-five and eighty-four, with 24.2 suicides per 100,000 persons. A slight decline is seen in people eighty-five and older with a suicide rate of 20.8, but the numbers increase dramatically for white men eighty-five and older with 66.3 suicides per 100,000 persons (Barrow, 1990, pp. 222–223). This sharp suicide rate increase for white men, eighty-five and older, is generally attributable to difficulties faced in affecting a successful transition from the workplace setting, on which their self-esteen is often dependent, to retirement in which they are frequently faced with dependency relationships, especially if they require major medical assistance. Another factor includes widowhood; whereby, the widower is faced with extreme loneliness, a typical situation if the diseased wife was the principal facilitator of social relationships. Based on projected population increases for elderly persons sixty-five and older, it is reasonably assumed that the suicide rate will increase accordingly. Elderly alcoholics experience numerous losses, losses associated with the aging process and with their addiction to alcohol.

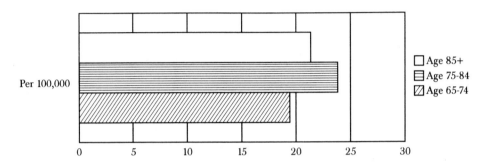

Source: Statistical Abstract of the United States, 1990, 110th ed. Washington, D.C., Department of Commerce, Bureau of the Census, p. 86, chart 125.

Kinney and Leaton (1995) also draw attention to the disproportionately high suicide rate among the elderly:

> Suicide among the elderly is a very big problem. Of those who commit suicide, 75% are over age 65. The rate of suicide for those over 65 is 5 times that of the general population. After age 75, the rate is 8 times higher. In working with the elderly a suicide evaluation should not be neglected because so many depressions are masked. (Kinney & Leaton, 1991, p. 328)

To appreciate the steadily increasing elderly population in the United States, refer to 1940, when merely 6.8 percent of the population was sixty-five and older; in 1990 it was 12.7 percent of the population; in 2040 it is estimated to increase to 21.7 percent; and in 2090, 25 percent (Porterfield, & St. Pierre, 1992, p. 14).

The suicide rate is established by multiplying the number of suicides within a given population by 100,000 and then dividing this number by the actual population size. Hence:

$$\text{Suicide rate} \;=\; \frac{\text{Number of suicides} \times 100{,}000}{\text{Population size}}$$

For example, the National Center for Health Statistics reported that in 1994 the suicide rate for persons within the seventy-five to eighty-four age bracket was 23.4; that is, there were 23.4 suicides committed within a

100,000 population for the year 1994. Incidentally, the 23.4 is nearly double the United States overall suicide rate of 12.1 (Katzenbaum, 1998, p. 177).

SUICIDAL SITUATION

Bowlby (1980) predicts that people who suffer losses are apt to become depressed, and if their depression becomes chronic, the suicidal potential increases (Bowlby, 1980, p. 301). It is not uncommon for the elderly to experience several losses in rapid succession; but, sadly, too frequently many professionals lack the skills and patience to assist them through the difficult grief work. Without persistent, genuine encouragement, the needed grief work will be ignored. The predictable outcome, professionals forewarn, is depression, and most elderly suicides are attempted by depressives.

There are varied opinions among mental health experts concerning the antecedents of elderly suicide. Garden, Garrison, and Jain (1990) attribute the disproportionately high rate of elderly suicides to depression, widowhood, chronic illness, poverty, and alcoholism (Garden, Garrison, & Jain, 1990, pp. 1003–1005). Judith Stillion (1995), a recognized authority on elderly suicide, insists that elderly suicide has its antecedents in feelings of "loneliness, passivity, and despair." Stillion (1995) attributes the despair to not mastering Erik Erikson's stage of "integrity vs. despair," whereby elderly persons may feel a deep sense that their lives have been meaningless (Stillion, 1995, p. 194). Erikson's model postulates that there are seven specific stages through which a person evolves and masters to attain optimal emotional growth. That is, before the person is able to progress to a succeeding stage, he or she must first master the preceding stage. In theory, these stages occur at various junctures through the lifespan. The "integrity vs. despair" stage occurs in late adulthood and requires that the person attain a strong sense of well-being that his or her life has been fulfilling and meaningful. Without mastering this stage, the alternative is a sense of despair that one's life has lacked meaning and fulfillment. DeSpelder and Strickland (1995) maintain that widowers, especially those lonely and living alone, are prone to commit suicide, because they perceive their lives as meaningless and unfulfilling (DeSpelder, & Strickland, 1995, p. 194).

WIDOWHOOD: AN ANTECEDENT TO SUICIDE

Lopata (1977), generally considered a pioneer in successfully identifying problems facing widowhood, especially gender-specific losses, concludes that the major losses facing widows are usually income reduction, loneliness, and for the widower, emotional expression. Not surprising that in a society that extols the virtues of "stoic self-control," the male is discouraged from doing the vital grief work. Lopata (1977) writes that "American widowers have a much higher rate of mental breakdown, physical illness, alcoholism, suicide and accidents than do widows or married men" which may suggest that men, especially widowed men, encounter more difficulty grieving losses (Lopata, 1977, pp. 25–28).

Rational Suicide:

DeSpelder and Strickland (1995) suggest that older people, unlike the young whose suicidal attempts are often calls for help, have a genuine desire to commit suicide. For them, it may be a rational choice that is an alternative to the difficulties so characteristic of the aging process. The authors describe the double suicide that is more common among the elderly.

> Double suicides (a type of suicide pact) occur with greatest frequency among the elderly. The typical double suicide involves an older couple with one or more partners physically ill. Heavy alcohol use by one or both partners is also common. Such couples tend to be dependent on each other and isolated from external sources of support. There seems to be a "special chemistry" between couples who commit suicide together, with the more suicidal partner dominant and more ambivalent partner passive in the relationship. (p. 440)

There are those elderly persons who have discovered the aging process to be incongruent with the good life, especially the good life to which they may have become accustomed. The late Betty Davis, the illustrious vocal, free-spirited actress, once assured the TV audience during an evening talk show that "old age ain't for sissies." This forewarning was proclaimed after a stroke that left her with debilitating paralysis about four to five years before her death. It may cause one to ponder why so many elderly persons whose sentiments Betty Davis represented decide to end their lives. Gerontologists generally concur that increased longevity does not ensure the elderly a high quality of life. Although many elderly age gracefully in a lifestyle that lends itself to happiness and fulfillment, there are just as many impoverished, frail elderly who are not reaping the benefits of the so-called golden years. Robert Katzenbaum (1998), the insightful philosopher-writer and gerontologist, succinctly describes the plight of a growing number of elderly whose life's struggles have reached an intolerable level:

> There is the attitude that suicide is an acceptable, rational alternative to continued existence. It is a view often conditioned by adverse circumstances. "Life is not always preferable to death' is the thought here. Individuals do

not destroy themselves in hope of thereby achieving a noble postmortem reputation or a place among the eternally blessed. Instead, they wish to subtract themselves from a life whose quality seems a worse evil than death." (p. 191)

Physician-Assisted Suicide (PAS)

The term physician-assisted suicide (PAS) was coined to describe the work of Dr. Kervorkian, a Michigan physician who assisted in premature deaths of people with incurable, debilitating diseases. Opinions are sharply divided over the legitimacy of PAS, and the debate continues unabated as Kervorkian was convicted and imprisoned based mostly on questions raised when a PAS was taped and subsequently aired on the television program, "20-20." It is reported that the patient was not sufficiently ill to justify PAS. Because more than a third of the persons Dr. Kervorkian assisted to expedite their deaths were elderly, there raises the issue of self-determination. As professionals, are we obligated to embrace the cardinal value, self-determination?

This dilemma is further illustrated in the apparent contradiction between general public opinion and state laws governing assisted suicide. A poll conducted by the National Opinion Research Center reported that 62 percent favored either PAS or euthanasia if the patient is incurably ill (Cicirelli, 1998, p. 186). Oregon's Death with Dignity Act enacted in 1994, and the only state that permits "physician-assisted suicide in limited circumstances," may be struck down if the United States Senate follows the House of Representatives and votes to make assisted suicides unconstitutional (McMahon, & Kock., 1999, p. 21A).

THE DEPRESSION, ALCOHOL, SUICIDE INTERRELATIONSHIP

Fulop, Reinhardt, Strain, Paris, Miller, and Fillit (1993) insightfully understand the interplay between alcoholism, depression, and suicide when they write that "alcoholism and depression in the elderly result in serious complications and diminished functional status, as well as increased suicide risk and medical care utilization" (Fulop et al., 1993, p. 740). Rivers (1994, p. 47) calls attention to those depressed elderly, especially widowers, nursing home residents, and psychiatric patients, who resort to alcohol and/or suicide to escape from the emotional pain associated with losses. Researchers concur that suicide is high among alcoholics, and some even suggest it's "about 30 times greater than it is in the general population" (Schlaadt & Shannon, 1990, p. 184). Alcoholism is clearly a factor in the high elderly suicide rate (Richman, 1992). According to Rich, Young, and Fowler (1986) the overall suicide rate for men is 18.2; for women, 7.9; for persons 65 and older, the rate for men was 31.9 and for women, 15.9 (Rich, Young, & Fowler, 1986, pp. 577–582). Pfeiffer (1977, p. 357) reports that the suicide rate for white males aged 80-84 is 51.4 per 100,000.

FACTORS CONTRIBUTING TO HIGH SUICIDALITY

Crises/"Turning Points"

Late-life alcoholics commonly encounter turning points, or crises, in their lives wherein a deep sense of loss is felt. Rapid succession of losses is inevitably accompanied with loss of control in one's life. Without a sense that a person can control events, there develops a feeling of hopelessness and helplessness that nothing can be done to stop or alleviate the onslaught of losses.

Lack Control in Decision-Making Processes

Lacking control in their lives, elderly alcoholics' ambivalence about living or dying is likely to be strong. Coupled with ambivalence is the unwillingness to make decisions and to accept responsibility, thus resulting in unfinished tasks to make needed life changes. Lacking sufficient motivation to complete tasks is evident in the treatment plan where the client must be fully engaged. Elderly alcoholics who feel incapable of controlling and influencing their lives are apt to resort to suicide as a last desperate effort to regain a semblance of control in their lives. Owens (1994) expresses this need when she suggests that "choosing one's time and place to die is the ultimate expression of a need to control." She elaborates on the need for control for the recovering alcoholic when she writes that:

> For many people, their recovery program is based daily on sorting out,
> "Now who's in charge here? Who really has the control?" and letting go

when appropriate. This is what steps two and three and the serenity prayer are all about. Many people in recovery become very good at sorting out control issues in their everyday lives; but when it comes to something big, they try to take all the control back. When control has been a major issue in life and recovery, it may also be a major issue in facing death. For example, a person who is chronically or terminally ill may want to take back control and say, "I'll die when and how I choose." (p. 13)

Fields draws attention to the interrelationship between alcoholism and suicide. Considering the previous discussion concerning the role of control in suicide, it is understandable why a person who relapses from alcoholism recovery is highly vulnerable to committing suicide. For the alcoholic relapse represents for the alcoholic a complete loss of control and a profound sense of helplessness.

Increased Suicidality for Alcoholism Relapse

A case study that appears in Richard Fields' (1998) well-known text, *Drugs in Perspective*, documents the interrelationship between alcoholism relapse and suicide. It is understandable why a person who relapses from alcoholism recovery is vulnerable to committing suicide. For the alcoholic, relapse symbolizes a complete loss of control in one's life. "After years of successful treatment, what is there left in my life, but suicide?" Fields (1998, p. 142) insists that with persons whose suicidality is suspect the issue needs to be raised, because as the A.A. proverb warns, "Silence is the enemy of recovery."

Clinical Depression

Because many elderly alcoholics are clinically depressed, they become lethargic and dysfunctional in performing the simplest of self-help skills, such as self-grooming, bathing, and even eating, and their self-esteem is at the lowest ebb. For some elderly alcoholics, especially early-onset alcoholics who have experienced long durations of chronic alcohol consumption, there is an excellent likelihood that psychotic behaviors will be evident, including delusional and hallucinatory behaviors, disorientation, extreme mood swings characterized by deep depression and/or hostility, anger, and rage. The Centers for Disease Control and Prevention report that the "risk factors for suicide prevention among elderly persons differ from those among younger persons and include a higher level of alcohol abuse and depression" (*Suicide among older persons*, 1996, p. 33).

Unstable Lifestyle

For both early-life and late-life alcoholics, lifestyles tend to be unstable, often characterized by poor social interactions with other relatives or with their few remaining friends. For some, basic communication with others has stopped altogether.

Giving Away Possessions

Commonly, the suicidal person will start giving away possessions, indicative that suicide may be imminent. McIntosh (1985, pp. 288–293) asserts that "making a will under peculiar circumstances or giving away prized possessions (behavior that can be seen as 'putting one's affairs in order')" may be manifestations of suicidal ideation.

SUICIDAL PREVENTION

Mobilize Support

Because suicide is a high probability for the elderly alcoholic, immediate professional support is essential. For numerous reasons the elderly often receive inadequate social support, a significant factor in the overall suicidal scenario. Anomic suicide, a type of suicide coined and researched by Durkeim (1897/1951) is committed by persons who receive inadequate support "and meaning" from society. The professional will need to alert family members to the high suicidal potential of your client, and breach of confidentiality concerns may need to be secondary to your suicide prevention efforts, especially if suicide is imminent. Primarily because of the stigma associated with suicide, efforts to engage family members in the prevention process may be met with strong resistance in the form of denial that the person is suicidal. Ideally, family members' involvement in suicide prevention would be in the form of support. The professional's warm, caring, empathic relationship would also be immensely helpful in preventing a potential suicide. Robert Katzenbaum (1998) insightfully insists that,

> The companionship you offered a person during a crucial period or the confidence you displayed in a friend after he or she suffered a failure experience might have provided just enough support to dissolve a self-destructive pattern in the making. Whenever we bring sensitivity and a genuinely caring attitude to our relationship with other people, we may be decisively strengthening their life-affirming spirit. (p. 201)

Aside from using family members to prevent suicide, other resources should also be considered. The elderly frequently have spiritual needs that should be addressed, but too frequently mental health professionals have been inadequately trained in providing spiritual support, whereas religious leaders often lack the training in suicide prevention. Clearly the need exists for collaboration between religious and mental health professionals.

Nonjudgmental

Care should be taken not to superimpose your value system by stigmatizing suicide, because the suicidal person will very likely become defensive and carry out this threat and commit suicide as a form of rebellion. For similar reasons, do not make light of the suicide threat. The adage that "if he/she says he's going to do it, he won't because it's just manipulation" is a myth. Take the threat seriously.

Support the Reasons to Live

As previously mentioned, a sense of ambivalence is characteristic of the suicidal situation with part of the person wishing to live and part of the person wishing to die. It is important to focus on the many reasons that the person wants to live. By identifying the person's strengths such as being a good father, mother, grandfather, grandmother, a good friend, you draw attention for reasons to live and, too, you're working toward strengthening self-esteem and self-concept.

Do not Identify as the Rescuer

Because the suicidal person is characteristically indecisive, you need to mobilize the person to take personal responsibility and not to be indecisive in making decisions. By identifying as a rescuer, you are discouraging independent decision making and taking responsibility. In effect, you are reinforcing a dependency relationship that contributes to the person's loss of control.

Despite the difficulties often faced in the aging process, therapeutic intervention and support has proven in countless cases to be effective in thwarting suicide. Therapeutic intervention can mobilize support systems by focusing on client strengths to reinforce the ambivalent person's reasons to live and to instill a sense of control and independence, enhance self-esteem, and assist the client to work through loss-grief issues. The following anecdote demonstrates the efficacy of therapeutic intervention in this documented case study of a suicide pact involving an elderly couple beset with physical problems:

> With only three weeks of inpatient psychotherapy and drug therapy, the couple rekindled its taste for life. Several years later they continued to do well, living independently in the community and free of suicidal thoughts. This is but one of many examples that could be brought forward to demonstrate that a suicidal crisis can be overcome in later life as well as at earlier ages. (Katzenbaum, 1991, p. 178)

SUMMARY

This chapter called attention to the high rate of suicide among older people, especially older, white alcoholics. Examined were common suicidal situations, including depression, widowhood, chronic health problems, and especially alcoholism, which plays a prominent role among the elderly.

Different types of suicide were identified, which included physician-assisted suicide and rational suicide and explanations for their increase popularity. Next, factors contributing to high suicidality were examined, which included crisis situations, lack of control in making decisions, and alcoholism relapse.

GLOSSARY OF TERMS

Crisis: A "turning point" in one's life typically involving major loss.

Double suicide: Typically this is a pact between an elderly couple, whereby one or more partners is physically ill, and they resort to double suicide to end problems associated with their illness.

"Integrity vs. despair": A stage identified by Erikson in late adulthood emotional development that requires that one master a strong sense of well-being and that his or her life has been fulfilling and meaningful.

Physician-assisted suicide (PAS): Term popularized by Dr. Korvorkian in his role to expedite death in patients purportedly suffering from incurable diseases.

Rationale suicide: Characterized by people who prefer death to the prospects of suffering from debilitating diseases that commonly accompany the aging process.

Suicide: The act of intentionally killing oneself.

STUDY QUESTIONS

1. Describe a suicidal situation and what you can do as a counselor to prevent suicide in the recovering alcoholic.

2. How do you establish the suicide rate of a particular population unit?

3. What are your feelings regarding the practice of physician-assisted suicide?

4. What is the basis for the high suicide rate among alcoholics?

5. As a counselor working with a clientele who is ambivalent about whether to live or die, what intervention strategy would you use and why?

6. What are the potential pitfalls in identifying as a rescuer in working with the recovering elderly alcoholic who is suicidal?

REFERENCES

Bowlby, J. (1980) *Loss, sadness, and depression.* New York: Basic Books.

Cicirelli, V.E. (June 1998). View of elderly people concerning end-of-life decision. *Journal of Applied Gerontology, 17*(2), 186(18).

DeSpelder, L.A. & Strickland, A.L. (1995). R*eadings in death and dying: The path ahead.* Mountain View, CA: Mayfield Publishing Company.

DeSpelder, L.A. & Stickland, A.L. (1998). *The last dance* (5th ed.). Mountain View, CA: Mayfield Publishing Corp.

Devons, C.A.J. (March 1996). Suicide in the elderly: How to identify and treat patients at risk. *Geriatrics, 51*(3), 67(5).

Durkheim, E. (1897/1951). *Suicide.* Translated by Spaulding, J.A. &. Simpson, G.) New York: Free Press.

Fields, R. (1998). Drugs in perspective: A personalized look at substance abuse and use (3rd ed.). New York: The McGraw-Hill Companies, Inc.

Fulop, G., Reinhardt, J., Strain, T.J., Paris, B., Miller, M. R., & Fillit, H. (1993). Identification of alcoholism and depression in a geriatric medicine outpatient clinic. *Journal of the American Geriatrics Society, 41*(7), 737–741.

Garden, F.H., Garrison, S.J., & Jain, A. (1990). Assessing suicide risk in stroke patients: review of two cases. *Archives of Physical and Medical Rehabilitation, 71*(12) 1003–1005.

Katzenbaum, R.J. (1991) *Death, society, and human experience* (4th ed.). New York: Macmillan Publishing Company.

Katzenbaum, R.J. (1998). *Death, society and human experience* (6th ed.). Boston: Allyn & Bacon.

Kinney, J. & Leaton, G. (1995). *Loosening the grip: A handbook of alcohol information* (5th ed.). St. Louis, MO: Mosby-Year Book, Inc.

Lopata, H. (1977). Patterns of economic change surrounding death of a spouse. *The Humanist,* 25–28.

McIntosh, J.L. (April 1985). Suicide among the elderly: Levels and trends. *American Journal of Orthopsychiatry, 55,* 288–293.

McMahon, P. & Koch, W. (22 Nov 1999). Assisted suicide: A right or a surrender?" *USA Today, (22),* 21A.

Owen, P. (1994). *Understanding suicide and addiction.* Center City, MN: Hazelden Foundation.

Pfeiffer, E. (1977). Psychopathology and social pathology. In Birren, J.E. & Warner Schaie, K. (Eds.). *Handbook of psychology and aging.* New York: Van Nostrand Reinhold.

Porterfield, J.D. & St. Pierre, R. (1992). *Wellness: Healthful aging.* Guilford, CT: The Dushkin Publishing Group.

Quinnett, P. (1998). In Fields, R. (Ed.), *Drugs in perspective: A personalized look at substance abuse and use* (3rd ed.). New York: The McGraw-Hill Companies, Inc.

Rich, C.L., Young, D., & Fowler, R.C. (1986). San Diego Suicide Study. *Archives of General Psychiatry, 43,* 577–582.

Richman, J. (1992). *Suicide in the elderly.* New York: Springer.

Rivers, P.C. (1994). *Alcohol and human behavior: Theory, research, & practice.* Englewood Cliffs, NJ: Prentice-Hall.

Schlaadt, R.G. & Shannon, P.T. (1990). *Drugs: Use, misuse, and abuse* (3rd ed.). Englewood Cliffs, NJ: Prentice-Hall.

Stillion, J.M. Premature exits: Understanding suicide. In DeSpelder, L.A. & Strickland, A.L. (1995). *Readings in death and dying: The path ahead.* Mountain View, CA: Mayfield Publishing Company.

Suicidal Abstract of the U.S.: Chart 25. (1991). D.C., Department of Commerce, Bureau of the Census, 86. In Barrow, G.M. (Ed.). (1992). *Aging, the individual, and society* (5th ed.). St. Paul, MN: West Publishing Company.

Suicide among older persons–United States 1980–1992 (Centers for Disease Control and Prevention). (Feb. 21, 1996). *The Journal of the American Medical Association, 275*(7), 33.

Viorst, J. (1986). *Necessary losses: The loves, illusions, dependencies and Impossible expectations that all of us have to give up in order to grow.* New York: Fawcett Gold Metal.

Yesavage, J.A. (1995). Depression in the elderly. postgraduate medicine. In Buelow, G. & Herbert, S. (Eds.), *Counselor's resource on psychiatric medicines.* Monterey, CA: Brooks/Cole Publishing Company.

Chapter XIII

ON-SITE PROGRAM VISITS

I had an opportunity to interview staff at five elder-specific treatment programs to learn of their distinct features–four on-site interviews and one phone interview. Overall, I was struck with the dedication and passion with which these professionals provided services to an elderly clientele. The following facilities' descriptions will focus principally on the most salient features. I also conducted a phone interview with professional staff members at Amethyst, a gender-specific substance abuse program for women. After each facility description is a completed fact sheet with pertinent information specific to the treatment program.

COMMUNITY OLDER PERSON ALCOHOL PROGRAM (COPA) TORONTO, ONTARIO

COPA was established in 1983 to serve hard-to-reach elderly persons who experienced substance abuse–related problems. Unlike most treatment programs, COPA is designed to treat people in their own homes and does not require its clients to acknowledge substance abuse as the primary problem. The primary, presenting problem may be considered financial or marital, and substance abuse-related problems may be considered secondary. Unlike the traditional treatment approach, clients are not required to admit to being addicted to either alcohol or other drugs; treatment goals, therefore, do not necessarily include sobriety. The COPA philosophy stresses that by alleviating or eliminating the presenting problem, in effect, you will work toward problem resolution of the secondary problem of substance abuse.

Within a block of the University of Toronto campus, I was engaged in a spirited interview with COPA's first director, Margaret Flower, a registered nurse.

Because COPA's primary distinguishing feature seems to be its "harm reduction" approach, Flower emphasized that a "harm reduction" approach focuses on the reduction of the risks and harm associated with the addiction. She used as an example the elderly alcoholic with high blood pressure who conceivably could die from the effects associated with physical withdrawal from alcohol. M. Flowers (personal communication, July 28, 2000) suggested that:

> You may want to look at tapering if there is the likelihood of sudden withdrawal for a person with a history of physical problems. I may instead suggest that we work on this together with maybe one drink a day. Or, I may suggest trying sobriety for a week. But, if he drinks and is discouraged; I then say to him, "But you were about to do it at 90 percent of the time," and he feels good. I need to add that if the client decides to try sobriety, the nurse will visit his home everyday and check his blood pressure and look for other signs of physical withdrawal.

Although sobriety may not be the primary treatment goal at COPA, with other problems given higher priority, it was abundantly clear that the program's primary focus was to promote the improvement of the overall quality of life for the elderly client.

CHELSEA ARBOR TREATMENT CENTER (CATC)
ANN ARBOR, MICHIGAN

CATC is a joint treatment program between Chelsea Community Hospital that provides services, including inpatient detoxification, and the University of Michigan Health Services, where recovering elderly persons receive outpatient services, including counseling.

The Director of Clinical Services, Jeff Smith, a social worker by profession (personal communication, August 9, 2000), stresses the need to

> counteract the intense shame and guilt which is associated with alcoholism by using peer counselors, those who have been through the program. To reduce a sense of shame, they need to see it [alcoholism] as a disease, like diabetes that can be managed. By seeing alcoholism as an inherited disease, there is the likelihood that you'll minimize the shame and guilt. So, we use the Disease Model Approach, even though exposure to alcohol may very well have had an influence also.

CATC is a highly comprehensive treatment program that includes 14 days of inpatient detoxification, coupled with an additional 14 days of inpatient hospitalization to address medical problems that include dietary, pharmacological, and physical therapy services.

On hospital discharge, the recovering substance abuser receives outpatient services at the Older Adult Recovery Center (O.A.R.C.), with a multidisciplinary staff that provides individual, group, and family therapy to address such issues as addiction, aging, grief, and intergenerational family issues. An innovative peer group including successfully recovering elderly persons was organized to provide "support and camaraderie for newly recovering older adults."

OLDER ADULT ALCOHOL AND OTHER DRUG ABUSE (ADDA) SERVICES, APPLETON, WISCONSIN

Treatment involves two distinct phases on outpatient basis: Phase 1 includes individual and group counseling and therapy, education in substance abuse, health clinic participation, and social and recreational activities. Client participation in Phase 1 is for approximately two months. Phase 2 also includes individual and group counseling and therapy with an emphasis on relapse prevention. Phase 1 and Phase 2 include health care, exercise classes, educational opportunities, and recreational activities. Specific issues in both phases address the physical aspects of aging, loneliness and loss, fixed incomes, independence, and quality of life.

I found the comprehensive, vast array of services as the most striking feature of the overall treatment. B. Lutzewitz (personal communication, August 17, 2000) points out that:

> one reason that we have treatment at the Community Center is to make available to the participants the many activities such as social recreation, a program for the visually impaired, a YMCA program designed for an aging population, Adult Day Care; Burn-out Prevention Services, Caregiver Stress Prevention, Peer Counseling; friendly visitors, and to facilitate a dual diagnosis group.

Ms. Lutzewitz stresses that one of the primary obstacles to successful recovery relates to a strong sense of shame and guilt to which she attributes several factors. She believes that it is necessary to emphasize the disease model; that is, alcoholism is due to a genetic predisposition and not a "character disorder." She believes that the stigma associated with alcoholism and "ageism" contribute to a strong sense of shame and guilt. She further alludes to the stigma of being "gay." Often gay persons are "homophobic" themselves, and this will influence their self-esteem and self-concept."

Because recovering alcoholics need a reasonably healthy self-concept and self-esteem, it makes perfect sense that strategies be integrated into the overall treatment plan to remove conditions that contribute toward people not feeling good about themselves. Also considering the interdependent inter-play between the mind and body, it seems that the comprehensive services and activities provided at ADDA serve to promote healthy self-concepts.

AMETHYST

Amethyst, founded in 1984, is an alcohol and drug treatment program specifically designed to serve women and their families. To address individ-ualized needs, each client joins one of the five clusters:
• More Mature Women Who Use and Abuse Crack Cocaine
• Younger Adult Women Addicted to Crack Cocaine
• Women Addicted to Prescription Drugs
• More Mature Women Who Abuse Alcohol
• Substance Abusers with More Severe Mental Health Problems
Women assigned to Cluster 4 are typically between ages of forty and sixty-five and are alcohol dependent. Because many of these women lack ade-quate support systems as a result of marital divorce/separation and/or estrangement from their adult children, the treatment is especially geared toward developing self-help support systems. Because of the numerous loss-es experienced by this client population, grief therapy is provided. Many of the clients have been subjected to physical and sexual abuse, so a major seg-ment of the treatment focuses on developing a healthy self-concept. According to clinic social worker, Ginny O'Keefe (personal communication, June 8, 2001), "ninety-eight percent of the women have some type of abuse issue, and it is a relapse trigger that has not been addressed." Co-social work-er, Sara Niemeyer (personal communication, June 8, 2001), added that "for older women, it is especially challenging in getting them to talk about their families because of the traditional value of keeping things within." A trauma counselor is assigned to support clients to work through these issues. Gretchen Clark, another member of the social work team, stated that "we are a model program for drug and alcoholism treatment, and I have never seen anything like it as far as capacity and length of stay. By capacity, we can serve 101 women and their children in any given day."

A unique feature of Amethyst's treatment is the integration of five levels through which the client progresses:

Level 1: The goal is to break the denial that women have about their addiction. If the client does not see her addiction as a primary life problem, then cognitive and behavioral changes will not occur.

Level 2: During this phase, more emphasis is placed on self and career/job exploration. This phase continues with education on addiction concepts with an emphasis on relapse prevention. Group counseling focuses on values, feelings, communication, diversity, and barriers to self-sufficiency.

Level 3: This phase addresses the ongoing recovery issues each client faces as she begins to juggle full-time work and/or school. Family skills, time, and financial management skills are also program components.

Level 4: Clients begin to move from the safety net of treatment to a more independent way of life. Care is given to relapse prevention and developing a sober support system.

Level 5: This is the phase in which clients complete their education, work skills are strengthened, and women start to progress in their jobs. Women now have a foundation for lifelong sobriety, healthy relationships, and economic independence.

OLDER ADULT PROGRAMS, HANLEY-HAZELDEN CENTER
ST. MARY'S WEST PALM BEACH, FLORIDA

Four years after a three-day "Professionals in Residence Program" tenure with the Older Adult Program component, I interviewed Carol Colleran, the Older Adult Program Director.

Colleran stressed the importance for professionals who provide treatment to older adults to understand a value system that accepts and does not question authority. The benefit in adhering to a traditional value system is that "a high percentage will follow such recommendations as aftercare; but a negative feature "relates to older adults' general reluctance to share feelings."

Like other interviewees, Colleran also believes that "harm reduction" strategies have an appropriate place in treating older adults. She maintains that "abstinence is not necessarily an immediate goal and that realistically allowances need to be made for lapses and relapses." I had an opportunity to observe the rapport that quickly developed between members of the Alumni Support Group and current patients. The Alumni Support Group members, comprised of forty to forty-five members, meet once a week between 10:30 and 11:45 to offer encouragement and direction for current patients. After the group meeting, the support continues as they engage in spirited discussions over lunch. Colleran correctly points out that it is essential for the professional staff "to understand that food is important to older adults."

SUMMARY OF INTERVIEWS

Appearing as the most common themes emerging from the interviewees were the use of "harm reduction" strategies and the adherence to a traditional value system. Gleaned from the literature and the interviewees, there is clearly a new school of thought that "lapses" and relapses are normal and expected events in the alcoholism recovery process and that scolding, punitive reactions to these transgressious will only discourage the elderly alcoholic in continuing recovery efforts. A realistic treatment philosophy will likely bring about more favorable treatment outcomes.

Another emerging theme relates to a traditional value system that the elderly steadfastly embrace. With a clear understanding of its positive and negative effects, counselors can improve treatment outcomes. As Colleran insightfully suggested, because the elderly do not question authority, they are more apt to accept aftercare treatment services. As a challenge to attain successful treatment outcomes, the elderly embrace a value system that encourages the repression of feelings, a predictable source of depression. The creative counselor will need to skillfully use intervention strategies that encourage a healthy, outward expression of clients' feelings.

CASE STUDIES

The following are actual case studies that represent a wide range of client types, issues, and situations that the professional counselor is likely to face in his or her practice.

Case Study 13.1
Mr. & Mrs. S

Mr. and Mrs. S, both age 61, are successfully recovering alcoholics and next month will mark their fifth anniversary. They began recovery together and feel very proud of their success, but in recent months, they feel their recovery is threatened because of additional stress in their lives. Mr. and Mrs. S are first-generation Japanese who have lived in the United States for ten years and recently obtained U.S. citizenship.

For the past six weeks, Mr. S's widowed mother has been visiting from Japan. Mr. S has invited his mother to move into their household on a permanent basis. Although Mrs. S has empathy for her mother-in-law's loneliness and need for a support system, she has found living with her to be insufferably stressful. Her mother-in-law tends to control the household and is demanding. This living arrangement has caused considerable marital strain. Although Mr. S feels a strong obligation to care for his mother, his wife feels threatened by her mother-in-law, who she feels is "taking over my house and responsibilities." Despite feelings of shame and reluctance to disclose personal family problems, they both have agreed to seek alcoholism counseling for fear of relapsing.

Case Study 13.2
Mrs. W

Mrs. W is a 73-year-old African-American woman who lives with her daughter and ten-year-old granddaughter. Mrs. W has been widowed for five years and had the primary responsibility of bringing up her six children by working as a maid and receiving public assistance that allowed them to survive some very difficult times. Three of her children are married and have children living anywhere from 12-20 driving hours from her. Her one son was killed in a prison riot that occurred two years ago. Her youngest daughter visits regularly and lives in a nearby town.

Mrs. W does not receive a pension, and her only means of support is her monthly social security check, which is turned over to her daughter to help with the family's living expenses. She has very little money to spend on herself, because her daughter has complete control over expenditures. Mrs. W's only form of social life is her friendship with a 75-year-old-man who lives alone in a nearby apartment.

On a daily basis, she and Mr. R meet at his house to watch TV and drink bourbon and coke (their drink of choice). This relationship has been ongoing since they first met at the Senior Community Center about eight months ago. Her daughter has not been very concerned because, "after all, at her age, that is her right," and, furthermore, it is less work for her if she spends most of her time with Mr. R. At one point, her daughter was going to suggest that her mother move in with Mr. R, but that would put the social security check in jeopardy.

Mrs. W's youngest daughter, a school teacher, expressed concern about her mother's drinking to her older sister who tried to assure her that their mother's drinking is not a cause for concern. However, on three occasions in a two-week period, the youngest daughter has seen her mother inebriated after all-day drinking bouts with Mr. R. The daughter is concerned because her mother has high blood pressure and is diabetic. She is unsure about how to handle this situation. She is torn between concern for her mother's welfare and not wanting to interfere with her mother's newfound social life, which she seems to be enjoying. She has contacted a substance abuse clinic to seek advice.

Case Study 13. 3
Mr. N

Mr. N's four children are concerned that their father, age 63, refuses to heed their pleas that he be treated for alcoholism. "Mexican-American men are very proud and independent," offers his son. The son has approached an alcoholism counselor who agreed to put together an intervention team for the purpose of influencing Mr. N to enter treatment for alcoholism. His son stated that he had two very close friends who were also concerned about his health and had tried to get Mr. N to talk to his Catholic priest about his drinking problems.

Case Study 13.4
Mr. G

Mr. G is a 67-year-old White-American man whose wife of 36 years died three months ago. His one adult child reports that he is depressed and drinks heavily and has requested an intervention, because many failed efforts to get him into alcoholism counseling have failed.

His son has disclosed that he has a long history of alcohol abuse, beginning when he was in his early teens. He also has had several major losses in recent years. His son was killed in an alcohol-related accident when he was age 64, and since his retirement from a factory job at age 65, his two brothers have died suddenly from short-term illnesses. In addition, his health has deteriorated in recent years, including back problems and diabetes. His son further disclosed that when he was married, he had an active social life, but he now prefers to stay home alone watching TV.

Case Study 13.5
Mr. W

Mr. W is a65-year-old retired naval officer. When Mr. W was a young boy, age six, his father committed suicide, forcing him to assume an adult role in his family. Mr. W was the eldest of four siblings, and his mother was rather passive. Mr. W, as a teenager, was considered responsible and mature beyond his years and the model child in his small community of 4,500 residents. After several years of assuming an adult role in his family, he decided to escape by joining the Navy.

Mr. W described military life as the "perfect haven for a drunk," because of the many military functions surrounded by alcohol and the wide acceptance of alcohol consumption. Mr. W was convinced that alcohol helped him with the stress of military life, especially with the need to adjust to a new environment each time he was reassigned to a new naval station. Mr. W said that he was reassigned six times in his first ten years of military life.

Mr. W rose rapidly in rank. He enlisted as a seaman recruit, but was soon sent to Officer's Candidate School (OCS). After OCS, he got orders for flight training and subsequently served as a pilot for 14 years. He flew several combat missions beginning with the Korean Conflict when he was assigned to South Korea for the last few months of the fighting. He also served for two years in Viet Nam, where he flew several combat missions. At the age of 39, he was stationed stateside, and despite the end of the Viet Nam conflict, he continued to drink to "calm his nerves" as he puts it.

At age 39, and after 21 years of military duty, he made an appointment with a naval physician to discuss his alcohol dependency. The physician assured him that there was no cause for concern, that his drinking consumption was far less than with most naval pilots, and that he was not an alcoholic. Mr. W was convinced that if a medical doctor said he was not an alcoholic, then he could safely continue enjoying his drinking. At age 40, Mr. W retired from the Navy after 22 years of honorable service and was offered to fly commercially as a civilian pilot. After 17 years of flying, he was forced to resign after several reports that he flew while intoxicated.

At age 61, Mr. W is now receiving alcoholism treatment at an outpatient clinic in the city where he has retired. After three weeks of sobriety, Mr. W is able to talk openly about his many years of alcohol abuse. He shared with his therapy group that as a commercial pilot, he would pray before take-off for a smooth, safe flight with no complications. He shared with the group that part of him denied alcoholism, while another part feared that his alcohol abuse would slow down his reaction time and "cause harm" to his passengers. Mr. W expressed remorsefulness to his fellow recovering alcoholics that his drinking behavior got out of hand and caused many problems for his three children who refuse to see him, because they are resentful that he did not provide a stable family life. Recently, he offered to meet with his divorced wife in hope that she would help him to establish improved relationships with his children. She refused to see him. Mr. W is very lonely and chronically depressed, and the only support he receives is from his therapy group and his alcoholism counselor.

Case Study 13.6
Mr. J

Mr. J is a 66-year-old Cherokee Indian who resides in rural northeastern Oklahoma. Mr. J has attended AA meetings for the past 25 years intermittingly. He has not been able to go beyond 30 days of sobriety. Each relapse has become more traumatic. Since he was in the U.S. Army, he has entertained suicidal thoughts but has never carried them out.

He is now in his second week of a residential treatment program and has accepted neither the alcoholism diagnosis nor the treatment, which he refers to as a "waste of time for me." He received a comprehensive physical examination by the facility's physician who diagnosed him with diabetes, high blood pressure, and anemia. He was quoted by his daughter as saying that "I don't care if I live or die. What's the use?"

Mr. J experienced numerous losses in his life, but most of them have occurred since his early sixties–his wife died three years ago. He tells his children that he is over the loss of his wife, but they say "that it is all talk." His son shared with the counselor that "he's just too proud to admit that he's not over the loss of my mother."

Case Study 13.7
Dr. S

Dr. S, a 61-year-old university professor, was advised by his dean to seek treatment for his alcoholism or his job would be in jeopardy. Reluctantly, he began attending A.A. meetings only to once again relapse as his drinking continued. Complaints from faculty and students that they are able to smell alcohol on his breath persisted. The dean again sternly forewarned him that his contract would not be renewed unless he demonstrated a genuine intent to stop drinking.

Dr. S does not believe that he is an alcoholic, even though he experienced difficulty stopping. To prevent others from smelling alcohol on him, he decided not to drink during the week, and to limit his drinking to weekends and only at his sailing club where there were no faculty or students. After two to three months of using this strategy to limit his drinking to weekends, he again was confronted by the dean, who said that there were reports of him drinking at his sailing club. In a desperate effort to stop the nagging complaints from the dean and to prove once and for all that he is not an alcoholic, Dr. S decided to go into residential treatment for alcoholism. He was convinced that they would not diagnose him as an alcoholic and that would be proof to his dean.

After several phone calls to various treatment programs, he selected one that accepted his insurance and had a relatively unrestrictive treatment regimen. He then applied for and received a 30-day medical leave to enter residential treatment. When the nurse identified his physical problems as withdrawal systems, he was able to at least tenuously accept his alcoholism diagnosis.

In treatment, Dr. S was learning about himself within the context of his addiction. His father was also alcoholic, and their temperaments were similar. They both had enabling wives who tolerated their alcohol abuse. In fact, Dr. S's wife would usually drink with him, even though she neither drank to excess nor exhibited any symptoms of alcoholism. On Sundays, Mrs. S would visit her husband. Dr. S's counselor, Mr. Jones, noted that during his periodic meetings with Mrs. S that she was a domineering presence who seemed to delight in belittling him. Dr. S, on the other hand, was receiving a good deal of supportive therapy and was beginning to improve his self-concept. At this time, Mrs. S has become increasingly critical of the treatment and suggested to her husband that he needed to stop treatment, because it was not helping. Mrs. S's enabling role seemed to undermine all of Dr. S's progress in recovery. Dr. S would progress during the week only to regress after seeing his wife on the weekends. With only 10 days remaining in treatment, Dr. S's counselor is faced with the challenge of keeping him in treatment.

Case Study 13.8
Dr. B

Dr. B is a white, 73-year-old, retired university professor, who has experienced difficulty maintaining sobriety since his first effort to recover when he was 55 years old. Dr. B was at one time a Vice President at a large Midwestern university when his superiors recognized that his problem drinking impaired his job performance. After several warnings to seek treatment or face dismissal, his drinking continued. At age 55, he was dismissed from his administrative position and reassigned to his original position as a teaching professor. With encouragement from friends and family members, Dr. B agreed to seek treatment at the public substance abuse center. After inpatient detoxification, he began receiving outpatient group counseling on a weekly basis along with periodic A.A. meetings.

Dr. B expressed discomfort with group counseling and the A.A. meetings. He complained to his wife that "I feel like a piece of discarded meat with those A.A. derelicts." As expected, he stopped going to A.A. and the weekly counseling sessions, because "I really don't think I need it anymore, and furthermore, it's not doing me any good." Recently, his family has influenced Dr. B to return to counseling.

Between ages 55 and 73, Dr. B intermittently attended A.A. meetings only when his drinking caused major problems. At age 65, he retired and moved to Florida with his wife. Recently, his wife died from complications related to surgery. Since her death two months ago, his excessive drinking has caused him major problems, from being arrested twice for DUI to health problems related to high blood pressure. He continues to grieve the loss of his wife of 47 years, and his drinking problems have escalated dramatically. Dr. B has decided to leave Florida and return to his hometown permanently. His closest friend and former university colleague has contacted the substance abuse program from where he once received help for advice as to how he can help his friend.

Case Study 13.9
Mrs. B

Mrs. B is a 67-year-old, Asian woman whose husband of 41 years died three months ago. Her two children have disclosed to the counselor that she is depressed, and her "heavy drinking started just after her husband died six months ago, and she never even touched alcohol before." They have also reported that Mrs. B has had numerous losses since her husband's death. She does not enjoy the financial stability she once had; two of her close friends have moved out of the state; her best friend died from complications associated with an operation; and her health has suffered recently, including a recent diagnosis of arthritis and high blood pressure.

Mrs. B has expressed ambivalence about accepting alcoholism treatment. To her children, she has agreed to treatment; but to her three siblings, one brother and two sisters, she has offered assurance that she will keep the problem within the family for resolution. Her brother and sisters embrace strong cultural traditions and believe it is a disgrace to disclose family problems to outsiders. Despite feelings of ambivalence, Mrs. B has agreed to meet with an alcoholism counselor on Monday of next week.

STUDY QUESTIONS

1. As a culturally sensitive counselor for Mr. and Mrs. S, what strategies will you use to allay feelings of shame in having disclosed intimate family problems?

2. Mr. W's youngest daughter approaches you for help with her mother's "drinking problems." As an alcoholism counselor, what assistance will you offer Mrs. W's daughter?

3. You are approached by Mr. N's children for assistance in getting their father to accept alcoholism treatment. What will you suggest to the children?

4. As Mrs. G's counselor, what approach will you use when you meet with her next week?

5. Mr. W's counselor has recently resigned to accept another counseling position, and you have been assigned as a replacement. Mr. W remains depressed and lonely, and he displays "dry drunk" behaviors and is very close to relapsing. What strategies will you use in working with Mr. W?

6. You have experienced difficulty in getting Mr. J to surrender to a "higher power," because, as he put it, "power is within oneself, not higher." What strategies will you use in his treatment plan?

7. You have been assigned to work with Mr. S, who has agreed to thirty days of inpatient residential treatment. Identify appropriate objectives to include in the treatment plan.

8. Identify those case studies that represent early-onset, late-onset, and intermittent alcoholism.

9. You have been assigned to work with Dr. B, because his former counselor thought that Dr. B needed a more task-oriented counselor whose counseling style might be more effective. You suspect that one problem may relate to his former counselor's no-nonsense approach that may have caused Dr. B to be defensive. What are some of the strategies that you will use to encourage Dr. B to remain in treatment?

10. With Mrs. B consenting to treatment, rather than trying to resolve her alcoholism within the family, she feels intense shame. As her counselor, what can you do to allay these feelings of shame?

11. What intervention strategies will you use to influence Mrs. B to accept alcoholism treatment?

Chapter XIV

FUTURE TRENDS

In opposition to federal money earmarked for drug treatment, John Ashcroft, President-elect Bush's choice for U.S. Attorney General, asserted that such federal expenditures should not further the "lowest and least" conduct.

Solomon, 2000

The final chapter will include issues that need to be addressed to effectively promote elder-specific treatment.

TRAIN PROFESSIONAL COUNSELORS IN THE AGING PROCESS

In anticipation of a dramatic elderly population increase during the first two decades of 2000, it is essential that health care professionals, especially alcoholism counselors, gain knowledge in the aging process to accommodate so-called baby-boomers. Training will need to provide for a comprehensive understanding of the aging process from several dimensions, including the psychological, social, physical, and spiritual. An understanding of how a major decline in physical and psychological functioning can precipitate the onset of alcoholism must be included in the training. Beresford and colleagues (1988) suggest that by the latter 1980s health care professionals had sufficiently progressed to serve an increased number of older people by "devoting both clinical and research resources to better understand the needs and problems brought on by the aging process." Yet, he cautions that:

Despite these accomplishments, little research effort has been directed at the intersection of these two great phenomena: aging and alcoholism. There are two main convergence points: the longitudinal effects of alcohol use or addiction with respect to the physiologic and psychological processes of growing older, and the here-and-now difficulties of an elderly subpopulation suffering from alcoholism. (p. 61)

193

One of the principal themes of this book was to address the need for health care professionals, especially alcoholism counselors, to acquire expertise in the aging process to understand its impact on alcoholism. A secondary theme relates to the need to recognize individual differences in the aging process. Chapter IV explores various age theories to assist in developing effective intervention strategies for inclusion into individualized treatment plans; that is, the individualized nature of the aging process may be better appreciated and understood through an understanding of the various aging theories (Adams & Hal, Winter 1988).

IDENTIFICATION OF ELDERLY ALCOHOLICS NEEDS IMPROVEMENT

Chapter V identified problems associated with current screening instruments that failed to identify elderly alcoholics. Through the combined efforts of health care providers and researchers, an instrument must be developed that includes elderly-relevant events that withstand the rigors of scientifically based validity and reliability testing. Medical health care professionals must become actively involved in identifying elderly alcoholics, especially physicians who can influence their patients to accept alcoholism treatment; but, first, physicians need to become well trained to recognize behavioral and physical signs that may be symptomatic of alcohol addiction (Camire, 2001). Of the 125 schools of Medicine in the United States, only three offer specializations in geriatrics.) Gerontologically based training needs to be integrated into medical school curricula, but training for current physicians must somehow be encouraged, if not mandated, through legislation, because medical physicians will continue to use their busy schedules as excuses to not accept training. In the meantime, numerous elderly alcoholics continue to be misdiagnosed with acute dementia, especially of the Alzheimer's variety, because physicians are untrained in differentiating between the two diseases.

Another resource to identify elderly alcoholics is through preretirement counseling programs generally offered in larger organizations. To encourage smaller, less-solvent work organizations to establish preretirement counseling, tax incentives should be considered. Senior community organizations must also assume a role in identifying elderly alcoholics for treatment. Atkinson, Ganzini, and Berstein (1992) offer suggestions for identification and prevention:

> Alcohol and drug dependence in the elderly can be reduced. Prevention should begin with public and private institutions, sponsoring better pre-retirement planning for employees' future roles and constructive use of time, including substance-use education. Retirement communities, and senior organizations and periodicals, can promote smoking cessation and moderation of alcohol use. Health caregivers and social caseworkers can provide advice and education on the adverse health and behavioral effects of alcohol and tobacco, and programs for smoking cessation and alcohol-use reduction can be made more easily accessible. (p. 544)

CULTURAL-SPECIFIC TREATMENT

The field of substance abuse counseling is currently in the process of developing practice methods to better individualize services to people of color and to other special populations, but our repertoire of information is grossly inadequate. In Chapter VI, "Special Populations," it was suggested that gender-specific socialization largely contributed to the development of the so-called machismo man who abuses alcohol to superficially maintain a semblance of male identity. Substantive, empirical research is clearly needed to better understand the interplay between gender-specific socialization and abusive drinking behaviors. Such research may also inadvertently answer the nagging question: Why are men typically the perpetrators in violent behaviors, specifically school violence? Surely, the professional counselor will not simplistically embrace the notion that genetics and/or biology alone explain violent behavior. Understanding the dynamics of male violence may also provide insight into "macholike" alcohol abuse.

Further research is needed to understand and to effectively intervene in treating the homeless alcoholic. Another client population in need of further research is the nursing home client where reportedly some 40 to 50 percent alcoholism rates exist, but substantive research studies to support these claims are seemingly absent.

Principles/Attitudes

Alcoholism counselors who assume a relatively sizeable elderly clientele must inculcate a code of ethics that dictates appropriate principles and attitudes to enhance successful treatment outcomes and ethical practice. Many helping professions have formulated core values specific to their profession. It would behoove alcoholism counselors, especially those who provide services to a largely elderly population, to develop their own (cardinal) values.

Intervention Strategies

For too long, alcoholism counselors have limited themselves in the use of treatment intervention strategies. Although the Twelve-Step Program has its benefits, it should not be considered solely at the exclusion of other potentially viable treatment modalities, including laughter therapy, biofeedback, relaxation therapy, life review therapy, and, of course, grief therapy. As a relatively new field of practice, substance abuse counseling has a unique opportunity to be innovative and provide new intervention strategies to contribute toward improving successful alcoholism treatment outcomes. Although the A.A.'s Twelve-Step Program benefited numerous recovering alcoholics, there are those who for various reasons benefit more from an approach that is more culturally specific. The counselor who typically is most familiar with varied cultural practices is in an ideal situation to develop intervention strategies that are culturally relevant in working with clients representing different cultures; therefore, with alcoholism treatment practice methods in the infancy stage of development, there is the potential for the counselor to develop culturally relevant treatment modalities.

GRIEF WORK

Various factors contribute to high relapse rate, but one that is commonly overlooked relates to clients' inability to accept themselves as alcoholics. Simply proclaiming to counselors and fellow recovering alcoholics that, "I am an alcoholic," is, at best, a superficial self-examination. The recovering alcoholic must transcend the cognitive, intellectual level of acceptance to fully internalize himself or herself as an alcoholic on a feeling, affective level. With the counselor's assistance, the client is able to attain a level of acceptance that is less transient and more permanent. The recovering alcoholic is assisted by the counselor to evolve from denial to acceptance on a feeling level, as opposed to a cognitive, thinking level that offers, at best, temporary sobriety.

Suicide

Clearly a need exists to conduct research studies to determine whether there is an interplay between relapse and suicide; that is, does relapse precipitate suicide? Considerable research findings conclude that a disproportionately high number of successful suicides involves alcohol abuse, but there is a dearth of research showing that relapse may precipitate suicide. The astute professional counselor understands that when clients express a profound sense of helplessness and hopelessness it is likely a danger signal that the suicidal potential is at a dangerously high level. But, what could provide a more helpless and hopeless state than to relapse after several weeks, or months, of successful recovery? To lessen the impact that relapse has on the alcoholic, it may be prudent to convey to the client that a lapse and/or relapse is part of the disease process, a form of harm reduction.

Harm-Reduction Strategies

From the elder-specific treatment facilities I interviewed, there emerged a resounding theme that harm reduction treatment strategies may be more effective and realistic for older recovering alcoholics than strict compliance to sobriety. That is, instead of insisting on sobriety as a precondition to receiving treatment, "smaller steps" leading to sobriety may be a more realistic treatment for an elderly client population that is apt to resent a seemingly harsh policy that insists on sobriety as a precondition to treatment. The use of incremental small steps may also be applicable in treating nonelderly clients. Margaret Flower, a nurse associated with a team of treatment specialists at the Community Older Persons Alcohol Program (COPA), in Toronto, Ontario, reports that a harm-reduction approach is an especially effective strategy in providing treatment services to an elderly addicted clientele.

PROMOTE ELDER-SPECIFIC TREATMENT

Despite the need for more elder-specific treatment facilities, its likelihood is bleak without the aggressive support from senior service organizations. Not even the American Association of Retired Persons (AARP), arguably the leading advocate for the elderly, has either the inclination or the clout to effectively spearhead such a movement. The elderly are conspicuously without a viable organization and leadership to support needed legislation and policy favorable to the 120 million elderly in the United States. The

Gray Panthers, a once-influential organization led by its late charismatic founder, Maggie Kuhn, was instrumental in promoting important legislation for the elderly in the 1960s and 1970s. Without an effective political force representing the elderly, the responsibility rests principally with the substance-abuse professional community to exert pressure to promote and develop elder-specific alcoholism treatment. Political pressure needs to be exerted on those who are responsible for formulating healthcare policies and services. To varying degrees of influence, targeted persons should include elected officials at the local, state, and federal levels, as well as hospitals, mental health administrators, and others in the health care hierarchy who wield power in the planning and decision-making processes.

Two formidable obstacles face proponents of elder-specific alcoholism treatment. First, the prevailing attitude in the United States favors earmarking substance-abuse treatment expenditures to the addicted youth who presumably, because of enhanced longevity, are a more prudent investment. This ageist attitude unfortunately is rampant and indelibly engrained into the psyches of those who make major decisions in the healthcare sector.

The second obstacle relates to a policy issue concerning supply and demand. That is, should substance-abuse expenditures be appropriated for treatment and prevention or law and order–related activities to control the supply and demand of substances? The Drug Enforcement Administration, clearly the greatest recipient of drug monies, has traditionally argued that to curtail substance abuse, it is necessary to attack the supply side, whereas the treatment community advocates for prevention (education) and treatment to reduce the demand. About 75 percent is appropriated for curtailing the supply, whereas only about 25 percent is targeted for demand reduction. The supply and demand debate continues as the so-called "War on Drugs" rages on ineffectually. Although the supply-side argument is directed toward the curtailment of illicit drugs, it has an adverse effect on alcoholism treatment, because fewer monies are available when the disportionate emphasis is on cutting supply.

Before effective promotion of elder-specific alcoholism treatment can occur, treatment must be viewed as a basic right and not as a privilege reserved for the glorified youth who offer greater productivity in the workplace.

EPILOGUE

At this very moment as I complete this book, the Bush Administration is working feverishly to develop a coalition of Republicans and Democrats to support legislation that would provide for faith-based social services. Despite concerns that there likely will be efforts to exclude non-Christians, people of color, gays and lesbians, and the homeless from services, this may be a realistic source of sponsorship and funding for elder-specific treatment for thousands of alcoholics.

Lutheran Ministries, for one, has established a solid reputation in the provision of social services, including guardianship for the elderly and work with youth gangs to name but a few of the notable services under the auspices of Lutheran Ministries. Of particular significance, services have been provided to a clientele inclusive of diverse cultures, races, and religions. One such sponsored service that provides substance abuse treatment for the elderly is featured in Chapter XIII, the Older Adult and Other Drug Services in Appleton, Wisconsin.

If, in fact, exclusionary practices ensue, these situations can be resolved in the courts. In the meantime, this may be an opportune time to establish needed sponsorship and funding for elder-specific alcoholism treatment through the Lutheran Ministries and other interested denominations. I have plans to approach the Lutheran Ministries Florida/Gulf Coast Region for the very purpose of encouraging sponsorship and funding in needed alcoholism treatment for an elderly population.

REFERENCES

Atkinson, R.M., Ganzini, L., & Bernstein, M.J. (1992). Alcohol and substance-use disorders in the elderly. *Handbook of mental health and aging* (2nd ed.). New York: Academic Press, Inc., pp. 515–555.

Beresford, T.P., Blow, F.C., Bower, K.J., Adams, K.M., & Hall, R.C.W. (Winter 1988). *Psychosomatics, 29*(1), 61.

Camire, D. (June 14, 2001). Survey finds Americans hope to live to be 100 years old. *Pensacola News Journal*, Pensacola, FL. Gannet News Service, p. 3

Schonfeld, L., & Dupree, L.W. (1991). Antecedents of drinking for early- and late-onset elderly alcohol abusers. *Journal of Studies on Alcohol, 52*(6), 587.

Solomon, J. (December 8, 2000). *Bush's choice for AG praised confederate war heroes.* Pensacola, FL: Pensacola News Journal.

APPENDIX

SUMMARIES OF INTERVIEWED ELDERLY-SPECIFIC TREATMENT FACILITIES

Institution:___Amethyst, Inc._____
Address:___527 South High Street_____
City:___Columbus_____ State:___OH___ Zip Code:___43215___
Telephone/TTY:_(614) 242-1284_____ E-mail address:_____
Toll-free No.: (___)_____ FAX No.: (614) 1285_____

Self-Description: Amethyst was founded in 1984 by a group of women who recognized that women recovering from alcohol and drug addiction need long-term treatment and support. This support includes a safe and drug-free environment in which women and their families can make permanent life changes. In addiction to treatment for addition, women receive permanent housing, counseling for trauma issues, case management, support with education and employment, family programming, and management of mental health issues.

Treatment Philosophy: Amethyst's approach to recovery is gender-specific and incorporates the Relational Cultural Model into our practices. This model recognizes that women build on and develop in relationship to other people. To meet the gender-specific needs of women at Amethyst, we create a safe, supportive, nurturing, and woman-centered environment that encourages trust, bonding, and connection. Our program helps women learn how to develop positive connections to themselves, peers, family, the workplace, and the community as a whole.

Family Program: Amethyst's extensive family program is geared toward breaking the cycle of generational addiction, violence, poverty, and homelessness. Children and youth living with their mothers at Amethyst learn about the disease of addiction and begin to heal from the trauma they have experienced as a result of the disease. Emergency babysitting and childcare are provided for children under age six. All families are linked to primary health care providers, and all women in treatment at Amethyst participate in parenting classes.

Position on 12-Step Involvement: All participants are required to actively participate in peer-support networks.

Position on Confrontation: With a foundation in the Relational Cultural Model, staff and peers at Amethyst use confrontation in an environment of safety and respect. While dealing with difficult issues and patterns of unhealthy behavior can require confrontation, it is not done at the expense of the dignity of the client or in a way that hinders positive connections with staff or peers.

Additional Characteristics: Amethyst has created a community of recovery where women in treatment live in the same apartment community providing peer support and an environment of safety and sobriety. For many women, this is the first time they have lived somewhere that they and their children know the neighbors and feel safe. Of most importance, perhaps, is the long-term commitment that Amethyst has to participants. Over 35% of women at Amethyst have voluntarily participated for more than one year. This long-term stability and support undoubtedly has a positive impact on each woman's ability to make permanent life changes supportive of her recovery.

GENERAL:

Number of beds:	100 units/slots
Detox available:	No
No. dual diagnosed:	85% (not SMD)

• Current (2001) Admissions:

Total Annual Admits:	90 women
Average Length of Stay	11 months (range 0–48 months)
Percent of Women	100%
Percent of 55 and older	3%
Receiving psychiatric medication in addition to detoxification:	N/A

• Admissions Procedures:

Night Admission available:	No
Weekend Admission available:	No

SPECIAL POPULATIONS:
FACILITY HAS SEPARATE PROGRAM FOR:

	Yes	No
Anger management/conflict resolution	X	
Codependency	X	
Depression	X	
Domestic violence	X	
Family	X	
Geriatric		X
Grief and loss	X	
Men		X
Women	X	
Psychiatric (dual diagnosis)	X	
Other:	X	

PAYMENT INFORMATION:

Self-pay cost per month:	0
Public assistance coverage may be accepted:	Yes
Medicare coverage accepted:	N/A
Insurance coverage verified before admission:	Yes
Follow-up care:	Yes

LICENSING AND ACCREDITATION:

Licensed by:	Ohio Department of Alcohol and Drug Addition Services
Type of License:	Provide intensive outpatient and inpatient services
Accredited by:	N/A

Prepared by (optional):

Lori Criss	Associate Director	9/12/01
Name	Title	Date

Please return completed form to:
Dr. Michael Beechem, Professor
Department of Social Work
The University of West Florida
11000 University Parkway
Pensacola, Florida 32514

SUMMARIES OF INTERVIEWED ELDERLY-SPECIFIC TREATMENT FACILITIES

Institution: Chelsea Arbor Treatment Center–
                     Older Adult Recovery Center (OARC)
Address: 955 W. Eisenhower Circle Street, H.
City: *Ann Arbor (In-patient Chelsea)*   State: _MI_   Zip Code: 48103
Telephone: (800) 328 3261   E-mail address: jsmith@cch.org
Toll-free No.: (800) 328-6261   FAX No.: (734) 665-6487

Self-Description: Inpatient Detox and Treatment, Outpatient Day Treatment, Intensive Outpatient, Outpatient Treatment for adults age 55 and over with drug and alcohol problems and their families. Age-specific A.A. meetings on site. Peer counselor involved in all aspects of treatment. Medicare and other insurance accepted.

Treatment Philosophy: Addiction is a chronic, primary, progressive brain disease that manifests itself differently in each individual. Individual treatment planning is required. Twelve Step participation is important for recovery. Age is no respecter of the disease and older adults deserve an opportunity for recovery. There is no such thing as "a last remaining pleasure" for someone with this brain disease. But, it is treatable for older adults with understanding of the particular challenges of aging and by approaching the older adult with respect.

Family Program: Family appointments necessary. Family education series once per month. Family can be defined broadly and includes all types of support of relationships.

Position on 12-Step Involvement: Twelve-Step meetings are highly encouraged. We have A.A. meetings that appear to appeal to older adults on site. We offer a group that studies the writings and philosophy of twelve-step groups. We do not exclude someone from treatment if they refuse to go to twelve-step meetings. We work to match the most external support with each client.

Position on Confrontation: We have adopted the principles of motivational Interviewing that essentially encourage the individuals to motivate themselves into recovery. Traditional confrontation does not work well with older adults. Older adults have a lot of important life experience that can be channeled and brought to bear in service of their recoveries.

Additional Characteristics: Outreach collaboration with two local aging agencies. Travel all over the country to present workshops on how to set up systems in communities to motivate older adults into treatment. twenty Peer Counselors work in the program—each recovering and have gone through the OARC.

GENERAL:

Number of beds:	1–6
Detox available:	Yes
No. dual diagnosed:	Varies

- **Current (2001) Admissions:**

Total Annual Admits:	100 combined inpatient and outpatient
Average Length of Stay	Outpatients–16 days Inpatients–3 months
Percent of Women	55%
Percent of 55 and older	100%
Receiving psychiatric medication in addition to detoxification:	N/A35–40%

- **Admissions Procedures:**

Night Admission available:	Yes
Weekend Admission available:	Yes

SPECIAL POPULATIONS:
FACILITY HAS SEPARATE PROGRAM FOR:

	Yes	No
Anger management/conflict resolution	X	
Codependency	X	

Depression	X	
Domestic violence		
Family	X	
Geriatric	X	
Grief and loss	X	
Men		
Women		
Psychiatric (dual diagnosis)		
Other:		

PAYMENT INFORMATION:

Self-pay cost per month:	16 days about $9000
Public assistance coverage may be accepted:	Yes
Medicare coverage accepted:	Yes
Insurance coverage verified before admission:	Yes
Follow-up care:	Yes

LICENSING AND ACCREDITATION:

Licensed by:	Bureau of Substance Abuse Services
Type of License:	Full license
Accredited by:	JCALTO

Prepared by (optional):

Jeff Smith (sig)	Therapist	9/2/01
Name	Title	Date

Please return completed form to:
Dr. Michael Beechem, Professor
Department of Social Work
The University of West Florida
11000 University Parkway
Pensacola, Florida 32514

SUMMARIES OF INTERVIEWED ELDERLY-SPECIFIC
TREATMENT FACILITIES

Institution: Hanley-Hazelden Center
Address: 520 East Avenue
City: West Palm Beach   State: FL   Zip Code: 33407
Telephone: (561) 841-1000   E-mail address: _____
Toll-free No.: (800) 444-7008   FAX No.: (561) 841-1100

Self-Description: The Older Adult Program is designed to specifically meet the needs of older adults addicted to alcohol and/or prescription medication.

Treatment Philosophy: Our basic philosophy is dignity and respect. A warn, caring environment provides the setting for accurate and appropriate diagnosis, treatment, and continuing care.

Family Program: A three-day residential family program is provided. We also have a twice weekly, for three weeks, evening outpatient family program.

Position on 12-Step Involvement: We are a Minnesota Model 12-step-0based program.

Position on Confrontation: Older adults respond better to a less confrontive and more nurturing style of treatment.

Additional Characteristics: We treat all aspects of the older adult needs. We have a 24-hour staffed medical and treatment unit.

GENERAL:

Number of beds:	16 older adult beds
Detox available:	6 detox beds
No. dual diagnosed:	

• Current (2001) Admissions:

Total Annual Admits:	200–250
Average Length of Stay	30 days
Percent of Women	50%
Percent of 55 and older	All
Receiving psychiatric medication in addition to detoxification:	5%

• Admissions Procedures:

Night Admission available:	Yes
Weekend Admission available:	Yes

SPECIAL POPULATIONS:
FACILITY HAS SEPARATE PROGRAM FOR:

	Yes	No
Anger management/conflict resolution	X	
Codependency		
Depression	X	
Domestic violence		
Family	X	
Geriatric		
Grief and loss	X	
Men		
Women		
Psychiatric (dual diagnosis)	X	
Other:		

PAYMENT INFORMATION:

Self-pay cost per month:	$18–19,000
Public assistance coverage may be accepted:	No
Medicare coverage accepted:	No
Insurance coverage verified before admission:	Yes
Follow-up care:	Yes

LICENSING AND ACCREDITATION:

Licensed by:	Florida DCF
Type of License:	
Accredited by:	JCAHO

Prepared by (optional)

Carol Colhen	Director, Older Adult Program	9/2/01
Name	Title	Date

Please return completed form to:
Dr. Michael Beechem, Professor
Department of Social Work
The University of West Florida
11000 University Parkway
Pensacola, Florida 32514

SUMMARIES OF INTERVIEWED ELDERLY-SPECIFIC
TREATMENT FACILITIES

Institution: Lutheran Social Services – Side by Side AODA Program
Address: 820 W. College Avenue
City: Appleton   State: WI   Zip Code: 54914
Telephone: (920) 733-2860 ext. 12   E-mail address:
Toll-free No.: (   )   FAX No.: (920) 733-7321

Self-Description: Side by Side is designed for older adults who are in need of outpatient treatment services for alcohol or other drug abuse, or family members affected by AODA issues.   Housed at the Thompson Community Center.

Treatment Philosophy: To sensitively address the unique biological psychological and social issues of older adults, including physical aspects of aging, loneliness and loss issues, fixed incomes, and the economics of aging, independence, and quality of life issues.

Family Program: Side by Side offers weekly family groups as well as conjoint individual sessions to help educate and provide counseling for AODA issues affecting family and identified clients.

Position on 12-Step Involvement: Side by Side believes 12-step groups are a good support for older adults recovering from AODA, but individuals choose for themselves if it is right for them.

Position on Confrontation: Honesty and integrity are practiced by the members of the Side by Side program. Clients are encouraged to give feedback to each other in a helpful, caring, honest manner.

Additional Characteristics: Side by Side offers individuals the opportunities to re-engage in their community by becoming active in the Thompson Center's many and varied activities. The Thompson Center is a major hub of activity for older adults in this community and invites those who wish to join in.

GENERAL:

Number of beds:	N/A outpatient facility
Detox available:	No
No. dual diagnosed:	1

• Current (2001) Admissions:

Total Annual Admits:	37
Average Length of Stay	1 year
Percent of Women	20%
Percent of 55 and older	99%
Receiving psychiatric medication in addition to detoxification:	N/A

• Admissions Procedures:

Night Admission available:	No
Weekend Admission available:	No

SPECIAL POPULATIONS:
FACILITY HAS SEPARATE PROGRAM FOR:

	Yes	No
Anger management/conflict resolution		
Codependency		
Depression		
Domestic violence		
Family		
Geriatric	No	
Grief and loss		
Men		
Women		
Psychiatric (dual diagnosis)	No	
Other:		

PAYMENT INFORMATION:

Self-pay cost per month:	$900.00 per year
Public assistance coverage may be accepted:	No
Medicare coverage accepted:	No
Insurance coverage verified before admission:	No
Follow-up care:	Yes

LICENSING AND ACCREDITATION:

Licensed by:	State of Wisconsin
Type of License:	AODA Outpatient
Accredited by:	OCOA–National Concil of Accreditation

Prepared by (optional):

Rebecca Green, CADC III	Program Coordinator	9/2/01
Name	Title	Date

Please return completed form to:
Dr. Michael Beechem, Professor
Department of Social Work
The University of West Florida
11000 University Parkway
Pensacola, Florida 32514

BIBLIOGRAPHY

Abrams, R.C. & Alexopoulos, G.S. (1987). Substance abuse in the elderly: Alcohol and prescription drugs. *Hospital and Community Psychiatry, 38*(12), 1285–1287.

Adams, W.L. (1997). Interactions between alcohol and other drugs. In A. M. Gurnack (Ed.), *Older adults' misuse of alcohol, medicines, and other drugs: research and practice.* New York: Springer.

Adams, W.L., Yuan, Z, Barboriak, J.J., & Rimm, A.A. (Sept. 8, 1993). Alcohol-related hospitalizations of elderly people: Prevalence and geographic variation in the United States. *JAMA, 270*(10), 1222–1225.

Agarwal, D., Eckey, R., Harada, S., & Goedde, H. (1984). Basis of adelhyde dehydrogenase deficiency in Orientals. *Alcohol, 1,* CSAP (4), 111–118.

Alcohol and aging. (October, 1989). *Alcohol alert, (2).* National Institute on Alcohol Abuse and Alcoholism report (Al. Alert p. 3)

Alcohol and aging. (April, 1998) *Alcohol alert,* (40). National Institute on Alcohol Abuse & Alcoholism.

Alcohol and Hormones. (October, 1994) *Alcohol alert,* (26). National Institute on Alcohol Abuse & Alcoholism.

Allen, J.P. & Columbus, M. (1995). Assessing alcohol problems: A guide for clinicians and researchers. *The National Institute on Alcohol Abuse and Alcoholism,* 400–386.

Amodeo, M.A. (1990). Treating the late life alcoholic: Guidelines for working through denial, integrating individual, family, and group approaches. *Journal of Geriatric Psychiatry, 23*(2), 91–105.

Annis, H.M. (1990). Relapse to substance abuse: Empirical findings within a cognitive-social learning approach. *Journal of Psychoactive Drugs, 22,* 117–124.

Annis, H.M. & Davis, C.S. (1989). *Relapse prevention: The handbook of alcoholism treatment approaches.* New York: The Plenum Press.

As we grow older: Alcohol and medications. Pamphlet by Community Drug and Alcohol Commission, Pensacola, Florida.

Atchley, R.C. (1989). A continuity theory of normal aging. *The Gerontologist, 29,* 183–90.

Atchley, R.C. (1991). *Social forces and aging: An introduction to social gerontology* (6th ed.). Belmont, CA: Wadsworth Publishing Co.

Atkinson, R.M. (1991). Alcohol and drug abuse in the elderly. In R. Jacoby and C. Oppenheimer (Eds.), *Psychiatry in the elderly.* Oxford: Oxford University Press, 819–851.

Atkinson, R.M., Ganzini, L., & Bernstein, M.J. (1992). Alcohol and substance-use disorders in the elderly. *Handbook of mental health and aging* (2nd ed.). Academic Press, Inc., 515–555.

Atkinson, R.M. & Kofoed, L.L. (1982). Alcohol and drug abuse in old age: A clinical perspective. *Substance and Alcohol Actions/Misuse, V. 3,* 353–368.

Atkinson, R.M., Tolson, R.L., & Turner, J.A. (January, 1993). Factors affecting treatment compliance of older male problem drinkers. *Journal of Studies on Alochol,* 102–105.

Avis, H. (1996). *Drugs and life* (4th ed.). New York: WCB/McGraw-Hill.

Baer J. & Lichtenstein, E. (1988). Classification and prediction of smoking relapse episodes: An exploration of individual differences. *Journal of Consulting and Clinical Psychology, 56,* 104–110.

Barrow, G.M. (1992). *Aging, the individual, and society* (5th ed.), St. Paul, MN: West Publishing Company.

Beach, R. (Nov., 1999). Seminar at University of South Alabama, Hattiesburg, MS.

Beattie, M. (1987). *Co-dependent no more.* New York: Fiat Harper & Row.

Beaver, M.L. & Miller, D. (1985). *Clinical social work practice with the elderly: Primary, secondary, and tertiary Intervention.* Homewood, IL: The Dorsey Press.

Beechem, M. (1995). Developing a culturally-sensitive treatment plan in pre-hospice South Texas. *The Hospice Journal, 10*(2), 25.

Beechem, M. (1997). Beechem risk inventory for late-onset alcoholism. *Journal of Drug Education, 27*(4), 397–410.

Beechem, M., Anthony, C., & Kurtz, J. (1998). A life review guide: A structured systems approach to information gathering. *The International Journal of Aging and Human Development, 46*(1), 25–44.

Beechem, M. & Comstock, J. (1997). Teaching empathy skills to undergraduate social work students. *The Journal of Baccalaureate Social Work, 2*(2), 87–96.

Beechem, M., Prewitt, J., & Scholar, J. (1996). Loss-grief Addiction Model. *Journal of Drug Education, 26*(2), 183–198.

Bell, P., & Evans, J. (1981). *Counseling the black client: Alcohol use and abuse in Black America.* City Center, MN: Hazelden Foundation, CSAP 4.

Benjamin, A. (1981). *The helping interview* (3rd ed.). Boston: The Houghton Miffin Company.

Beresford, T.P. (1995). Alcoholic elderly: Prevalence, screening, diagnosis, and prognosis. In: Beresford, T. & Gomberg, E. (Eds.), *Alcohol and aging: Looking ahead.* New York: Oxford University Press.

Beresford, T.P., Blow, F.C., Bower, K.J., Adams, K.M., & Hall, R.C.W. (Winter 1988). *Psychosomatics, 29*(1), p. 61.

Berger, R.M. (1982). Gay and gray: The older homosexual man. Urbana: IL: University of Illinois Press. In Hooymonn, N.R. & Kiyak, H.A. (1988). *Social gerontology: A multidisciplinary perspective.* Boston: Allyn & Bacon, Inc.

Bienenfeld, D. (Aug. 1987). Alcoholism in the elderly. *American Family Physician, 36*(2), 163–169.

Biestak, F.P. (Feb. 1954). An analysis of the casework relationship. *Social Casework.*

Blake, R. (July 1990). Mental health counseling and older problem drinkers. *Journal of Mental Health Counseling, 12*(3), 354–367.

Blow, F.C.; Brower, K. J., Schulenberg, J.E., Demo-Damanberg, L.M., Young, K.J., & Beresford, T.P. (1992). The Michigan alcoholism screening test: Geriatric version instrument (abstract) Alcoholism. *Clinical and Experimental Research, 165*, 172.

Bowlby, J. (1980) *Loss, sadness, and depression.* New York: Basic Books.

Bowman, K.M. & Jellinek, E.M. (1941). Alcohol addiction and its treatment. In: E.M. Jellinek (Ed.), *Effects of alcohol on the individual, Vol. 1, Ch. 1.* New Haven: Yale University Press. Also in *Quarterly. Journal of Studies of Alcohol, 56*(2): 98–176.

Brigden, W. (1972). Alcohol cardiomyopathy. *Cardiovascular Clinics, 4*(1): 187–201.

Brod, R.L. & McQuiston, J.M. (1983). American Indian adult education and literacy: The first national survey. *Journal of American Indian Education, (1)*: 1–16.

Brown, B.B. (1982). Professionals' perceptions of drug and alcohol abuse among the elderly. *The Gerontologist, 22*(6), 519–524

Brown, S., Beletsis, S.G., & Cermak, T.L. (1989). *Adult children of alcoholics in treatment.* Deerfield Beach, FL: Health Comunications.

Brown, S.A., Vik, P.W., Patterson, T., Grant, I., & Schuckit, M.A. (Sept. 1994). Stress, vulnerability, and adult alcohol relapse. *Journal of Studies on Alcohol, 56*(5), 538.

Bullis, R.R. (1996). *Spirituality on social work practice.* Washington, D.C.: Taylor and Francis Publishers.

Burge, S.K. & Schneider, F.D. (January 15, 1999). Alcohol-related problems: Recognition and intervention. *American Family Physician.*

Butler, J.P. (1995). Of kindred minds: The ties that bind. In Orlandi, M., Weston, R., & Epstein, L. (Eds.), *CSAP 1: Cultural competence for evaluators.* Rockville, MD: U.S. Department of Health and Human Services.

Butler, R.N. (1975). *Why survive?* New York: Harper & Row.

Butler, R.N., Lewis, M., & Sunderland, T. (1991). *Aging and mental health: Positive psychosocial and biomedical approaches* (4th ed.). New York: MacMillan Publishing Company, 209.

Camire, D. (June 14, 2001). Survey finds Americans hope to live to be 100 years old. *Pensacola News Journal,* Pensacola, FL. Gannet News Service, p. 3

Carroll, C.R. (2000). *Drugs in modern society* (5th ed.). New York: McGraw-Hill.

Chafetz, M. (1983). *The alcoholic patient: Diagnosis and management, Vol. I & II.* Oradell, NJ: Medical Economics Company, Inc.

Chiauzzi, E. (1989). Breaking the patterns that lead to relapse. *Psychology Today, 23*(12), 18–19.

Cicirelli, V.E. (June 1998). View of elderly people concerning end-of-life decision. *Journal of Applied Gerontology, 17*(2), 186(18).

Clark, M. (1970). *Health in the Mexican-American culture.* Los Angeles: University of California Press.

Cockerham, W.C. (1991). *This aging society.* Englewood Cliffs, NJ: Prentice-Hall.

Coke P., & Twaite, T. (1971). Attitudes toward aging and the aged among Black Americans: Some historical perspectives. *Aging and Human Development, 3,* 66–70.

Corey, G. (1986). *Theory and practice of counseling and psychotherapy* (3rd ed.). Monterey, CA: Brooks/Cole Publishing Company.

Corey, M., Schneider, J., & Corey, G. (1993). *Becoming a helper* (2nd ed.). Pacific Grove, CA: Brooks/Cole Publishing Company.

Council on Scientific Affairs (1996) (1990). The world-wide smoking epidemic, *Journal of the American Medical Association, 263*, 3312–3318.

Cousins, N. (1986). *Human options.* New York: Berkley Publishing Group.

Covington, S.S. (1991). Awakening your sexuality: A guide for recovering women and their partners. San Francisco, CA: HarperCollins.

Cowgill, D.O. (1986). *Aging around the world.* Belmont, CA: Wadsworth Publishing Company.

Crandell, J.S. (1987). *Effective outpatient treatment for alcohol-abusers and drinking drivers,* Article 22. Lexington, MA: Lexington Books.

Crandall, R.C. (1991). *Gerontology: A behavioral science approach* (2nd ed.). New York: McGraw-Hill, Inc.

DeHart, S.S. & Hoffman, N.G. (1997). Screening and diagnosis: Alcohol use in older adults. In A. M. Gurnack (Ed.) (1997). *Older adults' misuse of alcohol, medicines, and other drugs: research and practice.* New York: Springer.

Denzin, N.K. (1987) *The recovering alcoholic,* Article 23. London: Sage Publications.

DeSpelder, L.A. & Strickland, A.L. (1995). *Readings in death and dying: The path ahead.* Mountain View, CA: Mayfield Publishing Company.

DeSpelder, L.A. & Stickland, A.L. (1998). *The last dance* (5th ed.). Mountain View, CA: Mayfield Publishing Corp.

Devons, C.A.J. (March 1996). Suicide in the elderly: How to identify and treat patients at risk. *Geriatrics, 51*(3), 67(5).

Devore, W., & Schlesinger, E G. (1996). *Ethnic-sensitive social work practice.* Needham Heights, MA: Allyn & Bacon.

Diagnostic and statistical manual of mental disorders (4th ed.). RT. (2000). Washington, DC: American Psychiatric Association.

Dowd, J.J. (1975). Aging as exchange: A preface to theory. *Journal of Gerontology, 30*(5): 584–594.

Doweiko, H.E. (1999). *Concepts of chemical dependency* (4th ed.). Pacific Grove, CA: Brooks/Cole Publishing Company.

Downs, Hugh. (September, 27, 2000). "20-20."

Dunlop, M.A. (1990). Peer groups support seniors fighting alcohol and drugs. *Aging, 361*, 28–32.

Durkheim, E. (1897/1951). *Suicide.* (Translated by Spaulding, J.A. &. Simpson, G.) New York: Free Press.

Edinberg, M.A. (1985). *Mental health practice with the elderly.* Englewood Cliffs, NJ: Prentice-Hall, Inc.

Ehmann, V.E. (1971). Empathy: Its origin, characteristics, and process perspectives. *Psychiatric Care, IX*(2), 76.

Everything about Kwanzaa. (March, 2001). http://www.tike.com/celeb-kw.htm

Falicov, C.J. (1982). Mexican families. In M. McGoldrick, J. K. Pearce, & J. Giordano (Eds.), *Ethnicity and family therapy.* New York: Guilford Press.

Fields, R. (1998). *Drugs in perspective: A personalized look at substance abuse and use* (3rd ed.). New York: The McGraw-Hill Companies, Inc.

Finlayson, R., Hurt, R.D. Davis, L.J., & Morse, R.M. (1988). Alcoholism in elderly persons: A study of the psychiatric and psychosocial features of 216 inpatients. *Mayo Clinic Proceedings, 63*(8), 761–768.

Fishbein, D.H. & Pease, S.E. (1996). *The dynamics of drug abuse.* Needham Heights, MA: Allyn & Bacon.

Fleming, M. & Manwell, L.B. (1999). Brief intervention in primary care settings: a primary treatment method for at-risk, problem, and dependent drinkers. *Alcohol Research and Health, 23,* 128–137. Retrieved at April 16, 2000 from FirstSearch database (WilsonSelect) Number BSSI00002888.

Flower, M. (1998). *Choosing to change: A client-centered approach to alcohol and medication use by older adults.* Toronto, Canada: Center for Addiction and Mental Health.

Freud, S. (1959). *The future prospects of psychoanalytic therapy.* In E. Jones (Ed.) Collected papers of Sigmund Freud Vol. 2, pp. 285–286, New York: Basic Books.

Fulop, G., Reinhardt, J., Strain, T.J., Paris, B., Miller, M. R. & Fillip, H. (July, 1993). Identification of alcoholism and depression in a geriatric medicine outpatient clinic. *Journal of the American Geriatrics Society, 41*(7), 737–741.

Gaitz, C.M. & Baer, P.E. (April 1971). Characteristics of elderly patients with alcoholism. *Archives of General Psychiatry, 24,* 372–378.

Garden, F.H., Garrison, S.J., & Jain, A. (1990). Assessing suicide risk in stroke patients: review of two cases. *Archives of Physical and Medical Rehabilitation, 71*(12) 1003–1005.

Gelfaud, D.E. (1994). *Aging and ethnicity.* New York: Springer Publishing Company.

Genevay, B. & Katz, R.S. (1990). *Countertransference and older clients.* Newbury Park, CA: Sage Publications, Inc.

Gilbert, M. (1991). Acculturation and changes in drinking patterns among Mexican-American women. *Alcohol Health and Research World, 15*(3): 234–238.

Goddard, L. (1993). Background and scope of the alcohol and other drug problems. In Goddard, L. (Ed.) *CSAP Technical Report, 6.* Rockville, MD: U.S. Department of Health and Human Services, CSAP 4, 11–18, 81.

Goldberg, H. (1976). The hazards of being male. In Staudacher, C., *Of men and grief.* New York: New American Library.

Goldberg, R. (1997). *Drugs across the spectrum.* Englewood, CO: Morton Publishing Company.

Gorski, T.A. (1986). Relapse prevention planning: A new recovery tool. *Alcohol Health and Research World II, 6,* 8–11, 63.

Gorski, T.A. (1990). The CE NAPS model of relapse prevention: Basic principles and procedures. *Journal of Proactive Drugs, 22,* 125–133.

Graham, K., Saunders, S.J., Flower, M.C., Timney, C.B., White-Campbell, M., & Pietropado, A.Z. (1995). *Addictions treatment for older adults.* New York: The Haworth Press, Inc.

Gray, M. (1995). African Americans. In Philleo, J. (Ed.), *Cultural competence for social workers: A guide for alcohol and other drug abuse prevention professionals working with ethnic/racial communities.* SAMHSA 4. National Clearinghouse for Alcohol and Drug Information 73 of CSAP 4, 73.

Hartford, J.T. & Thienhaus, O.J. (1984). Psychiatric aspects of alcoholism in geriatric patients. In J. T. Hartford & T. Samorajski (Eds.), *Alcoholism in the elderly.* New York: Raven Press

Havighurst, R.J., Neugarten, B.L., and Tobin S.S. (1968). Personality and patterns of aging. In B. L. Neugarten (Ed.), *Middle age and aging: A reader in social psychology.* Chicago: University of Chicago Press.

Helms, J.E., & Cook, D. A. (1999). *Using race and culture in counseling and psychotherapy.* Needham Heights, MA: Allyn and Bacon.

Hepworth, D.H. & Larsen, J. (1990). *Direct social work practice: Theory and skills* (3rd ed.). Belmont, CA: The Dorsey Press.

Herr, J.J., & Weakland, J. H. (1979). *Counseling elders and their families: Practical techniques for applied gerontology.* New York: Springer Publishing Company.

Hidalgo, H., Peterson. T.L., & Woodman, N.J. (Eds.). (1985). *Lesbian and gay issues: A resource manual for social workers.* Silver Springs, MD: NASW Press.

Higgins, J.P., Wright, S.W. & Wrenn, K.D. (1996). Alcohol, the elderly, and motor vehicle crashes. *American Journal of Emergency Medicine, 14,* 265–267.

Hirayama, H. (1987). Public policies and services for the aged in Japan. In Dobrof, R. (Ed.), *Ethnicity and gerontological social work.* New York: Haworth Press, Inc.

Hite, S. (1976). *The Hite report.* New York: Macmillan.

Holmes, K.A. & Hodge, R.H. (1995). Gay and lesbian persons. In Philleo, J. (Ed.), *Cultural competence for social workers: A guide for alcohol and other drug abuse prevention professionals working with ethnic/racial communities.* SAMHSA 4. National Clearinghouse for Alcohol and Drug Information, CSAP4, 200.

How to talk to an older person who has a problem with alcohol or medications. *Alcohol and Aging* (April, 1999). Center City: MN: Hazelden.

Huntington, D.D. (1990). Home care of the elderly alcoholic. *Home Healthcare Nurse,8*(5), 76.

Jacobs, J. (1993). Black America, 1992: An overview. In Tidwell, B. (Ed.), *The state of Black America.* New York: National Urban League, CSAP 4, 1–10.

Johnson, V.E. (1980). *I'll quit tomorrow: A practical guide to alcoholism treatment.* New York: Harper & Row Publishers, Inc.

Johnson, V.E., (1986). *Intervention: How to help someone who doesn't want help.* Minneapolis: MN: Johnson Institute QVS, Inc.

Joyner, C. (1991). The world of the plantation slaves. In Campbell, E., & Rice, K. (Eds.), *Before freedom came: African-American life in the antebellum South.* Richmond, VA: The Museum of the Confederacy, CASP(4), 51–99.

Jung, J. (1994). *Under the influence: alcohol and human behaviors.* Belmont, CA: Brooks/Cole Publishing Company.

Kalish, B.J. (September, 1973). What is empathy? *American Journal of Nursing, 73*(9), 1548–1551.

Kalish, R.A. (1985). *Death, grief, and caring relationships* (2nd ed.). Monterey, CA: Brooks/Cole Publishing Company.

Kart, C.S. (1990). *The realities of aging: An introduction to gerontology* (3rd ed.). Needham Heights, MA: Allyn & Bacon.

Katz, R.J. (1990). Using our emotional reactions to older clients: A working theory. In Genevay, B. & Katz, R.J. (Eds.), *Countertransference and older clients.* Newbury Park, CA: Sage Publications, Inc.

Katzenbaum, R.J. (1991) *Death, society, and human experience* (4th ed.). New York: Macmillan Publishing Company.

Katzenbaum, R.J. (1995). *Death, society, and human experience* (5th ed.). Needham Heights, MA: Allyn & Bacon.

Katzenbaum, R.J. (1998). *Death, society and human experience* (6th ed.). Boston: Allyn & Bacon.

Keefe, T. (1976). Empathy: The critical skill. *Social Work, 71*(1), 10–14.

Khantzian, E.J., Halliday, K.S., & McAuliffe, W. E. (1990). Addiction and the vulnerable self. In Straussner, S., & Zelvin, E. (Eds.), *Gender and addictions: Men and women in treatment.* New York: Guilford.

Kinney, J. (2000). *Loosening the Grip* (6th ed).. Boston, MA: McGraw-Hill Higher Education, 452.

Kinney, J. & Leaton, G. (1991). *Loosening the grip: A handbook of alcohol information* (5th ed.). St. Louis, MO: Mosby–Year Book, Inc.

Kinney, J. & Leaton, G. (1995). *Loosening the grip: A handbook of alcohol information* (5th ed.). St. Louis, MO: Mosby–Year Book, Inc.

Kola, L.A., Kosberg, J.I., & Wegner-Burch, K. (Winter, 1980). Perceptions of the treatment responsibilities for the elderly client. *Social Work in Health Care, 6*(2), 69–76.

Kubler-Ross, E. (1969). *On death and dying.* New York: MacMillan Publishing Co., Inc.

Kus, R. (1988). Alcoholism and non-acceptance of gay self: The critical link. *Journal of Homosexuality, 15:L,* 24–41.

Lang, R. (1983). Therapists' reactions to the patient. *The Technique of Psychoanalytic Psychology, 2,* 139.

Lawson, A. (1989). Substance abuse problems of the elderly: Considerations for treatment and prevention. In G. Lawson & A. Lawson (Eds.), *Alcoholism and substance abuse in special populations,* 95–113. Rockville, MD, Aspen Systems.

Le Marchand, L., Kolonel, L.N., & Yoshizawa, C.N. (1989). Alcohol consumption patterns among five major ethnic groups in Hawaii. In *Alcohol use among U.S. ethnic minorities.* National Institute on Alcohol Abuse and Alcoholism Research Monograph (18). DHHS Pub. No. (ADM)89-1435. Rockville, MD: National Institute on Alcohol Abuse and Alcoholism, 355-371.

Leipold, W.D. (1995). *Walk through the valley.* Independence, MO: Independence Press.

Levin, J. (1997). Psychodynamic perspectives on substance abuse men. In Straussner, S.L.A., & Zelin, E. (Eds.), *Gender and addictions.* Northvale, NJ: Jason Aronson Inc.

Levinthal, C.F. (1996). *Drugs, behavior, and modern society.* Needham Heights, MA: Allyn & Bacon.

Lewis, J.A., Dana, R.Q., & Blevins, G.A. (1994). *Substance abuse counseling* (2nd ed.). Pacific Grove, CA: Brooks/Cole Publishing Company.

Lewis, O. (1959). *Five families.* New York: Basic Books, 25–26.

Lieber, C.J. (1995). Disorders of alcoholism. *New England Journal of Medicine, 333,* 1058–1065.

Longres, J. F. (1974). Racism and its effects on Puerto Rican continentals. *Social Casework: 55:67–75.* CSAP 1, 124.

Lopata, H. (1977). Patterns of economic change surrounding death of a spouse. *The Humanist,* 25–28.

Lowy L. (1991). *Social work with the aging: The challenge and promise of the later years* (2nd ed.). Prospect Heights, IL: Waveland Press, Inc.

Lum, D. (2000). Social work practice and people of color: A process-stage approach. Pacific Grove, CA: Brooks/Cole.

MacKay, R.C., Carver, E.J., & Hughes, J.R. (Eds.). (1990). *Empathy in the helping relationship.* New York: Springer Publishing Company.

Mancall, P.C. (1995). *Deadly medicine: Indians and alcohol in early America.* Ithaca, NY: Cornell University Press.

Marlatt, A., & Gordon, J. (1985). *Relapse prevention.* New York: Guilford Press.

Marsono, L. (1993). Alcohol & malnutrition. *Alcohol World Health & Research, 17*(4), 284–291.

Maslach, C., Leiter, M.P. (1997). *The truth about burnout.* San Francisco, CA: Jossey-Bass Publishers.

Mason, B.J. & Kocsis, J.H. (1991). Desipramine treatment of alcoholism. *Psychopharmacology Bulletin, 27*(2), 155–161.

McIntosh, J.L. (April 1985). Suicide among the elderly: Levels and trends. *American Journal of Orthopsychiatry, 55,* 288–293.

McMahon, P. & Koch, W. (22 Nov 1999). Assisted suicide: A right or a surrender?" *USA Today, (22),* 21A.

McNeece, A.C, & DiNitte, D.M. (1994). *Chemical dependency: A systems approach.* Englewood Cliffs, NJ: Prentice-Hall.

McPerson, B. (December 8, 1999). *Vigil remembers homeless who did not survive.* Pensacola, FL: Pensacola News Journal.

McWilliams, C. (1968). North from Mexico: The spanish-speaking people of the United States. New York: Greenwood Press, CSAP, No. 1, 123

Mellinger, G.D., Balter, M.B., & Manheimer, D.I. (1971). Patterns of psychotherapeutic drug use among adults in San Francisco. *Archives of General Psychiatry, 75,* 385–394.

Miller, G.A. (1999). *Learning the Language of Addiction Counseling.* Boston, MA: Allyn & Bacon.

Miller, K.A., Stitt, J.B., & Ellis, B.H. (September, 1985). Communication and empathy as purcursors to burnout among human service works. *Communication Monographs, 55*(4), 750–765.

Moniz, C. (1994). Alcohol and bone. *British Medical Bulletin, 50,* 67–75.

Mooney, A.J., Eisenberg, A., & Eisenberg, H. (1992). *The recovery book.* New York: Workman Publishing.

Moran, J.R. & May, P.A. (1995) American Indians. In J. Philleo (Ed.), *Cultural competence for social workers: A guide for alcohol and other drug abuse prevention professionals working with ethnic/racial communities.* SAMHSA 4. National Institute of Alcohol Abuse and Alcoholism, No. 2, October 1986.

Owen, P. (1994). *Understanding suicide and addiction.* Hazelden Foundation.

Padilla, A.M. & Salgado de Snyder, V.N. (1995). Hispanics: What the culturally informed evaluator needs to know. In Orlandi, M.A. (Ed.), *Cultural competence for social workers: A guide for alcohol and other drug abuse prevention professionals working with ethnic/racial communities.* SAMHSA 1, U. S. Department of Health and Human Services.

Parette, H.P. , Hourcade, J.I., & Parette, P.C. (1990). Nursing attitudes toward geriatric alcoholism. *Journal of Gerontological Nursing, 16*(1), 26–30.

Pelletier, K.R. (1982). Mind as healer, mind as slayer: A holistic approach to preventing stress disorders. New York: Delta Publishing Co.

Perlman, H.H. (Ed.). (1969). *Helping: Charlotte Towle on social work.* Chicago, IL: University of Chicago Press.

Petronio, S., Alberts, J.K., Hecht, M.L., & Buley, J. (1993). *Contemporary perspectives on interpersonal communication.* Madison, WI: Brown & Benchmark.

Pfeiffer, E. (1977). Psychopathology and social pathology. In Birren, J.E. & Warner Schaie, K. (Eds.). *Handbook of psychology and aging.* New York: Van Nostrand Reinhold.

Philleo, J. (Ed.) (1995). Introduction. *Cultural competence for social workers: A guide for alcohol and other drug abuse prevention professionals working with ethnic/racial communities.* SAMHSA 4. National Clearinghouse for Alcohol and Drug Information, XIV.

Porterfield, J.D. & St. Pierre, R. (1992). *Wellness: Healthful aging.* Guilford, CT: The Dushkin Publishing Group.

Quadagno, J. (1999). *Aging and the life review course.* New York, NY: McGraw-Hill.

Quinnett, P. (1998). In Fields, R. (Ed.), *Drugs in perspective: A personalized look at substance abuse and use* (3rd ed.). New York: The McGraw-Hill Companies, Inc.

Raines, M. (1983). *Life transitions workshop* (unpublished). East Lansing, MI: Michigan State University.

Raschko, R. (1990). Gatekeepers: Do the case findings in Spokane. *Aging,* 361.

Redman, M.V. (December, 1985). The relationship between perceived communication competence and perceived empathy. *Communication Monographs, 52,* 337.

Relapse and craving. *Alcohol alert.* (October 1989). National Institute on Alcohol Abuse and Alcoholism, No. 6, PH 277.

Rich, C.L., Young, D., & Fowler, R.C. (1986). San Diego Suicide Study. *Archives of General Psychiatry, 43,* 577–582.

Richman, J. (1992). *Suicide in the elderly.* New York: Springer.

Riley, H. (1972). Attitudes toward aging and the aged among black Americans: Some historical perspectives. *Aging and Human Development, (3),* 66–70.

Rivers, P.C. (1994). *Alcohol and human behavior: theory, research, & practice.* Englewood Cliffs, NJ: Prentice-Hall.

Robertson, N., (Feb-Mar 1991). Under the influence: The intimate enemy. *Modern Maturity,* 27–28, 30, 65.

Robinson, J. (1990). *Monograph.* In Genevay, B., & Katz, R.S. (Eds.), *Countertransference and older adults.* Newbury Park, CA: Sage Publications, Inc.

Rogers, C. (1975). The necessary and sufficient condition of therapeutic personality change. *Journal of Consulting Psychology, 22,* 95–103.

Russell, D. (1986). The Secret trauma: Incest in the lives of girls and women. New York: Basic Books. In Straussner, S., & Zelvin, E. (Eds.), *Gender and addictions: Men and women in treatment.* New York: Guilford.

Saghir, M. & Robins, E. (1973). *Male and female homosexuality.* Baltimore: Williams & Wilkins. CSAP, 200.

Schlaadt, R.G. & Shannon, P.T. (1990). *Drugs: Use, misuse, and abuse* (3rd ed.). Englewood Cliffs, NJ: Prentice-Hall.

Schlaadt, R.G. & Shannon, P.T. (1994). *Drugs: Use, misuse, and abuse* (4th ed.). Englewood Cliffs, NJ: Prentice-Hall.

Schneider, J. (1984). Stress, loss and grief: Understanding their origins and growth potential. Baltimore: University Park Press.

Schonfeld, L. (Jan./Feb. 1991). Research findings on a hidden population. *The Counselor,* 20–26.

Schonfeld, L. & Dupree, L.W. (1990). Older problem drinkers–long-term and late-life onset abusers: What triggers their drinking? *Aging, (361),* 5–9.

Schonfeld, L. & Dupree, L.W. (1991). Antecedents of drinking for early- and late-onset elderly alcohol abusers. *Journal of Studies on Alcohol, 52*(6), 587.

Schonfeld L. & Dupree, L.W. (1991). Treatment alternatives for older abusers. In A. M. Gurnack (Ed.) (1997). *Older adults' misuse of alcohol, medicines, and other drugs: research and practice.* New York: Springer.

Schonfeld, L., Dupree, L.W., Rohrer, G.L., & Glenn, F. (1995). Age-specific differences between younger and older alcohol abusers. *Journal of Clinical Geropsychology, 1*(3).

Schuckit, M.A. (1977). Geriatric alcoholism and drug abuse. *Gerontologist, 17*(2), 168–174.

Selzer, M.L. (1971). The Michigan alcoholism screening test (MAST): The quest for a new diagnostic instrument, *American Journal of Psychiatry, 3,* 176–181.

Shipman, A. (1990). Communities aren't Helpless: Outreach to older workers works. *Aging* (2nd quarter), 18–32.

Siegel, J.S. & Davidson, M. (1984). Demographic and socioeconomic aspects of aging in the United States: Current population reports, special studies series P-23, No. 138. Washington, DC: U.S. Department of Commerce, Bureau of the Census.

Silverstein, O. & Rashbaum, B. (1994). *The courage to raise good men.* New York: Penguin Books, 231.

Simmons, L.W. (1945). *The role of the aged in primitive society.* New Haven, CT: Archon Books.

Smith, D.M. & Atkinson, R.M. (1997). Alcoholism and dementia. In A. M. Gurnack (Ed.) *Older adults' misuse of alcohol, medicines, and other drugs: research and practice.* New York: Springer.

Smith, J.W. (1982c). Neurological disorders in alcoholism. In Estes, N.J. & Heinemann, M.E. (Eds.), *Alcoholism development, consequences, and interventions.* St. Louis: Mosby.

Solomon, J. (December 8, 2000). *Bush's choice for AG praised confederate war heroes.* Pensacola, FL: Pensacola News Journal.

Stachler, C. (1991). *Men and grief.* Oakland, CA: New Harbinger Publications, Inc.

Stahler, G.L. & Stimmel, B. (1955). *The effectiveness of social interventions for homeless substance abusers.* Binghamton, NY: Haworth.

Standridge, J. (Nov. 1998). *Alcohol abuse in the elderly.* Internet article: http://www.sma.org/medbytes/gm_9.htm.

Staudacher, C. (1991). Men & grief: A guide for men surviving the death of a loved one, A resource for caregivers and mental health professionals. Oakland, CA: New Harbinger Publications, Inc.

Stiff, J.B., Dillard, J.P., Somera, L., Kim, H., & Sleight, C. (1988). Empathy, communication, and prosocial behavior. *Communications Monographs, 55,* 198–213.

Stillion, J.M. (1995). Premature exits: Understanding suicide. In DeSpelder, L.A. & Strickland, A.L. *Readings in death and dying: The path ahead.* Mountain View, CA: Mayfield Publishing Company.

Straussner, S., & Zelvin, E. (1997). *Gender and addictions: Men and women in treatment.* New York: Guilford.

Suicidal Abstract of the US: Chart 25. (1991). D.C., Department of Commerce, Bureau of the Census, 86. In Barrow, G.M. (Ed.). (1992). *Aging, the individual, and society* (5th ed.). St. Paul, MN: West Publishing Company.

Suicide among older persons–United States 1980-1992 (Centers for Disease Control and Prevention). (Feb. 21, 1996). *JAMA, 275*(7), 33.

Teusch, R. (1997). Substance-abusing women and sexual abuse. In Straussner, S., & Zelvin, E. (Eds.), *Gender and addictions: Men and women in treatment.* New York: Guilford.

The big book: The basic text for alcoholics anonymous (3rd ed.). (1976). New York: Alcoholics World Services, Inc.

The Man who invented Kwanzaa. (January, 1998). *Ebony,* p. 118.

Twelve steps and twelve traditions. (1997). New York: Alcoholics Anonymous World Services.

U. S. Bureau of the Census. (1991). The Hispanic population in the United States: March 1990. *Current Population Reports,* Series P-20, No. 449, Washington, DC: U.S. Government Printing Office, CSAP 4, 45.

U.S Bureau of the Census. (1993). Population projections of the United States by age, sex, race, and Hispanic origin, 1993-2050. *Current Population Reports,* 25–1104. Washington, D.C.: U.S. Government Printing Office.

U. S. Bureau of the Census. (1995). *Sixty-five plus in the United States.* http://www.census.gov/socdemo/agebrief.html.

Vaillant, G.E. (1983). *The natural history of alcoholism.* Cambridge, MA: Harvard University Press.

van Wormer, K. (1997). *Alcoholism treatment: A social work perspective.* Chicago: Nelson-Hall Publishers.

van Wormer, K. (1997). *Social welfare: A world view.* Chicago: Nelson-Hall Publishers.

Vega, W., Gil, A., & Zimmerman, R. (1993). Patterns of drug use among Cuban-American, African-American, and White Non-Hispanic boys. *American Journal of Public Health, 83*(2) 257–259.

Victor, M. & Martin, J.B. (1991). In Wilson, J.D., Braunwald, E., Isselbacher, K. J., Petersdorf, R.G., Martin, J.B., Fauci, A.S., & Root, R.K. (Eds.). *Harrison's principles of internal medicine* (12th ed.). New York: McGraw-Hill, Inc.

Viorst, J. (1986). *Necessary losses: The loves, illusions, dependencies and Impossible expectations that all of us have to give up in order to grow.* New York: Fawcett Gold Medal.

Wallace, B.C. (1989). Psychological and environmental determinants of relapse in
crack cocaine smokers. *Journal of Substance Abuse Treatment, 6,* 95 106.

Wallace, G. (2001). *Does patriarchy exist in alcoholics anonymous: The fight for social justice continues.* 18th Annual Baccaleaureate Program Directors Conference at
Destin, Florida, 2001.

Wanigaratine, S. (1990). *Relapse and prevention.* London, England: Blackwater
Scientific Publishers.

Wegscheider-Cruse, S. (1989). *Another chance: Hope and health for the alcoholic family*
(2nd ed.) Palo Alto, CA: Science and Behavior Books, Inc.

Weiner, H.D., Wallen, M.C., & Zankowski, G.L. (1990). Culture and social class as
intervening variable sin relapse prevention with chemically dependent women.
Journal of Psychoactive Drugs, 22, 239–248.

West, H., Dupree, L. & Schonfeld, L. (1988). The A-B-C's of drinking behavior:
Training elderly alcohol abusers in the analysis of drinking behavior. *FMAI
Publication Series.* Gainesville, FL: Florida Mental Health Institute, The University
of South Florida.

Worden, J.W. (1991). *Grief counseling and grief therapy: A handbook for the mental health
practitioner.* New York: Springer Publishing Company. Alcohol and hormones.
(October 1994). *Alcohol Alert.* National Institute on Alcohol Abuse and
Alcoholism, No. 26, 352.

Yamamoto, J., Lee, C., Lin, K., & Cho, K. (1987). Alcohol abuse in Koreans.
American Journal of Social Psychiatry, 4(210–214). CSAP 4, 116.

Yesavage, J.A. (1995). Depression in the elderly. Postgraduate medicine. In Buelow,
G. & Herbert, S. (Eds.), *Counselor's resource on psychiatric medicines.* Pacific Grove,
CA: Brooks/Cole Publishing Company.

Zastrow, C. (1992). *Practice of social work* (5th ed.). Pacific Grove, CA: Brooks/Cole
Publishing Company.

Zimberg, S. (1978). Treatment of the elderly alcoholic in the community and in an
institutional setting. *Addictive Diseases: An International Journal, 3(3),* 417–427.

BIBLIOGRAPHY